Form of Life:
Agamben and the Destitution of Rules

ENCOUNTERS IN LAW AND PHILOSOPHY
SERIES EDITORS: Thanos Zartaloudis & Anton Schütz

This series interrogates, historically and theoretically, the encounters between philosophy and law. Each volume published takes a unique approach and challenges traditional systemic approaches to law and philosophy. The series is designed to expand the environment for law and thought.

Titles available in the series

General Advisor
Giorgio Agamben

Advisory Board
Clemens Pornschlegel, Institut für Germanistik, Universität München, Germany
Emmanuele Coccia, Ecole des Hautes Etudes en Sciences Sociales, France
Jessica Whyte, University of Western Sydney, School of Humanities and Communication Arts, Australia
Peter Goodrich, Cardozo Law School, Yeshiva University, New York, USA
Alain Pottage, Kent Law School, University of Kent, UK and Sciences Po, Paris
Justin Clemens, University of Melbourne, Faculty of Arts, Australia
Robert Young, NYU, English, USA
Nathan Moore, Birkbeck College, Law School, University of London, UK
Piyel Haldar, Birkbeck College, Law School, University of London, UK
Anne Bottomley, Law School, University of Kent, UK
Oren Ben-Dor, Law School, University of Southampton, UK

edinburghuniversitypress.com/series/enlp

FORM OF LIFE: AGAMBEN AND THE DESTITUTION OF RULES

Gian-Giacomo Fusco

EDINBURGH
University Press

Edinburgh University Press is one of the leading university presses in the UK. We publish academic books and journals in our selected subject areas across the humanities and social sciences, combining cutting-edge scholarship with high editorial and production values to produce academic works of lasting importance. For more information visit our website: edinburghuniversitypress.com

© Gian-Giacomo Fusco, 2023

Edinburgh University Press Ltd
The Tun – Holyrood Road
12(2f) Jackson's Entry
Edinburgh EH8 8PJ

Typeset in 11/13 Palatino by
Cheshire Typesetting Ltd, Cuddington, Cheshire, and
printed and bound in Great Britain

A CIP record for this book is available from the British Library

ISBN 978 1 4744 6092 7 (hardback)
ISBN 978 1 4744 6094 1 (webready PDF)
ISBN 978 1 4744 6095 8 (epub)

Contents

Preface

At the time of the completion of this book, the world is undergoing perhaps the worst crisis since World War II. A global-scale pandemic has struck our polities, dramatically exacerbating the flaws of the form of life under the political regimes of late capitalism. Although pandemics are part of the accidents and conjunctions that have constellated human history, the one we are currently going through has found governments and communities almost entirely unprepared. We are experiencing an epochal event that is gradually marking a cognitive threshold in the twenty-first century and compels us, once more, to put into question the legitimacy of the pillars sustaining modern society.

The history of modern times is the history of the intensification of the tendency to master, control and manage the world's contingency through the creation of political/economic institutions and the development of science and technologies. The machinery which we used to call the 'State' and capitalism as the leading form of the social organisation of exchange and access to resources have been the instruments that the modern mind perceived as producing endless security and prosperity. But as has become clear, the anxiety that led humans to live under the yoke of an almighty bureaucratic-techno-economic structure is itself reproducing social and environmental catastrophes. The fetishes of security and prosperity are generating, as a paradoxical collateral effect, a mounting unmanageable disorder. When a machine created and nurtured to produce a specific performance ceases to perform its function, contesting its adequacy and legitimacy becomes urgent.

This book is written in the conviction that Giorgio Agamben's work is still an excellent interpretative means to radically critique our forms of living and to think towards a coming politics and ethics outside the catastrophic distortions of (bio)power. With an over four decades-long conceptual excavation of the Western political tradition, Agamben has shed renewed light on some of the basic categories through which we have traditionally understood life as human social animals. He has drawn a method of interpretative paths, traced by rigorous archaeological research whose explicit ambition is to liberate something that rested covered and crystallised in the forms of our thought. Yet the intention of Agamben's philosophy is neither to amend the defects of certain theories or institutions, nor to lay the ground for the constitution of a new political form: any politics to come should not strive to conquer power or manage it towards further or better emancipation. No power is good in itself, and none can be reformed towards becoming good, this is the stark message underlying Agamben's reflections.

The *Homo Sacer* project has been explicitly oriented by the search for a way of conceiving the destitution of the apparatus of power. Through the elaboration of concepts like use, inoperativity, poverty – to name a few – Agamben has directed his gaze towards an ethos outside the receptacle of state politics and economic government. The concept of a form-of-life – to which this book is devoted – is the centre of gravity around which Agamben has advanced his attempts to think of an alternative politics. Such a notion encapsulates the idea of a life that has deposed its bonds with the institutional structures of sovereign, legal and economic powers; and for which modes, acts and ways of being are always possibilities and never predetermined obligatory patterns. A form-of-life is the living dimension that is disclosed when the *rules* that make up our life into forms of life are destituted and rendered inoperative.

Reading a text invariably involves a risk of misinterpretation or, worse, misappropriation. This is even more true for a work like Agamben's that covers several decades, and that ranges from linguistics to theology, from political theory to jurisprudence, from philosophy to art and aesthetics. His stylistic choices and methods often built on the idea of what he calls a paradigm, and on the practice of philosophical archaeology following in the steps of Michel Foucault, make his writing often allegoric and at times arcane. Any failure to grasp the intentions and proposals of Agamben's texts not only derails the hermeneutic practice underlying the interpretative endeavour: it also distorts the thoughts and writings of an author who focuses immense attention on style and accuracy. Keeping faith in Agamben's propositions, the chapters of this book in their singularity as well as synergy try to trace and further develop some central themes and notions of his philosophy, putting them into contact and some contrast with wider ongoing debates over radical emancipatory politics. In so doing this book aims to offer, at least, an idea of how Agamben's works might be a strategic resource towards thinking against the tragedies of our present.

~ * ~

Every intellectual endeavour is as much a product of individual sensitivity as an offspring of a community of minds. The 'acknowledgements' moment of a book positions the author and its work within a collective, whose definition however is always partial: in the end, naming all the persons, authors, institutions, that have directly or indirectly contributed to the composition of a book is impossible.

There are, however, people and institutions that have accompanied me in the making of the manuscript that really ought to be mentioned. I am extremely grateful to the series editors Thanos Zartaloudis and Anton Schütz for their invaluable support and advice throughout the different stages that led to the publication of this book. During the last few years, I have greatly benefited from enthusiastic and inspiring discussions with Cosmin Cercel, Przemysław Tacik, Rafał Mańko, Alexandra Mercescu, Simon Lavis, Tormod Otter Johansen, Dimitris Kivotidis, Ceylan Begüm Yıldız, and all the members of 'Nomos: Centre for International Research in Law Culture and Power'.

Elements of my doctoral dissertation survive in this book. So, I must express my gratitude to Kent Law School and its vibrant community for having made that project – and then this book – materially possible.

Abbreviations

CA   *Creation and Anarchy: The Work of Art and the Religion of Capitalism*
CC   *The Coming Community*
HS   *Homo Sacer: Sovereign Power and Bare Life*
MWC *The Man Without Content*
MWE *Means Without End: Notes on Politics*
N   *Nudities*
TO   *The Open: Man and Animal*
P   *Potentialities: Collected Essays in Philosophy*
Pr   *Profanations*
Pul *Pulcinella: Or, Entertainment for Children*
HP   *The Highest Poverty: Monastic Rules and Form-of-Life*
K   *Karman: A Brief Treatise on Action, Guilt, and Gesture*
KG   *The Kingdom and the Glory: For a Theological Genealogy of Economy and Government*
Sat *The Signature of All Things: On Method*
SE   *State of Exception*
SL   *The Sacrament of Language: An Archaeology of the Oath*
TTR *The Time That Remains: A Commentary on the Letter to the Romans*
UoB *The Use of Bodies*
WA   *What is an Apparatus? And Other Essays*
WDP 'What is a Destituent Power?'
WoM 'The Work of Men'

To Lucia, Dora Luce and Joshua

Introduction

The world is like a ride in an amusement park, and when you choose to go on it you think it's real because that's how powerful our minds are. The ride goes up and down, around and around, it has thrills and chills, and it's very brightly colored, and it's very loud, and it's fun for a while. Many people have been on the ride a long time, and they begin to wonder, 'Hey, is this real, or is this just a ride?' And other people have remembered, and they come back to us and say, 'Hey, don't worry; don't be afraid, ever, because this is just a ride.' And we ... kill those people. 'Shut him up! I've got a lot invested in this ride, shut him up! Look at my furrows of worry, look at my big bank account, and my family. This has to be real.' It's just a ride. But we always kill the good guys who try and tell us that, you ever notice that? And let the demons run amok ... But it doesn't matter, because it's just a ride. And we can change it any time we want. It's only a choice. No effort, no work, no job, no savings of money. Just a simple choice, right now, between fear and love.

Bill Hicks

Pulcinella's mask

In 2015, Giorgio Agamben published a book dedicated to Pulcinella, a mask of the 'Commedia dell'Arte'. The volume is structured as an exegetical journey through the images that Giandomenico Tiepolo (the son of the more famous Giambattista) devoted to the figure of Pulcinella included in a series of frescoes and in an album of 104 tables titled *Divertimento per li Regazzi* [Entertainment for Children].[1] Originating as a classical character of Neapolitan puppetry, the mask of Pulcinella is present, with variations, in the collective imaginary of other European traditions.[2] Despite its enduring and articulated representations, the definition of its substantial traits is anything but easy. Pulcinella is, in fact, a weak subject, a figure of metamorphosis, a hybrid identity in constant transition. Benedetto Croce, in this respect, argued that 'Pulcinella does not designate a particular artistic personage but rather a *collection of personages*, bound together only by a name, and ... a black half-mask'.[3] In the end, Pulcinella is purely and simply its mask; the unitary function of a lack of identity: a fickle container, chiselled with different traits (a mask, a dress, the hat, a stick, the strident voice). Pulcinella, Agamben writes, 'is not a noun: it is an adverb ... it is neither a character nor an identifiable type'; indeed, its mask is the aggregation 'of all the features that characterize the personages of comedy' (Pul, 49).

The ambiguity of Pulcinella's being is expressed in its name, which evokes animality and substantial sexual uncertainty. 'Pulcinella (from *pullecino*: chick) is a gallinaceous being, a type of flightless bird: this is also attested by the squeaky voice – similar to Donald Duck's – used by puppeteers when they make him talk' (ibid., 45). And the fact that the name is inflected in the feminine (the diminutive of *pullecino* is normally *pulleciniello* rather than *Pulcinella*), exposes its uncertain sex. Although usually represented as male – in Tiepolo's drawings, for example, urinating while standing – the presence of swellings in its body – something like humps or breasts (we cannot be sure about this), makes its identity even more ambiguous. The figure of Pulcinella, Agamben claims, creates a sort of short-circuit in the classic conception of the human as a self-centred subject: its body 'is no longer, as in Western metaphysics, the animal presupposed to the human. It breaks the false articulation between the simply living being and the human, between the body and *logos*' (ibid., 117). Pulcinella is truly and simply a mask that does not hide a subject-holder: it is an indifferent, anarchic being – a creature of pure possibilities whose existence is nothing other than the sum of its vague modalities.

For Agamben, Pulcinella has a decisive political connotation, which he illustrates by reflecting on the historical moment in which Tiepolo devoted himself to the Neapolitan mask. The painter turned on the figure of Pulcinella at the twilight of the Republic of Venice, about the time when the Great Council decided on its own extinction, abandoning the Serenissima to the control of Napoleon (who eventually handed it over to the Habsburgs a few months later). That Tiepolo initiates these works immediately after the collapse of the Republic of Venice is certainly not accidental. However, this should not induce us into imagining these works as a sort of escape route, due to disaffection and disillusionment with historical reality. Indeed, Agamben claims, Tiepolo turned his attention to Pulcinella, not for leisure, but to point out the importance of a figure who can survive the end of an era and its politics.

In a time in which the human seems to have reached its 'historical telos', when there is 'nothing left but the depoliticization of human societies by means of the unconditioned unfolding of the *oikonomia*' (TO, 76), Agamben (like Tiepolo) turned his gaze to Pulcinella. This mask that embodies the spirit of comedy appears as a paradigm through which to think another life and another politics, amid a catastrophe that earthly powers, instead of managing, are aggravating. Yet, a reflection on the end of times that elects such a figure as a companion is anything but apocalyptic. Pulcinella is what shies away from tragedy. Being singular and plural, a collection of characters gathered around a name and a mask, places it in a zone of irresponsibility in which acts, and gestures have value in themselves and cannot be imputed or captured in a normative system. Pulcinella represents the figure of the possibility of another life and another politics: one that emerges out of the destitution of the traditional categories through which the West has imagined its political, social and juridical uniqueness. The non-subject of Pulcinella, the lack of purpose of its acts, offers us the chance of thinking a way out; and indeed, its motto 'is *ubi fracassorium, ibi fuggitorium* – where there is a catastrophe, there is an escape route' (Pul, 43).[4]

Hodology

Perhaps there is nothing more indicative for the correct comprehension of Agamben's political proposal than the obstinacy with which he has depicted our time and our lives as an endless catastrophe that, from whatever angle it is viewed, seems to offer no genuine way out. In a recent short volume, which collects some contributions inspired by the COVID-19 pandemic crisis,[5] he has adopted the metaphor of a house burning down. 'Everything I do is meaningless if the house burns down. And yet as the house is burning one must carry on, as usual, doing everything with care and precision, perhaps even more scrupulously'; it may be the case, Agamben goes on, 'that life disappears from the earth, that no memory of what has been done for better or for worse, will be left. But you carry on as before; it is too late to change; there is no more time.'[6] But which house is burning? Or in other words: who/what is the subject/object of the seemingly irreversible catastrophe of our time? Here Agamben's answer cannot be more explicit: Western civilisation, whose anxiety for endless security, progress and prosperity, coupled with the mighty powers of technology, has produced a self-inflicted catastrophe. Now that the house is burning down, the structural architectonic problems become evident. At the same time, it is too late to save it; the instruments at our disposal can only patch up the ruins, transforming the blaze into an endless disaster.

Agamben is not new to the gloomy characterisation of the present. He did not hesitate, for instance, to describe the current form of political powers as hell on earth. Ingrained on the normalisation of crisis, imposed as a standard mode of administration and the 'complete juridification and commodification of human relationships', the government of humans assumed for him the guise of a perpetual economic managerial enterprise. And as he claims, there is only one institution that 'knows neither interruption nor end: hell'.[7] What makes the present truly infernal is our apparent sense of impotence in facing it; the impossibility to envision a way out, the fact that 'things continue as they are',[8] even when a system of supposedly efficient rules and procedures, instead of fulfilling the purposes for which it has been created, cannot do anything but reproduce its errors and horrors. The sovereign law, the mundane embodiment of universal rationality, has become the fabric of its own uselessness. And the tragedy is that we cannot see anything outside the horizon of our institutional limits.

We are living, Agamben claims, in a post-historical time, 'in which every dialectic is abolished, and the Great Inquisitor watches over so that the Parousia is not produced in history' (KG, 8); where every political option must be subsumed under the dusty category of modernity – democratic liberal state, law and capitalism. Every possibility to even allude to another politics seems excluded from the comfort zone of our form of life – which sadly, but not unpredictably, is failing on all its promises of endless happiness, peace and security. In the end, as Mark Fisher has brilliantly explained, our contemporary culture is essentially anachronistic, marked by an unapologetic slow cancellation of the future, with a consequent prevalence of nostalgia, retromania fetishism and lowering of expectations.[9]

Yet, more than signalling pessimism, such a lugubrious characterisation of the present epitomises a conscious strategy of adherence to our own time. To be contemporary to an epoch, to understand its most intimate meaning, we need to hold our gaze firmly to perceive, not its light, but rather its darkness. 'The ones who can call themselves contemporary', Agamben writes, 'are only those who do not allow themselves to be blinded by the lights of the century, and so manage to get a glimpse on the shadows in those lights, of their intimate obscurity' (WA, 45). Looking into the darkness of our time does not mean plodding along in the absence of any light. What we usually call darkness is simply a reaction of our vision to the absence of light. Darkness is the vision of light in its potential: and its invocation is functional to the search for a different light of the present. 'We can have hope only in what is without remedy'; only in the contemplation of what is irreparable, we can see a 'passage outside the world' (CC, 101).

Far from dismissing any form of redemption, Agamben's works are constantly permeated by the search for a way out. The archaeology of Western philosophical, political and juridical traditions that has occupied much of his research, aimed to investigate and destabilise some of the original categorial structures of our form of life. This archaeological dimension runs in parallel with a hodological one that coincides with the constant search for another way – a *hodos* – another politics and another life in common. As Agamben maintains, 'it is the existence today of something like a *hodos* or a way that we seek to interrogate, by asking ourselves whether the track that seems to have been interrupted or lost can be taken up again or instead must be definitively abandoned' (UoB, 114). In the urgency of the 'catastrophe' in which we are living the signatures with which we have informed our life must be 'revisited without reserve' (HS, 12); and indeed, the *magnum opus* that goes under the title of *Homo Sacer*, responds to the necessity to imagine radically different strategies, whose definition is the eminent task of any coming politics.

The destitution of life

In *The Use of Bodies* – the volume that marks the conclusion (or the abandonment, as Agamben says) of the *Homo Sacer* project – Agamben's archaeological-hodological path[10] undertakes a decisive development with the introduction of the notion of destituent potential. Such a concept represents a pivotal complement to his theory of inoperativity: in a sense, it condenses the logic underpinning all those practices and paradigms that Agamben has considered as exemplars of inoperative politics.[11] From the Latin *destituo*, destituent potential refers to the very possibility of contemplating the deactivation of the *rules*, institutions and signatures forming the varied biopolitical apparatuses that performatively shape human subjectivities. Destituent potential must not be considered as the negative moment or presupposition of every constituent/ creative act. The affirmation of a destituent potential points to the liberation of something already present: it is the gesture that deposes a condition of subjection to power, to open a path of 'becoming' other out of what we already are.

Form-of-life is the technical term with which Agamben encapsulates such becoming. 'The constitution of a form-of-life', he claims, 'fully coincides, with the destitution of the social and biological conditions into which it finds itself thrown' (UoB, 277); it represents what remains after the biopolitical machinery of the West has been rendered inoperative. Even though Agamben considers the idea of a form-of-life as the 'guiding concept and the unitary center of coming politics' (ibid., 213), a univocal and programmatic definition of such a term is lacking. As often happens with Agamben's terminology, this lack is a result of his style of thought, which is more oriented towards allegoric explanations than prescriptive or apodeictic determination, especially when it comes to practical/strategic options. Nonetheless, one thing is certain: the idea of form-of-life intersects all the main concepts and notions he has included as part of his philosophical/political vocabulary, such as inoperativity, use, poverty, potentiality. Thus, the proposition that governs this book is that form-of-life in a sense represents the centre of gravity around which Agamben has developed all his attempts at conceiving ways of destituting the structures of power. And the conceptual perimeter of such a notion, which this book aims to analyse, defines a space of possibilities in which different emancipatory strategies can be conjured up.

To get a better sense of what a form-of-life is, it is worth looking at where it first appeared, that is, in the short essay titled 'Form-of-Life', eventually included in the volume *Means Without Ends. Notes on Politics*. Here form-of-life is defined as a 'life that can never be separated from its form, a life in which it is never possible to isolate something such as naked life'; a life 'directed toward the idea of happiness', and emancipated 'from any sovereignty' (MWE, 3–7). This concept responds directly to Agamben's critique of sovereign power and law. As is well known, at the core of the *Homo Sacer* project, stands a conception of sovereignty as an apparatus whose scope consists of capturing life in its mechanisms. 'The sovereign', Agamben writes, 'decides not the licit and illicit but the originary inclusion of the living in the sphere of law' (HS, 26), which is obtained through the separation of a bare life and the socially, politically and legally qualified life.

What seems to be at stake in this operation is something akin to what Roman jurisprudence referred to as the institution of life [*vitam instituere*].[12] As Pierre Legendre explains, this notion nominates the distance that separates the law from any naturalistic determination of the human. The instituted life is the symbolic-linguistic dimension that is established with and through the polity, according to which all members should live.[13] It represents a proper *second birth*: the first is the biological one which associates the human with the animal world; the second birth is human life instituted through rules structured through language and speech and enshrined in the law that guarantees such a differentiation.[14] In becoming a social-speaking animal, humans undergo a fictitious separation according to which the biological-natural substance of the living becomes isolated as a prerequisite and placed as a separated substance-presupposition of the legal-institutional form.

For Agamben, such a separation boils down to a strategic political function and meaning according to which, what is divided (the biological-natural dimension of living) is what allows the unity of the subject to be constituted, as a hierarchical and oppositional articulation between bare life and the socially and legally defined forms of life. The many different 'forms of life abstractly recodified as social-juridical identities (the voter, the worker, the journalist, the student, but also the HIV-positive, the transvestite, the porn star, the elderly, the parent, the woman) … all rest on naked life' (MWE, 6–7). To the extent that 'the fundamental activity of sovereign power is the production of bare life' (HS, 181), which represents the 'ultimate subject' (UoB, 209), the instituted form of life through which humans experience their being-human as members of one or the other human community has as its core (as its foundational presupposition) bare life – that is to say, the natural bodily life as exposed to the absolute power of the sovereign. The subject of rights – with its peculiar existence, identities and social-legal roles – exchanges its degree of formalised freedom, recognition and legal protection with the possibility of having what makes its very person revoked – or, at the extreme, annihilated.

The sovereign power that sustains the unity of political communities, appears to Agamben not as founded on a pact, but rather on the production of bare life, 'which is kept safe and protected only to the degree to which it submits itself to the sovereign's (or the law's) right of life and death' (MWE, 5). Paradoxically, Agamben claims, the docile citizen who passively accepts doing whatever 'he is asked to do inasmuch as he leaves his everyday gestures and his health, his amusements and his occupations, his diet and his desires, to be commanded and controlled in the smallest detail by apparatuses, is also considered by power a potential terrorist' (WA, 22–3), to be eliminated when necessary. Our docile subjectivities are structured upon a scission and

8

re-articulation – produced and presupposed by the very governmental machine – between bare life and a composite set of abstract identities, established and governed by social, legal and economic systems. And the task for the coming politics is to revoke such separation: that is to think towards becoming truly ungovernable. The constitution of a form-of-life defines the moment in which the fracturing of life has been rendered inoperative; it encapsulates the impression of the possibility of another life in which the isolation/separation of bare life is no longer possible.

But thinking a form-of-life necessitates the abandonment of the classic categories of Western modern law and politics. The political ethos of a form-of-life is essentially opposed to state politics and the economic governmentality, and it constitutes itself through specific practices that aim at rendering inoperative the multiplicity of forms of life composing our subjective identities, opening them up to renewed uses. A form-of-life names a mode of living free from specific determination, where all the schemata of our subjectivities are deactivated from their *vis obligandi* and used simply as habits. Here, form-of-life is not the refusal of every praxis, but a critique of the totalising claims attached to the structures forming our (collective and individual) identities. A life that has deposed its bond to pre-determined rules is a way of living that is never exhausted by the definitional operation of social and juridical roles and rules.

We could consider the process of destitution of life as a form of de-subjectification. As Judith Butler puts it, the performance of power consists in '*forming* the subject', through a process of subjection – our being dependent 'on a discourse we never chose but that, paradoxically, initiates and sustains our agency' – [15] that makes our selves somehow coercively shaped in the forms we become accustomed to. In establishing itself at the moment in which the many different categorial apparatuses (and discourses) underpinning our forms of life are detached from their operativity, a form-of-life is revealed through a movement opposite to that of subjection. And this necessarily implies a sort of ontological break and the rethinking of the epistemic bases upon which power and human subjectivity have been conceived. Indeed, ontology, for Agamben, is not an 'innocuous academic discipline', but rather 'the fundamental operation in which anthropogenesis, the becoming human of the living being, is realized' (TO, 79). It represents the source of meanings for the auto-comprehension, for the action and interaction of humans as living beings, which 'has constituted for centuries the fundamental historical *a priori* of Western thought' (UoB, 112). Therefore, politics entails necessarily ontological assumptions. And at the same time, for Agamben, each ontology cannot but implicate a politics since the scission of life – the relation of the exception – on which the *polis* is established and reproduced is the concrete transposition (as an order of things and men) of something thought at the level of ontology. As a result, the contemplation of a form-of-life must pass through the critical re-working of the ontological tradition.

The ontological-biopolitical machine

Here, then, is the signature motif of Agamben's philosophy: the way in which we experience our lives is the product of a dispositive (or machinery) that is at the same time ontological, linguistic and political. It works by generating divisions, categorisations, separations, inclusions and re-appropriations. As far as we look back the dispositive is in motion, and even though it has assumed different guises, its core logic has remained somehow intact: the exception.[16] For Agamben, the 'the structure of the exception' – a 'strategy' according to which something is divided, excluded and 'pushed to the bottom', and through this exclusion, included as a 'foundational element' – appears as laying down the '*archè*, in the juridico-political tradition as much as in ontology' (UoB, 264). This structure is a common element of several experiences that Agamben has analysed throughout his work. The *polis* – as in the first volume of the *Homo Sacer* series – is founded on the scission and re-articulation of life in *zoē* (animal life) and *bios* (a politically qualified life). The 'human' is defined through the exclusion-inclusion of *animality*; the law through the exclusion-inclusion of anomy and violence (ibid., 264–5).

The contiguity of ontology and politics occurs on the terrain of the relation of the exception, whose *archè* is located by Agamben in that apparatus of scission of being that Aristotle has codified in the *Categories* [2a 10–15], where he has advanced the distinction between 'prime' and a 'secondary' essence [*ousia*]. The prime essence [*hypokeimenon*: the subject, what 'lies below', 'under', 'at the base'] refers to what an entity *is* – what is expressed by the singularity of the name. The secondary essence, instead, is a predicative being – what *is said* of it.[17] Such a classification underpins every ontological difference and, Agamben claims, made Western philosophy interrogating being (and life) beginning always from a division (ibid., 115). This distinction transposes in ontological terms a fundamental feature of language, that is the promiscuity of the meaning of the verb 'to be', which 'has a double meaning': the first 'corresponds to a lexical function, which expresses the existence and reality of something ("God is," that is, exists), while the second – the copula – has a purely logico-grammatical function and expresses the identity between two terms ("God is good")' (ibid., 117–18). To predicate – 'to say' – is always to say something of a subject. The act of the predication presupposes the existence (the *being*) of its subject. Secondary essence – what is said of something – in this light, presupposes the existence of a primary essence – as the subject of the predication. For this reason, Agamben claims that 'the subjectivation of being, the presupposition of the lying-under is therefore inseparable from linguistic predication, is part of the very structure of language and of the world that it articulates and interprets' (ibid., 118). The presuppositional logic that Agamben sees as the core element of the structure of the exception, is an epiphenomenon of the possibility of taking place of language.

For Agamben, the Aristotelian ontology assumed the form of an ontological-biopolitical machine that had an enduring effect in the formation of Western culture. Such a dispositive has left its traces in the way in which the human has been envisaged in its biological, social and political dimension. As Agamben maintains, according to the axiom formulated by Aristotle in the *De anima* [415b 13] ('Being for the living is to live, *to de zēn tois zosi to einai estin*) what holds on the level of being is transposed in a completely analogous way onto the level of living': as for being, also living is said in many ways ... and here as well one of these senses – nutritive or vegetative life – is separated from the others and becomes a presupposition to them. Nutritive life thus becomes what must be excluded from the city – and at the same time included in it – as simple living from politically qualified living. Ontology and politics correspond perfectly (ibid., 129).

To the extent that every predication on an entity presupposes a subject – as a non-linguistic existent element – political life too is organised upon a division of different spheres of life, one of which is excluded and posed at the base – subjected – of the *polis*. For these reasons, Agamben claims that 'the ontological apparatus, which articulates being and puts it in motion, there corresponds the biopolitical machine, which articulates and politicizes life' (ibid., 205).

The place of this dual articulation/separation is *logos* (language and thought), which 'can divide what cannot be physically divided', that is, the different aspects of the life of human beings from its biological (animal) substrate. This 'logical' division makes possible the politicisation of the im-political life, that biological dimension the exclusion of which stands as a foundational element of human communal life. Accordingly, Agamben argues that 'politics, as the *ergon* proper to the human, is the practice that is founded on the separation, worked by the logos, of otherwise inseparable functions'; politics, therefore, 'appears as what allows one to treat a human life as if in it sensitive and intellectual life were separable from vegetative life', and since this is impossible in humans, of 'legitimately putting it to death' (ibid., 204). But this implies that the biological life (and life in general and perhaps even the concept of being), which polities try to govern and to take care of, is indeed an abstraction.[18] The apparatus of powers through which human beings are made into subjects does not consist in the domination of people by other people, but in the dominion of people by the abstract categories that they invented themselves, which throughout history somehow assumed their autonomous operativity. The investigation of ontology is for Agamben functional to grasping the logic underpinning such a form of abstract domination and to think a political/ethical way of deactivating its operation.

Potentiality

In the essay *On Potentiality* Agamben writes: 'I could state the subject of my work as an attempt to understand the meaning of the verb "can" [*potere*]. What do I mean when I say: "I can, I cannot"?' (P, 177) As has been observed, potentiality – what one can or cannot – is perhaps the central concept (or idea) of his work, the one that has oriented its speculation over the many different spheres of philosophy and culture – from aesthetics to ontology and politics.[19] Agamben has developed his idea of potentiality through an original reading of book *Theta* of the *Metaphysics*, where Aristotle advanced and explained the ontological difference between potential (*dynamis*) and act(uality) (*energheia*) – which should be regarded as the second arm of the ontological-biopolitical machine. As Aristotle states, being 'sometimes means being potentially, and sometimes being actually', and accordingly we can say that one sees, or one can use knowledge both potentially and actually.[20] While the act refers to the actual doing or being something – for example, to actually see – the potential mode of being refers to the possibility of actually seeing. The potential corresponds to the sphere of the *faculty* of an entity to do something and to 'assume a determinate – an actual – form'.[21]

Aristotle separates the faculty (or power) to do and to be – to see, to hear, to use knowledge, to be an architect – from its actual manifestation – seeing, hearing, using knowledge, being an architect. To *have the faculty to do*, is different from doing: one has the capacity/faculty to see, even when not seeing. By the same token, an architect does not cease to be an architect when not actually practising his knowledge and profession. Therefore, what human beings have in the form of a faculty is a 'privation' [*sterēsis*], which attests the presence of a habitus [*hexis*] that is (actually) not in act.[22] In other words, to have a 'potential, to have a faculty' means 'to have a privation' (ibid.); potentiality therefore refers to the non-actual existence of what can exist.

As a modality of being, potentiality has a dual character that makes it both active and passive. If potentiality is only the potential of doing or becoming, if it exists only to pass to the act, then there would be no possibility of the privation [*sterēsis*] that is the basis for human beings to state 'I can', be or do, this or that.[23] Aristotle expresses this with the term impotentiality [*adynamia*] that is a privation contrary to potentiality: 'all potentiality is impotentiality of the same and with respect to the same' (ibid., 182). And, Agamben maintains, 'beings that exist in the mode of potentiality are capable of their own impotentiality; and only in this way do they become potential' (ibid.). Impotentiality here does not mean the absence of potential, but the possibility not to act; to every potential, therefore, belongs its im-potential: the possibility not to.

The *fil rouge* that connects the many Agambenian declinations of such a concept is the consideration of potentiality as the innermost character defining the human. 'There is in effect something that humans are and have to be', Agamben writes in *The Coming Community*, 'but this something is not an essence nor properly a thing: It is the simple fact of one's own existence as possibility or potentiality' (CC, 42). What differentiates humans from other living beings is that they 'are capable only of their specific potentiality' (P, 182). Being entities of pure potential, humans are defined by an essential lack of vocation and destiny. And this represents for Agamben the ground on which the question of ethics and freedom arises and should be interrogated. The 'abyss of potentiality', he claims, is the root of human freedom: to be free 'is not simply to have the power to do this or that thing, nor is it simply to have the power to refuse to do this or that thing' (ibid.). Humans can define themselves as free only to the extent to which they are capable of their own impotentiality, of the privation of any specific determination. And for this reason, something like ethics and politics, as a problem of what can and cannot be done, should and should not be done, could be raised. Differently than animals for which it is possible to 'develop only the infinite repeatable possibilities fixed in the genetic code', human beings are in the existential condition of having the capacity of paying attention to what has not been written, to somatic possibilities that are arbitrary and uncodified and free from any genetic prescription.[24] And to the extent that the problems of a human ethos and political life emerge out of such potentiality of being, for Agamben, the question of an alternative politics can only be posed by considering potentiality as the most proper sphere of the human.

The history of human cultures and institutions narrates the gestures with which humans have been constantly separated from their intimate potential, which through the development of metaphysical/normative apparatuses has been constantly informed, removed, and kept as a hidden foundation of our forms of life. The fact that the social sciences relentlessly expose is that the institution of life, which sustains the experience of the human as a social (speaking) animal, corresponds to the legislation of the potential, exercised through the creation and imposition of categorial devices that tends to attach humans to specific vocations, models and images, making what they *can/cannot*, into *must/must not*. The human world is covered with signs and signatures, and as Agamben's philosophical archaeology has shown with an abundance of detailed investigations, the categories that have from time to time been established for rendering human life intelligible and governable, corresponds to power in its existential effectivity. They are, in a sense, the real abstractions informing human life. And for Agamben, the task for the coming politics consists in the liberation of the potential embedded in any form of life, through the destitution of the abstract forms with which we have thought our life-systems. Form-of-life as a life of the potential is the dimension that opens up when the faith and the imaginary qualities that cultures attach to the signatures of power, are deposed.

Anarchy

It is certainly true that, as Adam Kotsko claims, 'we can't expect any kind of political program from Agamben'.[25] However, to the extent that his philosophical archaeology, is also a hodology, the *pars destruens* and the *pars construens* of his research are conflated into one encompassing strategy of pointing a way out, while digging into the history of culture and institutions. Perhaps, the basic hallmark of Agamben's political proposal is that theory and practice cannot be kept separate as two moments in which one (theory) orients and grounds the other (praxis); which would be conversely the actualisation/constitution of a potential (theoretical) programme. As Kotsko put it, 'It can't be a matter of getting away from abstract concepts and into lived experience, because for Agamben, our life and our politics play out precisely at the point of intersection between life and abstraction, between the human-animal and language'.[26] But such a reluctance to undertake an elaboration of a political strategy is not simply a philosophical or an aesthetic-stylistic choice; rather it should be considered itself as a political stance.

Implicit in Agamben's ideas of destituent potential and inoperativity is the deactivation of the *archè* of power. And to the extent that he has conceived anarchy as an absence of *archè* (an-archy), of commands and principles, his political proposal tends essentially to anarchy, since it aims at destituting the different *archai* that command and rule our forms of life. Therefore, the elaboration of a political recipe or strategy would contradict the very purpose of his thoughts, since the normativity generally embedded in every strategy would pose itself as a principle or command. For Agamben, 'Anarchy can never be in the position of a principle' (UoB, 276). Anarchy is a condition in which every principle – intended as origin and command – is deactivated; in which all forms of being are never in a prescriptive-transcendental position in need of actualisation, but are always possibilities, simple ways of living.

Agamben's anarchic and anti-normative way of doing philosophy is perhaps the biggest hurdle one is facing in the investigation of his political propositions. Such a tonality is permeating all his more politically oriented works, and it is expressed in the methodological adoption of 'paradigms'. Agamben intends a paradigm as a singular historical fact, figure, or practice (the *homo sacer*, the *Muselmann*, the camp, the feast, etc.) that serves to analogically illuminate the connection between a larger series of phenomena, events and practices that would otherwise remain obscure. As he writes, a 'paradigm is a form of knowledge that is neither inductive nor deductive but analogical. It moves from singularity to singularity' (Sat, 31), and cannot aprioristically and normatively rule over how historical facts should be interpreted, and actions, oriented. Agamben's works could be described as a rather extreme form of paradigmology for which the study of specific historical events, aimed at the discovery of the signatures shaping the Western conception of law, politics and more generally of philosophy, do not assume a normative character. Much like an example, the elaboration of a paradigm is not of immediate practical use to draw a rule or a norm analogically; indeed, by moving from singularity to singularity it makes 'every singular case into an exemplar of a general rule that can never be stated a priori' (ibid., 22).

Akin to the literary device of the allegory, paradigms aim at rendering indirectly explicit a concealed concept or a practice, which is left to be de-codified and somehow interpreted rationally. Although he sometimes does come back to the examples he has deployed in his extensive oeuvre, Agamben never endeavours to make them more intelligible by way of adding self-interpretations. On the contrary, he has constantly treated his works as something to be abandoned (UoB, xiii) and left so to speak for free interpretative use for others. By leaving his research to be eventually completed by others, Agamben has in a sense marked the task of a philosophy to come, that is to keep on questioning the metaphysical structures on which the architecture of powers is built, towards their destitution. And in a sense, this book responds to such an invitation.

~ * ~

The idea from which this book takes its cue is that the notion of form-of-life makes up the nodal point in which some of the most prominent concepts of Agamben's political vocabulary intersects, forming a kind of coherent-albeit-not-systematic proposal. In the following, I will proceed through a preliminary recollection of the idea of form-of-life (Chapter 1), before looking into a range of themes and concepts that are functionally linked to it, such as destituent potential (Chapter 2), work (Chapter 4), common (Chapter 5) and anarchy (Chapter 6). The question of law and Agamben's critique of the juridical will be kept under special consideration (Chapter 3). If anything, with the idea of form-of-life, he aims to bring to the fore a sense of human life as not instituted, as not subjected to law's work. Clearly, this selective approach to Agamben's extensive body of works will leave some of the core elements of his thought untouched. Effectively, this book does not claim to offer a comprehensive introduction/exposition of Agamben's opus.

Agamben's more politically oriented works, imbued as they are by ontological terminology and centred on the idea of inoperativity, have always tended to polarise readers. Some dismissed them as overly impractical, utopian or nihilistic. Others praised them not only for their diagnostic relevance, but also for their intrinsic although indirect political potential – and this book is aligned with this latter approach. It is true that Agamben constantly falls short of responding to the much-needed question of 'what is to be done?' Indeed, for him, the crucial question to answer would rather be how is it to be done? And yet there is a kind of eerie enthusiasm and hope in Agamben's prose that repeatedly peaks through his paradigmatic philosophy. It is because he invites us to take into serious consideration the radical contingency and groundlessness of the present and the constitutive potential for re-inventing a world by simply living a life. However, here is precisely the problem of Agamben's political proposal. The idea of redemption through destitution and inoperativity to undermine the current dominant regimes is somehow frustrated by his reluctance to elaborate it in normative terms. In a sense, this book aims at doing what Agamben refrained from doing, compensating his perspective by employing others' perspectives. Of course, this is not going to be an attempt at filling gaps or amending lacunae; rather it will be a matter of trying to cross the boundaries inside which Agamben has placed his philosophy.

Except for Chapter 1, which lays the foundation of the others, the book follows two lines of enquiry: the interpretative reconstruction of some of the concepts associated with the notion of form-of-life; and the attempt at thinking ways in which they might be used to inspire emancipatory theories and practices. The trajectory of this book is therefore rather methodological: the exegetical consideration of specific themes central to Agamben's work will be placed in relation to wider debates on radical political strategies to think towards a form of collective life liberated from the yoke of sovereign/legal violence and capitalist economic dominion. Though this might be an attractive option, this work will not present Agamben *stricto sensu* as a thinker of and for a revolution – by his own admission, he is not a strategist, and his works never purported to advance prescriptions or recipes for political struggles.[27] Rather, making *use* of the openness and incompleteness of his work, this book will try to expound the prefigurative political potential of Agamben's philosophy.

Notes

1. Agamben renders this formula as the subtitle of his book.
2. See Horvath (2010); Fava (2015).
3. Croce (1899: 2).
4. In a sense, this motto is a reformulation of the verses *Wo aber Gefahr ist, wächst Das Rettende auch* [where danger grows, grows also saving power] from Friedrich Hölderlin's *Patmos*. Hölderlin is one of those figures who has accompanied Agamben constantly in his works. In 2020 Agamben has published a volume titled *La follia di Hölderlin. Cronaca di una vita abitante (1806–1843)*, which marks a further decisive development. See Agamben (2020b).
5. In a series of short interventions posted in his blog *Una Voce* hosted by 'Quodlibet' publisher's website and eventually included in two short books (2020; 2020a), Agamben advanced a stark critique of the governmental reaction to the COVID-19 pandemic – from lockdowns to the widespread use of vaccination certificates. His position diverged radically from the attitude common to most intellectuals and scholars who, in one way or another, tended to justify the evident infringement of fundamental liberties constitutionally granted and protected, as a reasonable reaction to the pandemic emergency. Although pretty much in line with his most popular writings (and in a sense highly predictable) Agamben's opinions have been labelled as irrational, dangerous and somehow akin to a conspiracy theory. This book does not devote specific reflections of his pandemic writings, not because of a strategy of avoidance, but simply because it was largely conceived and written before the COVID-19 pandemic.
6. Agamben (2020: 7).
7. Agamben (2012: 40–1).
8. Whyte (2013: 4).
9. The return of fascist languages and fascist political styles is not simply a peculiar fetish for vintage politics, but rather they are a predictable response to a lack of imagination

towards alternatives. In the end, fascism has been one of the few successful answers to the crisis of capitalism and the failure of liberal democracy that Europe has known.

10. Cinquemani (2019).
11. *Inoperativity* is among the fundamental notions of Agamben's political vocabulary. The themes of a politics to come and of an alternative form-of-life is interrogated starting from the idea of inoperativity. More on these issues in Chapter 2.
12. Such expression is present is the *Digest* I, 3, 2 and is attributed to Marcianus: *Lex est. cui omnes obtemperare convenit; tum ob alia multa: tum vel maxime eo, quod omnis lex inventum ac munus Dei est: decretum vero prudentum hominum, coercitio eorum, que sponte, vel involotarie dlinquantur; communis sponsion civitatis, ad cujus prescriptum omnes, qui in ea republica sunt, vitam instituere debent.*
13. Legendre (1999: 106–8).
14. Legendre (2001).
15. Butler (1997: 2).
16. On this point see UoB, 115–34; 263–79.
17. See Aristotle (1991: 4).
18. Agamben (2020: 14).
19. See de la Durantaye (2009); Salzani (2013).
20. Aristotle (1991: 68).
21. Altini (2014: 21).
22. Ibid., 32.
23. Ibid., 33.
24. Agamben (1995: 95).
25. Kotsko and Dickinson (2015: 243).
26. Ibid., 244.
27. Agamben (2004; 2020d).

One
Form-of-Life

We fill pre-existing forms and when we fill them we change them and are changed.

Frank Bidart

Form(s) of life

'All living beings are in a form of life, but not all are (or not all are always) a form-of-life. At the point where form-of-life is constituted, it renders destitute and inoperative all singular forms of life' (UoB, 277). Among the sparse definitions of the concept of form-of-life that can be found throughout Agamben's oeuvre, this is certainly one of the more incisive: it includes references to some of the central terms of his philosophical-messianic[1] vocabulary (inoperativity and destitution) and shows how the technical term 'form-of-life' should be understood dialectically against its counterpart 'form of life'. The interrogation of what distinguishes (and unites) the two is therefore crucial, since the constitution of a form-of-life has as its object the plurality of forms of life structuring human subjectivities. The comprehension of such an operation must pass, logically, through the scrutiny of the definition of form of life. Indeed, within the couple of hyphens separating the words 'form' 'of' 'life' seems to lie a large part of the whole Agambenian political proposal.[2]

In the short essay 'Form-of-life' (published in 1993 in *Futur Antérieur*, and eventually included in the volume *Means Without Ends*), Agamben defines a form of life as the plurality of 'abstractly recodified socio-juridical identities (the voter, the worker, the journalist, the student, but also the HIV-positive, the transvestite, the porno star, the elderly, the parent, the woman) that all rest on naked life' (MWE, 6–7).

21

Western culture, for Agamben, produced (and continues to produce) a panoply of machines/apparatuses (from the ephemeral discursive/ontological categories to sovereign power and social-governmental dispositives) that constitute human subjectivities, through the division and separation of a foundational element, bare life and its re-articulation with another element: the plurality of forms of life. It is safe to say that 'form of life' is the technical term with which he condenses the idea of a 'qualified life' (*bios*) in its relation to the natural living substrate, as captured in the apparatuses shaping both human communal and individual identity (bare life).

The production of bare life, as the ground on which the plurality of the forms of our life lie, is the outcome of a mechanism of subjectification, triggered by the encounter of living substance with the variety of apparatuses of culture and power. The subject, Agamben claims, 'results from the relation, and so to speak, from the relentless fight between living beings and apparatuses', and even though the substances (or living beings) seem to coincide totally with their subjects, they do not overlap with them completely (WA, 14). The same living being is constantly the 'place' of a multiplicity of processes of subjectification, which all operates through the production of a foundational element: bare life. Subjectification, as a result, takes place through the division on the plane of human existence between forms of life and bare life. In such pairing, the latter represents what is presupposed by the former, as a foundational element and site of exercise of power. For this reason, Agamben concludes that bare life is the 'ultimate subject' (UoB, 209): the site upon which the plurality of forms of life are grounded.

But bare life is not a natural datum; rather it is the product of belonging to a community structured upon sovereign laws. It is the principle that a community is necessarily founded upon the obligatory adherence to institutions, rules, customs and authorities, and the duty not to infringe their dictates, which gives room to the emergence of bare life. One of the central tenets of the whole *Homo Sacer* project is the idea that traditional political aggregations (as we know them) are regimes established upon the sovereign right to decide and divide between the forms of life that are legally/institutionally recognised, protected and enforced, from those that must be excluded. Forms of life are the matrixes of communal and violent human political ordering, which, Agamben (inspired by Alain Badiou) claims is based not so much on a pact or a societal bond, but on the impossibility of its dissolution (CC, 86), as well as the sanction of the conducts negating the forms of life, recognised, protected and enforced by social and political institutions.

Agamben intends forms of life as the historical product of the contingent encounter between a living being and determinate sets of socio-juridical identities composing the substance of the institutional structure of polities. It follows that there is nothing natural in the forms of human life: 'human living', Agamben writes 'is never prescribed by a specific biological vocation nor assigned by any necessity whatsoever, but even though it is customary, repeated, and socially obligatory, it always preserves its character as a real possibility' (UoB, 208). Human life is intrinsically potential, un-formed, lacking pre-ordained (biological) structures; it is always open to the possibility of being otherwise. 'Human beings', he claims, 'insofar as they know and produce, are those beings who, more than any other, exist in the mode of potentiality' (P, 182).

What seems to be really in question in the notion of form of life[3] is something akin to what the tradition of philosophical anthropology[4] called 'institution'. As Arnold Gehlen, has sustained the human-animal is substantially a 'deficient being' [*Mängelwesen*],[5] in constant disharmony with the natural environment. Men, he argues, lack preordained (pre-codified) instincts, which in other animals frame a kind of perfect programme of actions to be undertaken in the presence of certain stimuli. Humans are not tied to a given environment since they are instinctually deficient and world-open.[6] While for the animal, 'instincts are the instincts of its organs, through which it has adapted to its environments' and following the predictable 'rhythm of Nature', for humans the instincts seem to be 'tailored to the unpredictable'.[7]

In Gehlen's anthropology, humans are destined to create their environment, to erect the world that could stabilise humans' formless instinctual nature. 'Culture' is the term that defines the 'closure' of the human environment. Intended as the sum of all those social products created to guarantee survival and subsistence, such as technology, religion, law, art and morality, culture reduces 'the contingency stemming from human biological deficiency'.[8] It inhibits and shapes human behaviour, and therefore has a restrictive (conservative) essence. Social structuring, familial ties, the law, the division of labour, state forms, government: these elements entered human *nature* and must be considered as facts of natural history that have oriented men's drives and needs for so long as to have become structures of human consciousness.

On the ground of the peculiar lack of a defining human nature, Gehlen introduces the notion of 'institution'. Thanks to the capacity of adaptation and elaboration of impulses embodied in cultural structures, human beings build upon the 'relative disorder'[9] of their environment: rites and schemes of conduct transmitted by social groups throughout generations. Forms of action are stabilised and reinforced by a process of institutionalisation that the members of a given community inherit as a 'stock of knowledge'.[10] The institutions of a given society – its organisation, law, customs, etc. – work as 'external supports' that harmonise and balance the many diverse needs of individuals. Institutions allow the self-standing of a community; they work as preordained instincts, permitting the establishment of a human communal environment. If the institutions of a given community are destroyed, the tendency to disaggregation and chaos that is characteristic of human nature is freed and the community is said to be destined to dissolution.[11] An institution, thus, 'crystallises and stabilises' in specific forms the 'human interaction, which emerges in a given geo-historical context, and creates an objective order'[12] of rules and the relative subjects.

Not unlike Gehlen's philosophical anthropology, Agamben conceives human life as formless and lacking vocations and orientations. It might be argued that with the notion of a form of life, he refers to the process of informing such formlessness through specific commands, fixed patterns of behaviour, institutions, norms, obligations and generally all the items that could be listed under the label of normativity. The concept of a form of life encapsulates the articulation between nature and culture: *bios* and *zoē*, *nomos* and *physis*. It refers to the merging of a 'form' as a lifeless norm, and 'life' as unformed existence, or as Agamben puts it: the 'capture of life in law' (HS, 26). From this point of view, the utmost operation of the sphere of normativity is the modelling (or institutionalisation) of life in specific forms coupled with the somehow collateral production of bare life (as the *locus* upon which sovereign violence is exercised, and the law enforced). A form of life represents the 'how' humans experience their selves and identities; it condenses the idea of the subject as the sum of all the dogmatic institutional constructs as articulated within a substrate of organic life – the body; the matter of biological life, which as Agamben argues is 'two-faced being' (HS, 125) – it is the bearer of the individual forms of life and the subject/object of the absolute sovereign power.

Here we are faced with the traditional Western understanding of the human as a composition of two substances (or natures) – one spiritual (or cultural) and one natural – or in the terms of Christian theology as a composition of 'matter and spirit in their unity'.[13] Implicit in this image is that the acquisition of human subjectivity (a personality) is dependent upon factors that turn out to be heteronomous with respect to the singularity of human bodily existence. And this is also expressed in the renowned Aristotelean definition of the human as a political animal [*politikon zōon*], which ultimately means that 'I am not human except insofar as I belong to a social group'.[14] The access to a human form of life and the gaining of the status of subject depends on our being part of a political community; it requires, as Alan Supiot argues, a third-party guarantor, which in modern secular society is the state's apparatus. Indeed, the state – he maintains – 'is the cornerstone of the organisation of the socio-political whole and is the immortal representative of the attributes of the human being'; the state is 'the ultimate guarantor of the legal personality of the real or fictive beings that are referred to it':[15] in the West, he goes on,

> there is no 'I' possible without an authority that guarantees this 'I', or, to put it in legal terms, without an authority that guarantees personal status. No one can make the sovereign gesture of altering their lineage, sex or age. Such issues have long been referred to religious authorities ... In the West, it is the State which is nowadays the ultimate guarantor of personal status; ... the identity of the mortal

human being still continues to be governed by an immortal and super-human subject. Even before arriving at the autonomy of the speaking subject through the heteronomy of language, the human being becomes a legal subject through the heteronomy of the law.[16]

The acquisition of a form of life is, therefore, dependent on the statement of an external authority (state sovereignty, the law, the *polis*), which guarantees the unity of the subject – the articulation of the natural substrate with the public-social-legal personality, which constitutes the form of a (subjected) life. Being a subject is being subordinate to an entity that is heteronomous to any natural/material substance. The status of a subject – its form of life – is the outcome of a sovereign decision (or the suspension of a decision) on whether a life must be recognised as worthy or capable of bearing rights, duties (offices) and a determinate form, or, on the contrary, whether it has to be excluded from the institutional forms the community.

~ * ~

The thought of a coming politics, for Agamben, necessitates considering anew the articulation between human life and its forms. And what he calls form-of-life is the guiding concept of such re-thinking. By virtue of living, human beings find themselves immersed in power mechanisms and apparatuses that seek to capture, rule and govern every single aspect of life – from the mere biological processes to tastes and desires – through coercive and violent calculation, producing controllable subjectivities (all resting on bare life). 'The constitution of a form-of-life', Agamben writes, 'fully coincides with the destitution of the social and biological conditions into which [human life] finds itself thrown' (UoB, 277). Calling for the emancipation of human life from the yoke of the traditional architecture of powers, the concept of form-of-life invites us to consider seriously a post-statist communitarian form, based simply on living-in-common and not on prescribed norms, law's commands, or identities, where life can never be separated from its form, or divided and isolated as bare life.

Monastic rules

Agamben's *The Highest Poverty: Monastic Rules and Form-of-Life* represents a decisive step in the delineation of the notion of form-of-life. The great novelty of monasticism, and what makes it of particular interest in his perspective, is the refusal to organise the life in common through the establishment of 'a legal framework that purports to protect, stabilise and defend it'.[17] Implicit in the refusal to adhere to legal codification as cement on which to ground a communal life is the renunciation of rules and modes of life without any principle of transcendent authority, other than the exemplary life of Christ. Rather than setting laws, monastic rules try to reach a new plane in which life and rule(s) overlap and become indeterminate. The form of communitarian living practised by monastic orders – which has its most articulated and notorious paradigm in the Franciscan rule – had therefore not only a material meaning but also a juridical and political one, which renders it, for Agamben, a paradigmatic example of the possibility of form-of-life that finds its perfection in overcoming the traditional structures of power, through the abolition of private ownership and the implementation of a nonjuridical conception of community belonging.

Born as a form of voluntary and solitary exile in the tradition of Eastern Christianity (mainly in Egypt), monasticism, Agamben claims, became, in a short time 'a model of total communitarian life' (HP, 9), structured upon the intensification of the regulation of almost every single aspect of the life of its members. Monastic rules permeated the whole existence of the monk, so much so that their labelling as *vita vel regula, regula et vita* and *forma vitae*, more than circumscribing a relationship between two terms, sanctioned their definitive indistinction and the establishment of a way of living in which rule and life are not distinguishable. Indeed, in these texts, Agamben sees a 'radical reformulation of the very conceptuality that up until that moment articulated the relationship between human action and norm, "life" and "rule"' (ibid., 4).

The life form that is at stake in the monastic rules centres on the cenoby: the site of a 'life in common' [*koinos bios*]. The communal habitation, Agamben observes, is the 'necessary foundation of monasticism' (ibid., 13). This aspect of the monastic life finds its paradigmatic expression in the *Book of Acts* where the life of the Apostles is 'described in terms of unanimity and communism' (ibid., 10): 'the multitude of believers – we read – had one heart and soul, and none of them claimed any of his property as his own: they held everything in common'.[18] The communal life, Agamben notes, has a crucial political character since it stands for the foundational element upon which monastic rule is established. The life in common of the cenoby is not the object that the rule must institute and govern; on the contrary, it is the rule that finds in the community of life its constitutive element. In the vocabulary of public law, the communal life of the cenoby functions as a constituent power (ibid. 58). But differently from the traditional idea of constituent power, which as Schmitt argued is held by the people, intended as a political subject with specific consciousness of itself,[19] the *koinos bios* has to be understood as the simple fact of living a life in common. What is presupposed by the monastic rule as a foundational element is nothing other than the fact of living a communal general (unspecified) life.

As Agamben argues, the community of life of the monks has not to be intended merely as the actual sharing of the same place. In the context of monastic literature, the *habitatio* [dwelling] also indicates a virtue and spiritual condition, manifested in the whole existence of the monks, passing from the clothing to working and spiritual activities. The strict regulation of the dress of the monks, for example, embodies moral values. 'The habit of the monk', Agamben writes, is a '*morum formula*, an example of a way of life', reflected in the single components of clothing: 'the small hood (*cucullus*) that the monks wear day and night is an admonishment to hold constantly to the innocence and simplicity of small children', while the 'short sleeves' of the tunic (*colobion*) signify 'that they have cut off the deeds and works of this world' and the small mantel 'symbolises humility' (ibid., 14). In this sense, the shape of the exterior vestments mirrors the interior, moral, way of being – the *habitus* as a habit. Along with a dress code, the monastic rule prescribed for moral and religious ends includes a strict temporal scansion of daily life that was termed *horologium* (clock). The activities of the monastery were organised according to a strict and rigid 'timetable' that made 'the whole life of the monk' to appear as shaped 'according to an implacable and incessant temporal articulation' (ibid., 21). The monk became a sort of living clock, whose existence coincided with the organisation of the ascertained time for prayer, labour and reading. 'In the cenobitic *horologium vitae*', Agamben suggests, 'time and life were for the first time intimately superimposed to the point of nearly coinciding' (ibid. 24), rendering the life of the monks indistinguishable from time as such and from the rules regulating it.

What is decisive, for Agamben, is that the hypertrophic regulation of the cenoby radically twists the way the relationship between rule and behaviour – law and life – has been traditionally understood. In the cenoby, he claims, the rule enters

> into a zone of undecidability with respect to life. A norm that does not refer to single acts and events, but to the entire existence of an individual, to his *forma vivendi*, is no longer easily recognizable as a law, just as a life that is founded in its totality in the form of a rule is no longer truly life (ibid., 26).

A rule that is simply lived that does not have any application to specific cases and therefore cannot be separated from the life it applies is destined to dissolve itself in the flowing of a *modus vivendi*. This aspect is what marks the substantial otherness of monastic rules for the law and juridical precepts; for monks, the rule does not refer to acts and events that must be regulated but coincides with their entire life.

The otherness of monastic life to the law was already clear to medieval jurists. Agamben, in this regard, refers to Bartolus' *Liber minoriticarum*, where the jurist claimed that the novelty of monastic order is so great that 'the *corpus iuris civilis* does not seem capable of being applied' to their form of life.[20] The embarrassment of legal thought confronting monastic rules is symptomatic of their somewhat ambiguous essence when compared with law's form. The presence of a precise set of penalties, among which the *excomunicatio* [excommunication] is the most severe, renders the determination of the nature of monastic rules even more complicated.

However, as Agamben notes, even if correlated with a system of penalties, 'in an epoch when punishments had an essentially afflictive character' the monastic rule seems 'to suggest that the punishment of the monks had an essentially moral and amendatory meaning, comparable to therapy prescribed by a doctor' (ibid. 31). The discussion on the legal or extra-legal nature of monastic rule, for Agamben, does not offer a viable solution to the question of their essence. 'What is decisive', he claims,

> is not so much the problem of the more or less juridi-cal nature of the rules ... but more generally that of the peculiar relation between life and norm that comes to be established in the rule. What is in question is thus not what in the rule is precept and what is advice, nor the degree of obligation that it implies, but rather a new way of conceiving the relation between life and law, which again calls into question the very concepts of observance and application, of transgression and fulfilment (ibid. 54).

The monk who promises to live according to the rule is not – as for the law – to 'obligate himself' to the 'fulfilment' of every letter of the rule: as long as the monk lives according to the customs of the monastery, in the case of omission of single aspects of the rule, he will still be considered as 'truly living the rule' (ibid., 55). Hence, Agamben sustains that the essence of the monastic condition is not substance or content, but a *habitus,* or form-of-life, in which rules are lived and not applied. What seems really in question in monasticism is not the enforcement of norms, but the monks' very form-of-life.[21]

What Agamben sees in the experience of monasticism is the paradigmatic example of an attempt at living a communitarian life without the mediation of a juridical/dogmatic apparatus, whose political meaning must be considered in the messianic context in which it has been conceptualised and put into practice. Following a thesis that has accompanied his interpretation of messianism, Christ (the Messiah) embodies the fulfilment and the end of all laws. Consequently, a life lived according to Christ's example cannot be informed and ruled by legal means: its form and content must be radically other with respect to any *nomos*. Therefore, it would be a contradiction in terms to model the messages of the Gospels in the form of the law. It follows the peculiar resistance of monastic orders in defining their form-of-life in juridical terms. Contrary to the law, which obliges the fulfilment of individual acts, monastic rule calls into question the entire way of life of the monk. The vow that the monk professes does not refer to their acts but produces a habitus or a form-of-life. Here, it is a life that produces a norm and not a norm that is applied to life; or rather, the rule does not simply apply to life, but remains immanent to it. It produces performatively the life that it is aimed at regulating while being determined by the life it assists in creating. The zone of indifference, between life and rule, in this way, deactivates the dichotomy of rule and life (or behaviour), which is structural to legal form and renders inoperative law's capture of life.

Constitutive rules

The opening of a space of indifference between norm and life represents the most novel and enigmatic aspect of the monastic rule. 'The cenobitic project – Agamben writes – by shifting the ethical problem from the level of the relationship between norm and action to that of a form of life, seems to call into question the very dichotomy of rule and life, universal and particular' (ibid. 72), through which we are used to consider both ethics and law. But what kind of rule is that which is indistinguishable from what or whom it is meant to rule? Agamben tries to answer this question by referring to what is known as *constitutive rule*, that is a norm that '[does] not prescribe a certain act or regulate a pre-existing state of things', but 'bring[s] into being the action or state of things' (ibid. 71) by itself.

Philosophers of language commonly place constitutive rules and regulative rules in opposition. In John Searle's words, regulative rules regulate 'antecendently or independently existing forms of behaviour; for example, many rules of etiquette regulate inter-personal relationships which exist independently of the rules', while constitutive rules 'do not merely regulate, they create or define new forms of behaviour'.[22] To explain the performance of these kinds of rules, and their power to constitute the reality they are called to regulate, Agamben looks to Wittgenstein's example of the game of chess. As Wittgenstein claimed, pieces like the king or the pawn consist of the sum of the rules defining their moves since 'chess is the game it is in virtue of all its rules'.[23] Here we are faced with the kind of rules that do not prescribe conduct, but produce entities and determine behaviours: 'a pawn is the sum of the rules for its moves: thus, the pawn does not follow the rule but is the rule' (UoB, 241). The concept of the constitutive rule seems to express the same indetermination between life and rule that defines monasticism, according to which 'rule is resolved without remainder into a vital praxis, and this coincides at every point with the rule' (ibid.).

The very idea of a constitutive rule, Agamben suggests, attempts to prove, 'something like a process of autoconstitution of being', the principle of the 'immanence of being to it-self'; the constitutive rule, he goes on, tries to convey 'this auto-hypostatic process, in which the constitutive is and remains immanent to the constituted' (ibid., 243), which finds its ultimate formulation in Spinoza's concept of *causa sui*. At the inception of his *Ethics*, Spinoza made use of such a notion to define the 'substance' (God), as auto-determined – as caused by itself. 'By that which is self-caused', he writes, 'I understand that whose essence involves existence or that whose nature cannot be conceived except as existing'.[24] In the idea of *causa sui*, essence and existence, thought and matter, coincide. The notion of constituent rule tries to express such self-constituting logic, according to which what is constituted remains immanent to the constitutive element, so much so, that it becomes indistinguishable from it. In this regard, the monk's form-of-life – much like the very existence of the pawn in a game of chess – coincides integrally with his *habitus*: it is, indeed, the sum of the constitutive rules defining his life.

Nevertheless, while apparently not presenting interpretative ambiguities, the concept of constitutive rule, Agamben claims, 'hides a difficulty' (ibid., 241), which makes it inadequate to express the immanence of the rule with a life. If considered as a formal set of commands, describing the structure of a game – the instructions of use – it is always possible for a constituent rule to be considered as separate from the plane of existence of what it constitutes. Agamben writes, the oft-invoked distinction between constitutive rule and pragmatic rule has no raison d'être. Every constitutive rule – the bishop moves in this or that way – can be formulated as a pragmatic rule – 'one cannot move the bishop except diagonally' – and vice versa. The same happens with grammatical rules: the syntactic rule 'in French the subject normally precedes the verb' can be formulated pragmatically as 'you cannot say *pars je*; you can only say *je pars.*' In truth, it is a matter of two different ways of considering the game – or language: one as a formal system that exists in itself (namely, as a *langue*) and another as a use or praxis (namely, as a *parole*). (ibid. 242)

As long as constitutive rules are considered from the point of view of their formal existence, as a set of rules defining determinate contexts and spaces of action, their supposed specificity disappears. Indeed, as Searle pointed out, constitutive rules are the matrix of institutions: 'institutional facts – he claims – are always applications of the form of the constitutive rule and institutions such as money, property and government are systems of such rules'.[25] From their formal structure and functions, constitutive rules *constitute* new realities and subjectivities, transcending any substantial relationship with what they constitute and rule.

A key point here that must be considered is that the very idea of 'rule', as a linguistic practice, can only re-propose the ontological device of the scission between essence and existence, which Agamben has defined as central to every ontological distinction. The logic of presupposition, with which the idea of a rule seems to be ingrained, is well expressed by Wittgenstein in paragraph 31 of the *Philosophical Investigations*:

Consider this further case: I am explaining chess to someone; and I begin by pointing to a chess piece and saying 'This is the king; it can move in this-and-this way', and so on. – In this case we shall say: the words 'This is the king' (or 'This is called "the king"') are an explanation of a word only if the learner already 'knows what a piece in a game is'. That is, for example, he has already played other games, or has watched 'with understanding' how other people play – and similar things. Only then will he, while learning the game, be able to ask relevantly, 'What is this called?' – that is, this chess piece. We may say: it only makes sense for someone to ask what something is called if he already knows how to make use of the name.[26]

The intelligibility of the idea of the king – of the words 'this is the king; it can move in this-and-this way' – presupposes something like the king from which it is possible to derive the rules (and the same idea) making up the king. In other words, the idea of the king, which as Wittgenstein claims is constituted by the rules of the game of chess, postulates the *subject*-king as existing in the outside world, as a connected but separated real reference.

In the above passage, Wittgenstein seems to suggest that this principle extends to other (if not all) linguistic elements: to ask what the name of a thing is presupposes the knowledge – and the existence – of something called 'name' and its use. The very same act of following a rule (for instance, following the rule of language, or of maths, etc.) presupposes the knowledge of what a rule is and the 'existence' of that rule as a stabilised custom and institution. To follow a rule, to make a report, to give an order, to play a game of chess, are customs (usages, institutions).[27] Only if we know how to deal with such customs, can we follow the related rules. Consequently, since the answer to the question on why rules are followed should be found on 'the outside', in the institutions and stabilised practices through which a rule takes its sense, acting according to a rule cannot be explained mechanically by referring to causes but can only be justified by referring to regularities: to custom and institutions, which remains in a way separate from the plane of living experiences – at the level of institutions. To recapitulate, the rule constitutes the ruled – the monk, the pawn, or the king – and can do this only by posing itself on a different level from the existence of the ruled. Norms, rules and laws presuppose the existence of customs and regularities; it is not possible to follow a norm, without something that makes following such a norm intelligible. We cannot follow a norm without the real concrete existence of that norm – as a fact, as a given institution or in other words as a 'regularity' giving the norm a meaning, which could be deduced or applied to specific subjects. For this reason, it could be argued that the rule presupposes the existence of the ruled, and what is ruled, in the moment of acting according to the rule is determined by it.

Yet there is a moment, Agamben claims, in which the rule and the ruled become in a way indistinguishable: if,

> we regard the game from the perspective of use and not from that of instructions, then the separation is no longer possible. On the pragmatic level, the game and the rule become indiscernible, and what appears in their becoming indeterminated is a use or a form of life ... In the same way, if we regard language from the point of view of grammatical rules, one can see that these define the language as a formal system while remaining distinct from it; but if we regard language in use (namely, as parole and not as langue), then it is just as true if not more so to say that the rules of grammar are drawn from the linguistic usage of the speakers and are not distinguished from them. (UoB, 242)

The moment of the use (and practice) deactivates in a sense the conception of the rule as an application of a principle to a single case. Of course, when we speak, play a game or follow rules, in other words when we act according to a certain norm, the rule and our behaviour enter a zone of indistinction. The rule is manifested in our action, and our action is the actualisation of the rule. In the moment of the use, the subject/object acting constitutes itself through the 'use' of a norm and, at the same time, the rule constitutes itself as rule by being used. For Agamben *use* is a key practical element to express the self-constituting logic (the Spinozian *causa sui*) of the ontology of immanence that is at stake in the idea of form-of-life.

Renouncing law

In the last section of *The Highest Poverty*, titled 'form-of-life', Agamben engages closely with the theory and practice of the Franciscan order, which represents, in his view, perhaps the most radical experiment in rethinking the relationship between law, rules and life. In the Franciscan literature, the syntagma *forma vitae* assumed the function of a proper technical term, in which the word 'form' is not something that is imposed on life but signifies a life that is simply its form. The reconciliation between life and rule happened for the Franciscans on the plane of life, rather than through an extreme intensification of discipline, as happened for other monastic orders. The rule of the friars minor is brief and concise, so much so that they seem not to obey a rule but simply live it. For the Franciscans, 'the traditional juridical idea of the observance of a precept is ... reversed. Not only is it the case that the friar minor does not obey the rule, but live it with an even more extreme reversal, it is life that is to be applied to the norm and not the norm to life' (ibid. 61).

As written in the *Regola Bollata* (1223) – the fundamental text of the Franciscan order – the scope of the rule is 'to live in obedience, in chastity, and without property' [*vivere in obedientia, in castitate, et sine proprio*].[28] The decisive corollary to the rule is the *abdication omnis iuris*, the radical renunciation of law, which Francis and his followers sustained as central for living according to the Gospels. This, in a way, is the greatest legacy of the Rule of Francis: the attempt at devising a form of life completely outside legal determinations and mundane powers, and the passage from the idea of a rule that defines itself negatively – through refusal or prohibition – to a 'form of law' whose task is the production of a specific form of life. Such a rule, instead of being simply prohibitive is intended as productive of some good: the form of life shaped according to the example of the Gospels, which is not grounded on the fear of punishment, but on the actual establishment of a way of life.[29]

What seems to be of most interest to Agamben in the Franciscan literature is the strategy that has been adopted to lay claim to the renunciation of living according to law. This strategy amounted to a proper ethical and political statement that put the order in a decisive tension with the Papacy, which at that time was always prone to reabsorb and regulate the novelty of monastic orders (and of other movements) into its juridical ranks. Most notably the friars minor defended their choice of embracing poverty and the subsequent renunciation of law, in economic terms, through the elaboration of a theory of the 'use of things' as separate from any property right, of the thing used. Crucial for such operation is the doctrine of the originary communion of goods, according to which property and all human law appeared with the Fall of Man. 'Just as in the state of innocence' Agamben writes 'human beings had the use of things, but not ownership, so also the Franciscans, following the example of Christ and the Apostles can renounce all property rights maintaining, however, the *de facto* use of things' (ibid. 113). Here, the renunciation of all kinds of property – and the revendication of poverty – implies the affirmation of a pre- or post-juridical way of life. The highest poverty [*altissima paupertas*] manifested in the 'use of things', epitomises in their perspective the 'form' of the renunciation of all the mundane law, and its establishment 'as a way of life' (ibid., 142).

To support and defend their renunciation of law, the Franciscans adopted a strategy that used juridical terminology to affirm, paradoxically, a form of life outside any juridical determination. As Agamben notes, 'what the Franciscans never tire of confirming … is the lawfulness for the brothers of making use of goods without having any right to them (neither of the property nor use)' (ibid. 110). Exemplary of such strategy, is the argument advanced by William of Ockham to legitimise the very practice of the use of things. Ockham begins by distinguishing between a natural right to use [*ius utendi naturale*] which is the one that all humans possess in case of necessity, from a positive right to use [*ius utendi positivum*] that is derived from certain human constitutions or pacts. For Ockham, the friars minor have no positive right to use the 'things' they have to use to survive. Instead, the brothers have permission to use things only for the time of extreme necessity;[30] 'they have renounced all property and every faculty of appropriating, but not the natural right of use, which is insofar as it is natural right, not renounceable' (HP, 114–15). Accordingly, Agamben argues, the friars minor, in order to legitimise their lawless life in poverty, proposed a substantial 'reversal and at the same time an absolutization of the state of exception' (ibid. 115). In the normal flow of their life, when positive laws are in force for all human beings, they do not possess rights, but only 'a license to use'; in the case of extreme necessity they enter in contact with the sphere of law, albeit natural and not positive. This implies that 'outside the state of necessity, they have no relationship with the law', and that 'what for others is normal thus becomes the exception for them; what for others is an exception becomes for them a form of life' (ibid.). To sum up, for Ockham the liceity of the Franciscans' poverty, and the consequent usage of things outside and against juridical determinations of property is legitimised by the licence or permission to *use*, which human beings possess naturally. This licence pertains to all humankind, and it is delegated – according to the originary communion of goods – to the common use of men together (and not to the use of individuals singularly). This is why those who live in a state of poverty, having renounced the right to property, have the natural 'right' to use things when it becomes necessary for living.

By differentiating the natural right to use in case of necessity and the positive right to use and to property, Ockham (and the Franciscans more generally) applied, reformulated and complicated the principle *in necessitate omnia sunt communia* [in the case of necessity everything is in common], with which medieval jurisprudence allowed the possibility of infringement of private property.[31] Borrowed from Roman law, this principle is present in various forms in medieval scholasticism, most notably in Gratian's *Decretum* in which it is formulated as follows: *In casu necessitatis omnia sunt communia, id est communicanda* [In the case of necessity all things are common, that means are to be made common], and it was used to a certain extent to justify (legally) poverty.[32] In this regard, Aquinas argues that theft is licit for a starving family since: 'in a condition of necessity, all things are in common'; and thus it is not a sin if someone takes something of another which necessity has made.[33] The use of things, for the poor, is not a crime as long as it is restricted to a situation of succour and necessity, since, in the words of Albertus Magnus, 'what is given to the poor it is ours and it is theirs: ours because of *dominium* [positive right] theirs because of a natural law [*iuris naturalis*], which put in common all good in case of necessity'.[34] Here, necessity – much like the state of exception – defines a juridical operator that permits the infringement of the right to (private) property, as sanctioned by positive law. And because of this, Agamben maintains, by legitimising their renunciation of law and poverty on the ground of necessity, the Franciscans remained somehow embroiled in a legal determination of their lawless life. Their strategy assumes the form of a juridical paradox: the legal justification of illegality. And in the end, this accounts for the most significant limitation of the Franciscan proposal (and its ultimate failure): by giving their renunciation of law in legal form and legitimacy, they made the *highest poverty* the outcome of a juridical strategy.

Let us now delve a little deeper into the principle according to which in case of necessity everything is in common. This precept articulates the capture by the law (or legalisation) of poverty and the possibility of *using things in common* outside and against private property. Necessity – what allows the possibility of 'legally' infringing the positive law of property – is the operator of such capture. For the law, the negation of property and the access to the common cannot have a legal form other than the exception (which is ultimately the negation of the legal form). Consequently, any positive 'normal' determination of poverty, use of things and common, cannot help but pass through the negation of the apparatuses with which law tries to capture its negation; or alternatively, as Agamben also suggested, through an act of profanation, that is through the 'restitution to common use' (Pr, 82) of things otherwise separated and fenced behind legal (but also political and economic) apparatuses.

The end of all lives

Although destined to fail, the Franciscans' attempt to live in poverty and renounce law as an instrument to structure a communal life is, for Agamben, still worth examining. Indeed, in the radicality with which the friars minor have pondered their *modus vivendi*, it is possible to trace the paradigm of what Agamben has termed form-of-life. In the closing of *The Highest Poverty*, Agamben looks into the work of Pierre Jean Olivi, a thirteenth-century Franciscan theologian. In his writings, Agamben finds a full expression of what, ontologically and existentially, the Franciscan *forma vitae* entails. Agamben here refers to Olivi's quaestio: *Quid ponat ius vel dominium?*, which includes an ontology of law articulated through an engagement with the problem of 'whether ownership or royal or priestly jurisdiction adds something real to the person who exercises them or to things or persons over whom they are exercised' (HP, 134). What is really in question in such texts is the explanation of all those objects like norms, rules and commands whose existence is dependent, not so much on their substances, but on their concrete effects. Olivi writes:

> Insofar as you can consider them with subtlety and clarity you will find that signification does not add to the real essence of the thing that is used as a sign anything other than the mental intention of those who have instituted it and accepted its validity and of those who accept it in action in order to signify and of those who hear it or receive it as a sign. But in the voice or gesture that are produced by the command of this intention, ... signification adds to the intention of the one signifying and to the essence of the thing that functions as a sign the habit of commanded effect ... and the command produced by the intention of the one who signifies.[35]

Those special objects, customs and institutions – like property and royal jurisdictions – are signs whose reality should not be doubted, but do not add anything 'essential' to their subjects. Here, as Agamben points out, we are faced with an 'ontology that is so to speak existentialist and not essentialist', according to which even though the 'real efficacy of rights and signs' is recognised as having a definite reality, they are nevertheless 'demoted from the level of essences and made to hold as pure effectualities that depend solely on a command' (ibid., 135–6), and its acceptance.

For Olivi, the whole realm of social practices, formed and informed by norms, rights and signs, exists only in the mental intentions of humans – in the form of 'collective intentionality and never at the level of essences'.[36] Accordingly, all social, political and legal phenomena are real in so far as they are efficacious. To speak of the reality of an office or royal power is to speak of their effects on the mind of humans: they are just signs – meanings, cultural formations, made real by their effects on the human mind and behaviour. Law's categories and norms, but also sacraments and offices, institutions and patterns of behaviour do not add anything essential to the subject to which they are referred; they exist only at the *existential level* as effects of signs (or as signature). Therefore, Agamben writes, 'the conflict with the law – or rather, the attempt to deactivate it and render it inoperative through use – is situated on the same purely existential level on which the operativity of law and liturgy acts', and the form-of-life the Franciscans tried to constitute is the 'purely existential reality that must be liberated from the signature of law and office or duty' (ibid., 136).

The theory and practice of the life of the friars minor is a paradigm for form-of-life, in that it represents one of the most radical attempts at overcoming the law as a form of regulation of human life, moving towards the establishment of a community of life not based on structures of power and violent coercion but the simple practice of use and poverty. However, such renunciation of law should not be seen solely from a political or juridical perspective. The liberation of life from the signature of law or duty is indeed a form of de-subjectification, which implies a renewed ethical and onto-logical conception of human life, based simply on living a life liberated from authoritative commands, rules and norms. But this necessitates the radical rethinking of the traditional relationship between the singularity of the subject and the many different signatures shaping our forms of life. And as Agamben points out the Franciscan form-of-life should be seen as the end of all lives (*finis omnium vitarum*), 'the final *modus*, after which the manifold historical dispensation of *modi vivendi* is no longer possible: the "highest poverty," with its use of things, is the form-of-life that begins when all the West's forms of life have reached their historical consumma-tion' (ibid., 143).

What does it mean for a life to be liberated from the signa-ture of law and duty? What form does a life that consists of the end of all lives in which Western culture has materialised itself have? The answer to these questions lies in Agamben's *use* of messianic theology. As Kotsko has noted, the Italian philosopher engages with the history of monasticism from the early stages to the Franciscan order, because he sees in such experience the manifestation of a truly messianic life.[37] The idea of liberation of life from legal determinations should not be seen as simply an opposition to legal instrumentality;

rather it is properly a strategy to deactivate the law, rendering it inoperative. Monastic communities did not simply oppose the law to overthrow its temporal dominion; their strategy was more akin to that of inoperativity, subtraction and 'destitution', which Agamben considers as the core political and ethical operation inaugurated by the thought of the messianic.

Of course, this does not come as a surprise. The problem of a coming politics and a renewed form of life, for Agamben, is challenged on the ground of the messianic. His reading of Paul's letters – mediated by Benjamin's anarchist political theology – remains at the heart of the definition of inoperativity and destituent potential. For Agamben, the messianic tradition offers the fundamental theoretical instruments for considering a redemptive political action that goes beyond the religious/theological context in which it has been elaborated: indeed, 'the messianic' he argues 'is always profane, and never religious'.[38] Albeit rooted in the Judaic and Christian tradition, Agamben's engagement with the messianic seeks to 'pass beyond the specificity of any particular religious tradition and to arrive at the conditions of a messianism implicit in any historical formulation of a Messiah figure', or of salvific forces more generally. The messianic, in Agamben, represents paradigmatically the logic underpinning any given redemptive event.[39] Consequently, the very definition of form-of-life, as the guiding concept of the coming politics, as the 'revocation of all factical vocations' (UoB, 277) (which Agamben repeats as a mantra) is modelled on that of (Pauline) messianic life, which he defines alternatively as the 'revocation of every vocation' (TTR, 23), the 'revocation of each and every concrete factical vocation' (ibid.), but also the 'revocation of every worldly condition' (ibid., 43).

What makes the idea of the messianic event particularly interesting, for Agamben, is its being the 'limit concept' through which 'religion confronts the problem of the Law' (P, 163). The coming of the Messiah is envisaged as provoking a radical transformation of all the mundane law (that of the exile or that of the Fall of Man) not simply through the imposition of a new law or the destruction of the old one, but through its 'fulfilling'. The Messiah brings back the law as it was before the Fall, at the same time opening a new world order. Messianism, accordingly, is 'animated by two opposed tensions: the first is a restorative tendency aiming at the *restitutio in integrum* of the origin, and the second is a utopian impulse turned instead toward the future and renewal' (ibid., 166). It entails a substantial paradoxical tension caused by the union of the ideas of the transformation of the 'actual' world, and the immanent opening of a new one: for the messianic 'another world' and 'another time' are present in this world and in this time.[40]

Agamben's use of such theologically profane tradition is guided by Paul's letters, which he considers the 'fundamental messianic text for the Western tradition' (TTR, 1). Central to such foundational text, he claims, is the question of the impact of the appearance of the Messiah on the world's normative ordering, which in the Pauline letters is expressed with the verb *katargein*. This term, Agamben notes, is 'a compound of *argeō*, which in turn derives from the adjective *argos*, meaning inoperative, not-at work (*a-ergos*), inactive' (ibid., 95). The Messiah, in Paul (1 *Corinthians* 15:24), 'will render inoperative [*katargese*] every power, every authority, and every potential' (UoB, 273). Although the verb is customarily translated as 'destruction' or 'annulment', Agamben points out how for Paul, the *Parousia* is not 'a matter of destroying the law, which is "holy and just," but of deactivating its action with respect to sin, because it is through the law that human beings come to know sin and desire' (ibid.). The coming of the Messiah produces a qualitative transformation of the law that is not abolished, but it is rendered inoperative, 'destitute of its power to command' (ibid., 274).

In the context of Paul's engagement with the Judaic tradition, such a messianic operation involves a material transformation of Jewish identity, which should pave the way for a new form of communitarian (Christian/messianic) life. As Agamben notes, the 'principle of the law' is 'division' (TTR, 47), and the grounding of Jewish law is made possible only through a clear-cut separation between Jews and non-Jews, between *Ioudaioi* and *ethnē*. Based on Pauline letters, the Messiah operates properly as a 'destituent potential' of the law that 'defines Jewish identity, without for that reason constituting another identity' (UoB, 274). The call to Christians to live under the law of the Messiah (what Paul calls the messianic vocation) should not be considered as the establishment of a new identity; rather, it manifests itself in the form of revocation and nullification of all identities. Exemplary of such logic are the oft-cited passages from 1 Corinthians, from which Agamben brought out some central aspects of his messianic-inoperative politics:

> If at the moment of your call you find yourself in the condition of a slave, do not concern yourself with it: but even if you can become free, make use rather of your condition as a slave.[41]
>
> I mean, brothers and sisters, time has grown short; what remains is so that those who have wives may be *as not* having, and those who mourn as not mourning, and those who rejoice as not rejoicing, and those who buy as not possessing, and those who use the world as not abusing.[42]

Agamben regards the *as not* as a deposition without abdication of all identities. The Messiah embodies a process of a transfiguration of all factual (juridical and social) conditions, which poses itself as a third element between the simple reaffirmation or restoration of the status quo and its radical abolishment. Living in the form of the Pauline 'as not', he claims, 'deactivates in the present all the juridical conditions and all the social behaviours of the members of the messianic community' (KG, 248), without grounding new singularities or communitarian identities.

The technical term describing the process of deposition of all identity characterising the Christian form of life is 'to make use' [*chresai*]. The form-of-life that Agamben draws from Pauline messianism is 'that which ceaselessly deposes the social conditions in which [one] finds itself to live, without negating them, but simply by using them' (UoB, 274); in an gesture of de-subjectification. In this regard he writes:

> The coming of the Messiah means that all things, even the subjects who contemplate it, are caught up in the as not, called and revoked at one and the same time. No subject could watch it or act as if at a given point. The messianic vocation dislocates and, above all, nullifies the entire subject. (TTR, 41)

The Pauline messianic call, in other words, conveys the idea of a form of human living in which individuals are not determined by their specific socio-juridical forms, but by their use. It is through a new use of the self that identities and, ultimately, the whole of the subject are deposed and a form-of-life is constituted. The messianic weak force eradicates every (f)actual identity restoring them to 'a place of pure potentiality beyond the reaches of any sovereign power'.[43]

From Agamben's profane perspective, the human condition that Paul's messianism purports coincides with a form of political redemption manifested in the new use of individual social/juridical statuses. The facts of being a slave, of having a wife, of mourning or rejoicing, are not something to abide by or adhere to, but living conditions to be used freely. From the perspective of the 'as not' the subject is displaced from its prescribed place in the world, making it possible to reside in it without becoming a term in it.[44] For the messianic life, every individual action becomes part of a multitude of potential possible worlds, instead of being the determination of *this* particular world.[45] And this makes of it – for Agamben – a profane paradigm of form-of-life that could interrupt the tragic flow of human life captured in the architecture of sovereign powers and law.

The Western biopolitical machine operates on the grounds of an idea of polity that presupposes forms of exclusion of specific forms of life, from the reality of the form(s) of life, protected and represented in the biopolitical body of the state. To resist such a form of politics, Agamben thinks it necessary to radically oppose the very production of personal identity; the process of subjectification that makes a community a community *of*.[46] Further, he claims, 'what the State cannot tolerate in any way … is that the singularities form a community without affirming an identity, that humans co-belong without any representable condition of belonging' (CC, 86). A form-of-life is the singularity that can never be represented as part of determined body political, for which all the social and juridical forms constitutive of a subjectivity are never a determination, but the objects of a free, unregulated use.

The slave

In *The Time that Remains*, Agamben turns on the Pauline use of the term 'slave', with which the Apostle introduced himself to the Romans. 'Paul called as slave of Jesus the Messiah' [*Paulos doulos christou Iēsou klētos*]; these are the words opening 1 *Romans*. Normally, slave (*doulos*) refers to the condition of the servant in its relation of subjection to the authority of the master. However, when read considering the messianic tone of Paul's message, the term assumes a different connotation. Agamben contends that the term slave here is 'used to express the neutralization that the divisions of the law and all juridical and social conditions, in general, undergo as a consequence of the messianic event' (TTR, 13), that is the peculiar transformation – nullification/ destitution – of all juridical and factical vocation that the messianic event produces. The messianic conception of the slave is further developed by Agamben in the first part of *The Use of Bodies*, devoted to the theorisation of slavery in Aristotle's *Politics* (and in antiquity in general). Here the figure of the slave is presented, paradigmatically, as the figure of a being of pure potentiality, with no defined vocation or identity, whose status is the proof of humankind's absolute faculty to cultivate a multitude of vocations in the form of the potential.

Aristotle defines the nature of the slave with the expression 'the use of the body'. In *Politics* we read:

> These human beings differ among themselves like the soul from the body or the human from the animal – as in the case of those whose work is the use of the body ... the lower sort are by nature slaves, for whom it is better to be commanded with this command.[47]

The relation between the master and the slave, Agamben writes, is of the same nature as that which separates and unites soul and body: 'the soul is to the body as the master is to the slave' (UoB, 4). The soul commands the body, as the master makes use of the slave. Central to the definition of the nature of the slave is the *ergon*, the work and proper vocation of humans, which Aristotle posed in the *Nicomachean Ethics*. Here, asking the question whether there is a vocation for humans, Aristotle affirmed that 'the work of the human being is the being-at-work of the soul according to the logos' (*ergon anthropou psyches energeia kata logon*).[48] Accordingly, the definition of the slave as that being whose work is the use of the body appears – Agamben points out – surprising, since for Aristotle the slave is and remains a human being. Implicit in a different definition of the nature of the human-slave is the possibility of a different form of purposeless being human (with no vocation), the political and ethical potential of which have been neglected (at best) or captured in the dreadful history of slavery.

Aristotle's definition of the nature of the slave concerns primarily the physical problem of slavery, that is the question of the very existence of the body of the slave. For Aristotle the essential trait of the slave's body is not deduced from some simple natural determinations, but conceived on the basis of its essential function. Agamben here refers to a passage in which Aristotle compares the slave to '*ktemata*, household equipment (tools, in the broad sense that this term originally had) and the instruments (*organa*) that are parts of the administration of a household' (ibid., 10). Instruments, Aristotle writes, are of different kinds, some of them possess a life, others do not, and the slave is in this sense an 'animate equipment' [*ktema ti empsychon*]. Thus, the slave, as a living instrument, is part of the equipment of the household, at a master's disposal. Yet, the instrument-slave is of a special, unproductive kind. Aristotle introduces another distinction: instruments like shuttles and plectra,

> are productive organs [*poietika organa*], while equipment is by contrast a practical [*praktikon*] instrument. From a shuttle, we get something else besides the use of it [*heteron ti genetai para ten chresin autes*], whereas of a garment or of a bed there is only the use [*he chresis monon*]. Further, as production [*poiesis*] and praxis [*praxis*] are different in kind, and both require instruments, the instruments that they employ must likewise differ in kind. The mode of life [*bios*] is a praxis and not a production, and therefore the slave is an assistant for things of praxis. Now 'equipment' has the same meaning as 'part' [*morion*, 'piece,' what belongs to an ensemble]; for the part is not only a part of something else

[*allou*] but totally belongs to it [*holos* – some manuscripts have *haplos*, 'absolutely,' or with a still stronger expression, *haplos holos*, 'absolutely and totally']. This same can be said for equipment. The master is only the master of the slave and is not [part] of him; the slave is not only slave of the master but is totally [part] of him. Hence, we see what is the nature [*physis*] and the potential [*dynamis*] of the slave: the one who, while being human [*anthropos on*], is by nature of another, is a slave by nature; and the one who is of another who, while being human, is equipment, that is, a practical and separate instrument [*organon praktikon kai choriston*].[49]

The slave, therefore, is a non-productive instrument that, unlike productive ones (like shuttles and plectra), does not produce, when put to work, anything except the simple use of the body. Much like the use of a bed or a piece of clothing, the use of the body of the slave is purposeless and must be understood not in a productive sense, but simply in a practical sense. And for this reason, the assimilation of the modern worker to the slave – for Agamben – should be reconsidered. As long as to work means to produce commodities (or value), the slave does not work.

   Though recognised in its instrumental existence, the body of the slave entertains with that of the master a relationship that decisively complicates its status. The assimilation to a *ktema* [equipment] makes of the body of the enslaved an integral part of the master, much like an organ. For this reason, Agamben argues that the slave 'is a part (of the body) of the master, in the "organic" and not simply instrumental sense of the term', so much so that the master/slave relationship is defined as a 'community of life' [*koinonos zoes*] (ibid., 13). For this reason, 'by putting in use his own body, the slave is, for that very reason, used by the master, and in using the body of the slave, the master is, in reality, using his own body' (ibid., 14). This means that the body of the slave does not belong to the slave, but is part of a community of life and is situated in Agamben's words in a 'zone of indifference between one's own body and the body of another' (ibid., 22). In the use of the body of the slave, the traditional categories with which the Greeks (and West more generally) have thought human life seems to be reshuffled. The body of the slave as 'animate instrument' is that mode of life that allows the political life to be lived (by the masters), which as a consequence appears situated at the threshold that separates and articulate *nomos* and *physis*, *zoe* and *bios*, the house and the city. 'The slave' Agamben writes, 'is the human being without work, who renders possible the realization of the work of the human being, that living being who, though being human, is excluded ... so that human beings can have a human life, which is to say a political life' (ibid., 23).

In a move that might appear counterintuitive, Agamben reads the Aristotelean slave as a paradigm of a form-of-life. He hypothesises that in the figure of the slave is expressed a form of a human being whose essence and existence are never restrained and actualised in specific forms, acts or vocations, but remains living in their own potentiality. The phenomenon of slavery carved out in the interstices of Greek antiquity, is an exemplary modality of a human condition, the investigation of which could be useful to think of a coming politics. 'The anthropology that we have inherited from classical philosophy', Agamben writes, is modelled according to the image of the 'free man', as part of a political community, exercising its *logos*, which involves, however, the exclusion of certain forms of life (the slave, the *homo sacer*, etc.) as a necessary condition (ibid., 20). From the point of view of the slave, then, human anthropology – but also the very ideas of politics and society – would have looked differently, probably more humane.

Let us now recapitulate the logical consequence of the notion of 'use of the body' and the peculiar status of slaves. As animate equipment, which stands in an organic relationship with the master, the slave when performing determinate actions is used by the master, who in the work of the slave has his own body in action. In the use of the body the master acquires the possibility of being such, and at the same time, the slave recognises itself as a slave through the subtraction of any possible claim to ownership of his/her own body or actions. In the moment of acting, enslaved human beings are acted-through by their masters, who are consequently the subjects to which the actions are attributed. Conversely, slaves are those beings whose existence is not defined by an actual status or identity, but by the subtraction of any positive characteristic from their actual form of life. 'Unlike the cobbler, the carpenter, the flute player, or the sculptor', Agamben writes, 'the slave, even if he carries out these activities … is and remains essentially without work'; contrary to those who are acting 'positively' according to a determined identity and social status, the *praxis* of the slave 'is not defined by the work that he produces but only by the use of the body' (ibid., 15).

No actions, no identity and no vocation belong to the slave. The instrumental essence of the slave makes *it* a being of pure potentiality appearing when all positive characters and forms of life are deactivated and left open to simple use. In the definition of 'use of body', Agamben envisages the possibility of form of life that resists the mechanism of sub-jectification remaining open (in contact) with its potentiality. Indeed, Aristotle denied slaves every positive subjectivity, which belongs only to the master. The action performed by the slave is not an expression of the simple contingent use of the body that does not exhaust itself in the act but remains open to a multiplicity of uses. For slaves, the revocation of any vocation is an actual way of life. They are in this sense the non-subject of a general life, underlying any possible acquisi-tion of subjectivities.[50]

Of course, for Agamben, it is not a matter of imagining the slave happy. His reading of slavery in antiquity must be con-sidered for what it is: an exercise in paradigmatic philosophy – which has near to no overlap with modern slavery and the discussion that animates its current understanding – that allegorically tries to highlight thought formations that could be of some help in imagining a politics to come. In the case of the slave, there exists the idea of a human condition with no determinate vocation, a being of pure potentiality, which in history assumed the legal form of institutionalised exploi-tation, exclusion from the realm of the 'person' and the reduction of the human to the status of thing. 'It is possible', Agamben claims, 'that the slave represents the capture within the law of a figure of human acting that still remains for us to recognize' (UoB, 23). Slavery is, in this sense, the outcome of a capture in the law of a human praxis – the institutionalisation of a segment of human potentiality, whose reification into a stable relation of power has transfigured it, making it to a certain extent unrecognisable.

But what is captured within the law? What is the figure of human actions that is transfigured in the legal form of slavery? Agamben tries to answer these questions by referring to the Marxist economist Alfred Sohn-Rethel (1899–1990), who maintained that in the exploitation of one human being by another the immediate relationship that humans maintain with nature is replaced by a relationship between humans. Sohn-Rethel, in this regard, writes that in the relation of exploitation:

> The productive relationship humans-nature becomes the object of a human-human relationship, is subjected to its order and to its laws and therefore 'denatured' with respect to the 'natural' state, by being subsequently realized solely according to the laws of the forms of mediation that represent its affirmative negation.[51]

In slavery, the relationship between master and nature is mediated by the relationship with the slave's body; and the body of the slave consequently becomes a medium (instrument). However, Agamben claims, it might be the case that 'mediating one's own relationship with nature through the relation with another human being' is 'from the very beginning what is properly human' and that slavery contains, therefore, a 'memory of this original anthropogenetic operation' (ibid.). Making use of one's relation with another in the exchange with the environment is not unnatural (or unhuman); on the contrary, it accounts for a *factum socialitatis* intrinsic in the becoming human of humans, which has no negative value in itself. 'The perversion', Agamben goes on, 'begins only when the reciprocal relation of use is appropriated and reified in juridical terms through the constitution of slavery as a social institution' (ibid.). Humans are those 'animals' who constitute themselves as ethical (and political) beings, precisely because their interaction with the environment they build, and shape is mediated by the relationship of *use* with other humans. In slavery, such a relationship becomes the object of a process of reification, which obligates and commands specific subjects to live in the condition of being exploited, used, abused and reduced to the status of things. And as long as the relationship of *use* of one's bodies, and the body of the other, remains the object of processes of appropriation and legal codification, what is substantially a social-natural datum decays into mere exploitation.

Here, Agamben's aversion to the law appears clearly. What is ultimately perverse in slavery is not the reciprocal use of bodies among human beings – which is part of human existence as a social animal – but its institutionalisation, and its capture in law's machinery, which corrupts an anthropogenetic element of human sociality, transforming it into an object of power relation. The legal codification of slavery is, from this perspective, the instrument through which something potentially gratuitous and free – the common and reciprocal use of bodies – is institutionalised, appropriated and transformed into an extreme form of brutal exploitation, which for centuries excluded specific subjects from the realm of the authentically qualified life, denying them not only access to social statuses but even the property of their own body.

The form of life of the slave represents something unsaid that is concealed in the folds of the history of juridical and political institutions, and whose existence is the attestation that a different form of life is possible. Agamben invites us to see the polities in which we are living as including (via its exclusion) the possibility of a community and a form-of-life without vocations and substantial identities that consequently is potentially shared by all, which accounts for a possible source of coming happy life. Covered up under the legal-institutional stratification and at the same time alien to social and legal codification, such a form of life finds in the use of the body of the slave a paradigmatic expression. For Agamben, the task before us is to liberate the slave's form of life from capture by the law.

Notes

1. Salzani (2013).
2. It must be noted that Agamben defines the hyphens in this way: 'the hyphen is, in this sense, the most dialectical of punctuation marks, since it unites only to the degree that

it distinguishes and distinguishes only to the degree that it unites' (P, 153).

3. In the twentieth century, beginning with Rudolf Kjellén's *Der Staat als Lebensform* (1917), and then with Ludwig Wittgenstein's *Philosophical Investigations*, the concept of form of life has been used in different ambits and with different meanings. Certainly, the notion of form of life is not of Agamben's original coinage. However, as we will see later in this chapter, what inspired the adoption of such a concept by Agamben is not so much twentieth-century philosophy, but earlier configurations including medieval monasticism.

4. The label 'philosophical anthropology' refers to a philosophical approach that, under the influence of phenomenology, tries to challenge the main questions raised by anthropological studies. It has emerged in Germany primarily thanks to the influence of the work of Max Scheler, Arnold Gehlen and Helmuth Plessner. See: Scheler (2009); Gehlen (1988); Plessner (1970). On 'philosophical anthropology', see: Cusinato (2008); Rasini (2008); de Mul (2014).

5. The term is taken from J.G. Herder who used it in his 1772 *Treatise on the Origin of Language*; see Herder (1986).

6. The idea of a peculiar inborn natural incompleteness of humans, can be traced back to the thought of Fichte, whose theories had a decisive impact on the development of 'philosophical anthropology'. See Tarizzo (2010: 56–7).

7. Gehlen (1988: 49).
8. Croce and Salvatore (2013: 42).
9. Fabini (1991: 56).
10. Croce and Salvatore (2013: 42).
11. See Gehlen (1961, especially Chapter 1).
12. Croce and Salvatore (2013: 43).
13. Supiot (2007: 27).
14. Stiegler (2009: 3).
15. Supiot (2007: 28).
16. Ibid., 21.
17. De Caroli (2016: 214).
18. Book of Acts (1988: 100).
19. Schmitt (2008: 75–6).
20. Bartolus (1555: 190).
21. Kotsko and Dickinson (2015: 8).
22. Searle (1969: 33).
23. Wittgenstein (2009: 86e).
24. Spinoza (2018: 1).
25. Searle (2018: 52).

26. Wittgenstein (2009: 19^e).
27. Ibid., 87^e.
28. Francesco D'Assisi (2004: 109).
29. Coccia (2006: 23).
30. Ockham (1963), as quoted in HP.
31. Tierney (1997: 73).
32. Couver (1961).
33. ... *in necessitate sunt omnia communia, et ita non videtur esse peccatum, si alicuis rem alterius accipiat propter necessitate sibi factam commune*: Aquinas q.66 art. 7 of *Summa Theologie*.
34. *Illud quod exhibemus miseris, et nostrum est, et suum est: nostrum per dominium, et suum per rationem debiti iuris naturalis, quod in necessitate communicat bona.* Albertus Magno (1894: 611).
35. Olivi (1945: 324); quoted in HP, 136.
36. De Caroli (2016: 220).
37. Kotsko and Dickinson (2015: 193).
38. Agamben (2004: 120).
39. Dickinson (2011: 87).
40. Zartaloudis (2011: 292).
41. 1 Corinthians 7:21 as quoted in UoB, 274.
42. 1 Corinthians 7:29–31 as quoted in UoB, 274.
43. Dickinson (2011: 89).
44. Prozorov (2014: 145).
45. Cristensen (2018).
46. Whyte (2010).
47. Aristotle, (1254b 17–20), as quoted in UoB, 5.
48. Aristotle (1098a 7), as quoted in UoB, 5.
49. Aristotle (1254a 1–17), quoted in UoB, 12.
50. Christiaens (2018).
51. Adorno and Sohn-Rethel (1991: 32), as quoted in UoB.

Two

The Theory and Practice of Destituent Potential

> Why bother to confront a 'power' which has lost all meaning and become sheer Simulation? Such confrontations will only result in dangerous and ugly spasms of violence by the emptyheaded shit-for-brains who've inherited the keys to all the armories and prisons.
>
> *Hakim Bey*

Politics of inoperativity

In two lectures delivered in 2013, Agamben introduced into his philosophical vocabulary the notion of destituent power – eventually reformulated in the book *The Use of Bodies* as destituent potential.[1] As the wording of the concept suggests, destituent power (or potential) represents ideally a third element with respect to the dialectic constituent/constituted power, with which modern political theory has thought the origin and the legitimacy of polities. Underpinning the adoption of such a concept stands Agamben's fundamental scepticism towards the very idea of constituent power. In the 'inevitable dialectic between constituent power and constituted power', he claims, 'a power that was only just overthrown ... will rise again in another form' (WDP, 70), with the same substance. Every effort to radically change a regime carried out under the banner of constituent power will end up recreating the same apparatuses of control and oppression that were the target of the exigency to change.

As Agamben sustained in the inaugural volume of his *Homo Sacer* series, no matter how it is thought, constituent power is destined to be embroiled in the logic of sovereignty and in that form of violence that preserve the law in its mythical foundation. The idea of a destituent power or potential is conjured up to think the breaking of the dialectic that connects constituent and constituted power. If constituent power relates to a mythical-transcendental origin, grounded on a supposed will of a specific agent (the people, the nation, etc.), destituent potential embodies the thought of a praxis that remains essentially immanent to the constituted order to unmaking it, to render it inoperative, without giving room to the transcendental space in which a new order of the same substance of the old one could be established as legitimate and enforceable.

The adoption of the term destituent potential is surely a key moment in Agamben's speculation over a politics to come, since it condenses the logic underpinning the practical horizon in which the deposition of the governmental machinery could take place. For Agamben, something like a coming (emancipatory) politics is not the teleological accomplishment of a planned process, nor the destruction/reconstruction of a world or a form of life but consists in rendering inoperative all those forces shaping human life, opening them to a different purposeless use. The destituent gesture, in this sense, is the one that strives to make inoperativity a concrete option. Inoperativity, Agamben claims, 'coincides completely and constitutively' with the destitution of the forms of life in which humans are living; and 'this destitution is the coming politics' (ibid., 74). The coming politics is therefore a politics of inoperativity,[2] which comes through and after the destitution of the apparatuses of power that make us subject to specific social and legal identities.

Agamben has delineated his concept of inoperativity through a fairly long series of paradigms: the *Sabbath* in Judaism and more generally what it is known in social sciences as *feast*; the empty throne; the practice of play; the operation of the *Messiah*; the contemplative life; etc. As Sergei Prozorov puts it, in its common use inoperativity does not refer to an 'absence of action and failure to function'; on the contrary inoperativity is the affirmation of 'a form of praxis that is devoid of any *telos* or task, [which] does not rely upon any essence and does not correspond to any nature'.[3] Against the pre-eminence that the Western tradition assigned to work and productivity as consubstantial to the image of the human, and against the idea of politics as something that has to be done and realised, Agamben opposes an ethical and political inoperative living freed from any assigned purpose, work and identity as the ground for a renewed form of community.

Much has been written on the concept of inoperativity, and it is not our task to retrace its genesis or its articulation.[4] What is instead interesting to note, is that despite its apparent abstractness, Agamben approached the thought of inoperativity because of a specific historical/political exigency. As he wrote in the introduction to Paolo Virno's *Convenzione e Materialismo. L'unicità senza aura,*[5]

> Throughout the 1970s, in Europe, a disillusioned but not hopeless generation appeared to lay claim to a form of politics intended not as an autonomous and totalitarian sphere, but as the ethical community of singularities; to a history conceived not as a linear continuity, but a history whose fulfilment has been deferred for too long; to a work not finalised by the production of goods, but to an inoperativity without ends, which nonetheless is not unproductive.[6]

Written in 1986, this passage includes one of the earliest occurrences of the term inoperativity in Agamben's oeuvre and clearly exposes the political significance of such a concept. Inoperativity here is the keyword of a political proposal that emerged out of the disenchantment with the conception of politics, that of the Liberal-capitalist and orthodox-Marxist, which in that period has once more revealed its frailties. Faced with the transformation of the labour–capital relationship, the gradual eclipse of the working class as political subjectivity, and the failure of the soviet political experience (which become obvious at this moment), the elaboration of a renewed strategy to think a different politics was an urgent need. In the 1960s and 1970s, a generation of scholars, which eventually had a long-lasting influence on revolutionary-emancipatory movements, advanced the concept of a politics of the common and of the singular against that of individualist universalism, and the idea of inoperative work as an anti-capitalist practice against labour. As Jason E. Smith noted, the influence of the experience of the Italian movement of *operaismo* (and

post-operaismo), played a central role in Agamben's development of a theory of inoperativity.[7] In the 1970s, Italy was a
privileged political laboratory for the formulation of theories
for radical-revolutionary transformations of capitalist society
alternative to the Marxist-Leninist tradition. Ideas such as the
refusal of work, not simply as a form of idealisation of idleness, but as a strategy to tear down the economic and political apparatus and the identities settled around the figure of
the workingman in a capitalist state, formed part of revolutionary strategies and vocabularies.[8] Inoperativity could be
regarded, at large, as Agamben's contribution to the need to
think through and against the entire cloud of modern political categories.

~ * ~

Although lacking a systematic definition, it is possible to
delineate some key tenets that inoperativity, as the form of
coming politics, and destitution, as its operative logic, entail:
(1) As we have seen in the previous chapter, Agamben thinks
the politics to come as opposed to the state's form and the
legal regulation of living. The community of singularities,
which is somehow the communal form that inoperative
politics establishes – as Agamben maintains in the *Coming
Community* – refuses and opposes the state's institution as
a political medium. (2) But inoperativity also involves a
remodelling of human action in a non-purposeful sense: it
calls into question the very essence of humanity as an assem-
blage of *animalia laborantia*, with the consequent critique of
the very concepts of work and production. (3) This aspect,
in Agamben's work, is linked to a substantial rethinking of
the ontological grounds on which the very question of the
human has been traditionally thought, favouring an ontology of potentiality over that of actuality and action. 'The only
coherent way to understand inoperativeness', he writes, 'is
to think of it as a generic mode of potentiality that is not
exhausted (like individual action or collective action understood as the sum of individual actions)' (HS, 62). (4) The
politics of inoperativity entails the abandonment of the metaphysical concept of the subject and manifests itself in destituent practices that liberate the potential immanent to every

institution, law's determination, and more generally to all human forms of life.

The logic of destituent potential

The words destitution and destituent derive from the Latin verb *destituo*, which means to leave alone, to forsake, abandon, desert.[9] While in English the term destitution refers principally to the sphere of poverty and dispossession, in Italian and French it has an eminent juridical connotation: *destituire* and *destituer*, are indeed technical terms describing the deposition or removal of someone from duty or an office. Destitute – as deposed – is the predicate that defines the moment of the separation between a subject and a given institution; the making of an institution subjectless and conversely of a subject institutionless.

Perhaps, Walter Benjamin's *Critique of Violence* – one of the key texts inspiring Agamben's philosophy – represents the first document in which the logic of destitution as a political strategy has been considered as a desirable emancipatory option. The essay moves from a radical critique of law in its genetic/vital dependency from violence: 'when the consciousness of the latent presence of violence in legal institutions disappears', Benjamin writes, 'the institution falls into decay'.[10] Law's violence is defined by Benjamin according to the well-known separation between law-making violence [*rechtsetzende Gewalt*] – that of revolutionary-constituent parties, serving as original mythical positing of the law – and law-preserving [*rechtserhaltende Gewalt*] – manifested in the whole set of institutions apt for the conservation of order. For Benjamin the law perpetually needs to monopolise violence, not simply to foster the security of its subjects, but first and foremost for the sake of its own self-preservation. The law cannot tolerate any form of violence other than its own: giving space to non-legal violence would open up the possibility of the re-emergence of the creational potential entailed in violence itself, threatening in this way the survival of the order. As Derrida put it, the violence that 'threatens law already belongs to it, to the right to law, to the law of the law, to the origin of law'.[11] Violence, in this sense, is always tied to the possibility of establishing a new order; and law's preserving of violence could be considered as a type of violence that has suspended its creative potential. Therefore, the passage from foundation to preservation appears as never definitive; indeed it inaugurates a dialectic movement between violent law-making and law-preserving – where the latter is usually invested with the vocation of preventing the former.

Benjamin's engagement with legal violence points towards the theorisation of a specific (non-legal) form of violence, called alternatively 'pure violence', 'divine violence', or 'revolutionary violence' that should function as a pure means to depose and destitute [*Entsetzung*] the mythic order of law. Benjamin identified this form of violence in what the French revolutionary syndicalist Georges Sorel had defined[12] as 'proletarian general strike'. While the political strike suspends labour only to obtain certain external concessions or a modification of working conditions, the proletarian general strike subverts an order and inaugurates a new reality, in which labour is totally transformed and not defended and imposed by state force. For Benjamin, the proletarian general strike can bring about the catastrophic – messianic – rupture, the interruption of the cycle of mythic forms of law that is the destitution (de-position) of the juridical order [*Entsetzung des Rechts*], with all the powers on which it depends, deposing (or destituting) state violence once and for all. Divine violence – in doing violence to the mythical violence of law – is capable of deposing the law, while remaining essentially alien to the actualisation and formalisation into a constituted order.

As such, the logic of destituent potential is essentially inconsistent with plausible and well-established principles of the grammar of political change. It does not fit with the modern political and juridical canon that sees any new accomplishment in the broader sphere of human social life as the realisation and constitution of orders. The image of a destituent potential is alien to that of constitution and institution, as creation and fixation of normativity into a legitimate order of rules. As *The Invisible Committee*, following Agamben's thinking, writes 'whereas constituent logic crashed against power apparatus it means to take control of, a destituent potential is concerned instead with escaping from it, with removing any hold on it which the apparatus might have'.[13]

In the struggle against the state and capital the destituent logic manifests itself as 'exit from capitalist normality [and] desertion from the crappy relations with oneself, others and the world under capitalism',[14] without however creating a new order of institutional/economic powers. Contrary to the constituent logic, which involves the idea of dialectical opposition to authority, 'in order to take possession of it, destituent logic obeys the vital need to disengage from it',[15] the destituent act does not have as a target the institution itself, but 'the need we have of it': its scope is not to fight but to neutralise, in a gesture that at the same times escapes the architecture of power and empties it of its substance and legitimacy.[16]

But the destituent gesture is not merely the opposite, or the negative side of the constituent act; what differentiates it is its nature and ontological status. In ontological terms, the idea of constituent power necessitates the thought of the constitution of the potential according to which an institutional order is realised (or formed) out of what is potentially possible at the constituent level through the action of a willing sovereign subject deciding on the actualisation and ordering of its potential. The destituent logic, instead, entails the thought of a 'potentiality without any relation to Being in the form of actuality' (HS, 47); that is a potential that remains alien and at the same time open to assuming actual forms, without being fully absorbed and exhausted in its formation. Not creation, but de-creation and de-institution; this is the core logic of destituent potential.

Constituent power has historically spoken about the origin, creation and legitimacy of law and political orders, and worked as the ontological foundation of polities. Constituent power has its origin in the existence of a 'people' with a given consciousness of itself, deciding on its fate and institutional forms. Implicit in the idea of constituent power is the thought of the grounding of an order (institutions, forms of life, laws, etc.), out of a transcended present. On the contrary, the destituent gesture remains immanent to a given order: without recreating anything, it allows the potential that is connatural to the fact of being human, to resurface. If the constituent logic is that of destruction/creation, that of destitution is liberation, exodus and abandonment. And if the constituent act refers to a willing subject, which can assume to itself the creational task, or is determined in the constituent process; the destituent potential is not an expression of subjectivity, it is indeed what comes forth after the subject is deposed.

As argued in the first chapter, Agamben finds the paradigmatic figure of a destituent potential in Paul's messianism; more specifically in those passages in which the Apostle speaks of the coming of the Messiah as the end or fulfilment of the law. As Agamben maintains, Paul intends the law, not as a text (the letters of the Torah), but as a normative device, which he also defines as the law of commands [*nomos ton entolon*]. The figure of the Messiah brings into question the very principle of access to justice through the accomplishment of the precepts of the law; that is the idea that justice consists in a *realisation* or *actualisation* of the law in a series of actions and works, which make the law effective. For this reason, to describe the end of the law, Paul uses the term *katargein*, which does not mean to destroy, but to render inoperative [*katargein* is the opposite of *energeo*, to actualize]. In this sense, the fulfilment of the law, of which the coming of the Messiah is a paradigm, should be intended not as 'realisation', but as de-realisation – or destitution.[17] In the messianic perspective, the law ceases to be something that should be realised in the acts of humans and for this reason is neither abolished nor complied with.

In a sense, what is at stake in the idea of a destituent potential, is the overcoming of the concept of actualisation (or realisation), which is dominating the Western conception of politics; that is the idea that political action and politics more generally, consists of the making 'real' (or actual) of an idea or a project, the translation into a reality of what is thought possible – which is in a sense the kernel of every political theory. Destituent is that potential that resists its realisation in a constituted order, and that, resting solely in itself, acquires the form of a de-creation. Here the concept of a messianic-destituent politics exposes both its potential and its substantial limit. In so far as the destitution operated by the messianic event consists neither in realising nor in the destruction of a mundane order, it remains trapped in its factual non-realisation. Indeed, as Benjamin writes, 'the Messiah himself consummates all history ... for this reason nothing historical can relate itself on its account to anything messianic. Therefore, the Kingdom of God is not the *telos* of historical dynamic: it cannot be set as a goal'.[18] Drawing on such a conception of the messianic, Agamben claims that all the secularised concepts modelled on it (Marxist classless society, revolution, anarchy) – 'are not something that could be posed as the end of a political action and realised through a revolution or a historical transformation'.[19] The error of modern revolutionary ideology, he goes on, is that of 'having flattened the messianic order on the historical', forgetting that to keep its efficacy, the messianic can never become an end to be realised.[20] When placed as something to be realised in the profane order of history, messianic ideas – as the history of the twentieth century teaches us – will tend to reproduce in different forms the same profane order. Here the limit of messianic-redemptive politics emerges with great clarity. If it cannot be realised in a profane-mundane order, if it cannot be managed through concepts and practices, what is the meaning of the messianic in politics? Perhaps, the messianic can operate only as a paradigm or as an example, that is as a rule or a command that cannot be expressed, but that allegorically should push us to rethink the immanent destitution of our life.

Precedents

Although the idea of radical destitution of social and political orders has often accompanied theories of revolution and the imaginative representation of transformative events, it has never had either dedicated literature, or an organic definition. Indeed, it has always been something like a shadow, or something unsaid, involved in the thought of epochal changes. The destitution of social and political systems, and their cultural structures (law, religion and economy), was a real possibility embedded in Marx' conception of the existence of the proletariat as a revolutionary class. And the extinction of the state (Lenin) or of the law as a form of regulation of human social life (Evgenij Pashukanis) was the logical consequence of such an idea.[21] Only recently the concept of a destituent power/potential has been the object of a more organic theorisation. Its first occurrence is included in the work of the

Argentinian militant group *Colectivo Situaciones*, which used it to understand theoretically the insurrectional events of 19 and 20 December 2001, which had a profound impact upon the Argentinian political system and its pervasive neoliberal agenda.[22] Subsequently, the term destituent power has been used to characterise the spirit of the revolts that took place in Paris' *banlieues* in 2005; becoming a key term in the writings of the Invisible Committee, which placed it at the core of their non-programmatic conception of revolution.

Many of the revolts and insurrections that occurred in the twenty-first century were destituent in their spirit. From the *que se vayan todos, que no quede ninguno* of the Argentinian *piqueteros*, to the Arab spring; from the urban turmoil in Paris in 2005[23] and Tottenham in 2011, to the Occupy movement and Gezi Park, what guided social uprisings was the desire to change the pitiful form of life that we are destined to live under our current capitalist regime. And when Agamben adopted it, the concept of destituent power had already a (short) history and a definition which he integrated into his political and ethical proposal, developing it decisively. In so doing, he has in a way revealed his proximity to specific forms of social struggle that have taken place in the last two decades, imposing a rupture on the vocabulary and the practices of modern politics.

Considered from a broader epochal/historical perspective, the emergence of the image of a power that instead of commanding its own institution, operates according to an opposite logic – that of destitution (or de-institution) – is a further signal of the delusional disorder affecting the sanctified categories of modern politics: that of the state, of popular sovereignty, of the market, and of liberal constitutionalism and democracy. What such an idea renders evident is not only a very reasonable ideological loss of faith in such principles; rather it exposes the substantial collapse of legitimacy of the capitalist biopolitical regime. The secularised orders of our democracies are considered legitimate not so much by reference to a theological-transcendent source, but through their capacity to fulfil their promises: ever-growing security and prosperity, or in other words better form(s) of life. The long sequence of crises that have characterised the first two decades of the twenty-first century, the often-violent imposition of neoliberal policies with the correlated anthropological model based on precarity and competition, and the now evident impact of our lifestyle on the environment at a global level, have exposed the systemic unsustainability of the dominant forms of government in accomplishing their supposed function. To pursue a radical change using the same categories and practices that led to the establishment of the regimes in which we are living reveals a contradiction in terms. The emergence of the idea of a destituent power is the logical outcome of the consciousness of such a loss of legitimacy and cannot but reaffirm such loss somehow positively. And as the Invisible Committee put it: 'to destitute power is to take away its legitimacy, compel it to recognise its arbitrariness, reveal its contingent dimension'.[24]

These ideas have been elaborated by the *Colectivo Situaciones* in their seminal work on the mass protest that disrupted Argentinian social and political life in December 2001, when thousands of people, sick of the deep economic crisis made worse by the intervention of the IMF, took to the streets of Buenos Aires breaking the state of emergency which the government had declared. President de la Rúa resigned, triggering a period of political instability and social experiments: assemblies were formed, and many bankrupt factories were taken on and managed directly by their workers. For the *Colectivo*, the two days of mass protest represented an event that turned out not to be fully comprehensible from the point of view of traditional modern political categories and Marxist/anarchist revolutionary thought. The destituent spirit of those days of revolt, has shaken the conception that every revolution consists of confronting a constituted order to a constituent power, in a dialectic movement that necessarily produces a sequence of events that from an initial revolt leads to a provisional government and, finally, to the constitution of a new order.[25] As the *Colectivo* writes, 'the movement of the 19th and 20th was more a de-instituting action than a classical instituting movement ... the sovereign and instituting powers (*potencias*) were the ones that became rebellious without instituting pretensions – as a doctrine of political sovereignty would expect – while exercising their de-instituting powers on the constituted powers'.[26] Contrary to what is usually understood as a revolutionary movement, the events of December 2001 did not intend to 'produce a "situation of situations," a centre replacing the centrality of the state it questioned'.[27] The operative logic underpinning that revolt was that of de-institution, and this required the postulation of a different way of conceiving the political praxis of social change.

More importantly, for the *Colectivo* destituent power is not expression of a given subjectivity (individual or collective): there is no actual conventional protagonist that could legitimately lay claim to means for destitution. Hence, the destituent movement is embodied in the presence of a multitude to which pertains a potential that is never exhausted and represented in the image of an acting subject. The destituent praxis is an attack on the very idea of representation as a guiding principle of liberal/capitalist democracy and as a form of organisation of movements. For the principle of representation is traditionally linked to the sphere of sovereign power and to the processes of institutionalisation of social and political subjectivities: in order to be understood as 'selves', subjects must possess the capacity of representing their image (often mythical or metaphysical) and the force to orient actions according to such an image.

The practice of a destituent potential assumes the guise of an ethical gesture, according to which the rendering inoperative of the forces shaping human lives constitutes immanently a renewed form of inhabiting this world. In *To Our Friends*, the Invisible Committee expresses this point clearly: the practices oriented to the destitution of power confront the architecture of capitalist society to *ethical truths*, intended not as 'truths about the world, but truths on the basis of which we dwell therein ... Truths are what bind us, to ourselves, to the world around us, and to each other. They give us entry into an immediately shared life'.[28] Of course, these truths speak to power of the 'disgust with the life we're forced to live'; indeed, what seems to be in question in the form of contemporary destituent insurrection is 'knowing what a desirable form of life would be, and not the nature of the institutions that would loom over it'.[29] The destituent gesture opposes to the institution of the living, an ethos and a form of life that resists the very idea of the institution. Withdrawal, abandonment, subtraction: the affirmation of the negative, or a positive passivity. When it is clear that nothing in the system and its institutional forms seems to be functional to the overcoming of the tragedy of our current form of life, the ultimate reasonable action is that of refusing to engage with it.

Insurrection

In *The Time that Remains*, Agamben very concisely suggests that the logic of inoperativity embedded in the thought of messianic redemption is somehow prefigured in Max Stirner's idea of insurrection (*Empörung*)[30] that, he claims, represents a possible 'ethical-anarchist' interpretation of the Pauline *as not* (TTR, 32). As Stirner writes in a well-known passage of *The Ego and Its Own*:

> Revolution and insurrection must not be looked upon as synonymous. The former consists in an overturning of conditions, of the established condition or status, the state or society, and is accordingly a political or social act; the latter has indeed for its unavoidable consequence a transformation of circumstances yet does not start from it but from men's discontent with themselves, is not an armed rising, but a rising of individuals, a getting up, without regard to the arrangements that spring from it. The revolution aimed at new arrangements; insurrection leads us no longer to let ourselves be arranged, but to arrange ourselves, and sets no glittering hopes on 'institutions'. It is not a fight against the established, since, if it prospers, the established collapses of itself; it is only a working forth of me out of the established. If I leave the established, it is dead and passes into decay. Now, as my object is not the overthrow of an established order but my elevation above it, my purpose and deed are not a political or social but (as directed toward myself and my ownness alone) an egoistic purpose and deed. The revolution commands one to make arrangements, the insurrection [*Emporung*] demands that he rise or exalt himself [*sich auf oder emporzurichtenl*]. What constitution was to be chosen, this question busied the revolutionary heads, and the whole political period foams

with constitutional fights and constitutional questions, as the social talents too were uncommonly inventive in societary arrangements ... The insurgent strives to become constitutionless.[31]

For Stirner, insurrections are individual-egoistic forms of disengagement (or subtraction), manifested in acts that have been voided of predetermined ends and that find their most proper cause in nothing other than the affirmation of humans' discontent with themselves. Revolutions, to the contrary, are political events whose scope is the creation of new arrangements and institutions, which necessitates strategies 'coordinated and oriented over the mid-to long term towards ultimate objectives'[32] to be realised. As Furio Jesi argues, what distinguishes insurrections and revolutions, is also a different experience of time: while the former 'suspends historical time [and] institutes a time in which everything that is done has value in itself, independently of its consequences and of its relations with the transitory of perennial complex that that constitutes history', the latter 'would, instead, be wholly and deliberately immersed in historical time',[33] as the realisation of an event according to determinate (and perhaps deterministic) historical coordinates.

Agamben did not further develop his engagement with Stirner and with the theory of insurrection. However, his comments are of particular significance for the understanding of the sense of his destituent political proposal at large. Saul Newman, in this respect, argues that the destituent logic is insurrectionary, and the insurrection as an 'autonomous form of political mobilisation and practice, which sets itself apart from the state'[34] and economic governmentality, is eminently destituent. An insurrection, he goes on, encompasses a set of practices aimed at the 'affirmation of the autonomy and singularity of the individual', which takes the form of a 'micro-political transformation of the self in relation to power'.[35] As such, insurrection is the 'political articulation of ontological anarchy: a form of praxis which is not overdetermined by a project or a *telos*, but which simply assumes and puts in practice the freedom that we already have'.[36] Contrary to the traditional understanding of revolution, as the realisation of a concept (of ideas), insurrection manifests itself in an exodus or withdrawal from the forces that tie ourselves to specific forms of life. The defining end of insurrections, thus, is not the creation of a renewed form of life, rather they go 'to the roots of our own subjectivity',[37] unsettling the constitution of the person, re-shaping it into what Agamben has called a form-of-life.

But what form might insurrections take considering Agamben's philosophy of destituent potential? Allegorically, or better paradigmatically, Agamben's works on monasticism, poverty, his critique of sovereignty and law, in a way mark the direction to be taken by any possible answer. Inasmuch as form-of-life is that living dimension that is established through the destitution of social and legal identities, we could call 'destituent insurrection' all those practices that from time to time can free up a space in which juridical and social determinations are rendered ineffective. As Simone Bignall puts it, the political praxis of a form-of-life entails the thought of 'expropriation and impropriety that is at once individual and collective' that 'renders the governmentality of law ineffectual or inoperative'.[38] And from this perspective, the example of the *highest poverty* that the Franciscans professed, which Agamben has proposed as a paradigm of a form-of-life, was first of all an attempt to live a life according to specific practices and communal organisation that would have rendered the need for the legal form useless, starting from the refusal of private property. What is certain is that the monastic attempt at creating a different communal way of living was a withdrawal from the economic and political structure of the profane order. Or, using Bifo Berardi's words, we could argue that the destituent insurrection 'will not be an insurrection of energy, but an insurrection of slowness, withdrawal, and exhaustion. It will be the autonomization of the collective body and soul from the exploitation of speed and competition'.[39]

The destituent insurrection appears as a practice of withdrawal from an unbearable present, whose direction and purpose are not determined by a pre-established image of the future. It comes about from the radical desire to change and to open an unbounded and unformed space in which to think and practise different ethics and a different life. In this regard, the *Colectivo Situaciones* has defined insurrectionary ethics as a form of *self-affirmed marginalisation*, which implies two strategic moments: a resistant *subtraction* – from state and capital – and creative *self-affirmation*. Such a practice involves the subtraction from the norm, and an affirmation of new modes of life: 'it is not a struggle "against" the norm, to abolish it or substitute something else for it. It is not a matter of "changing the norm" for another, because what is being refused is not the specific normative content but rather the normative function itself'.[40]

We are used to thinking about insurrections in a derogatory manner, as synonymous with violence, disorder and anarchy. From the point of view of political history, the eminent transformative practice has always been a revolution – with its correlate ontological ground of the constituent power. However, we are living in a time in which revolutions, as the radical transformation of the totality of social and political relations, do not seem viable. Reality has reached a level of complexity that we lack the intellectual instrument to think it as a totality. As the Invisible Committee write, the 'traditional revolutionary program involved a reclaiming of the world, an expropriation of the expropriators, a violent appropriation of that which is ours, but which we have been deprived of'; and it is exactly on this point that revolutions appear obsolete: the dominion of capital and political-economic forces has pervaded every aspect of human existence:

> from being an exploitation of the existing forms of life, it has transformed itself into a total universe. It has configured, equipped, and made desirable the ways of speaking, thinking, eating, working and vacationing, of obeying and rebelling, that suit its purpose. In doing so, it has reduced to very little the share of things in this world that one might want to reappropriate. Who would wish to reappropriate nuclear power plants, Amazon's warehouses, the expressways, ad agencies, high-speed trains, Dassault, La Defense business complex, auditing firms, nanotechnologies, supermarkets and their poisonous merchandise? Who imagines a people's takeover of industrial farming operations where a single man plows 400 hectares of eroded ground at the wheel of his megatractor piloted via

satellite? No one with any sense. What complicates the task for revolutionaries is that the old constituent gesture no longer works there either.[41]

Insofar as the biopolitical dominion with its processes of commodification and expropriation invaded the whole of our worldly existence, there is no world or life to appropriate or to re-constitute. The only radical (revolutionary) option that remains is the destituent gesture. An act of disengagement, of exodus, which is also a positive affirmation of a communal form of living: 'the destituent gesture is desertion and attack, creation and wrecking, and all at once, *in the same gesture*'. [42]

Disobedience

In a series of articles and books,[43] the Italian historian of political ideas, Raffaele Laudani, attempted to frame the question of destituent power in terms of disobedience. This endeavour is predicated on the idea that disobedience, 'as an act of agency expressing a clear political intention',[44] represented the somatisation of a foundational aporia lying at the core of modern politics: one that combines, on the one hand, a conception of the subject hinged upon the ideas of moral autonomy and intrinsic (quasi-absolute) freedom, and on the other obedience to a sovereign law as the necessary prerequisite of political communities. As Laudani writes, the aversion of authorities

> is the starting point of the modern Subject, the act that allows an individual to leave the state of 'minority' in which he has lived until that moment and to finally live an adult, free, and rational existence. However, at the same time, modern politics is built as a will for order that, in the absence of a transcendent objective foundation, must artificially construct obedience. This is only possible drawing from these same principles of liberty, autonomy, and self-determination that motivate disobedience.[45]

In this sense, modern political theory strives to find a compromise between the need to preserve the autonomy of the subject (and its natural reluctance to be governed), and the necessity to establish obedience to the law. According to Laudani, two strategies have been adopted to achieve this compromise: 'the contract, with which the instances of freedom, autonomy, and self-determination that fuel diso-bedience are transformed into a "voluntary servitude" under the state' and the creation of the colony 'as a qualitatively different political space of the state, in which disobedience is physically and theoretically externalized'.[46]

The most vivid representation of such a paradox is exem-plified by Étienne de La Boétie's *Discourse of Voluntary Servitude*.[47] Here, sovereign power is exposed in its substan-tial precarity as deprived of any transcendent foundation and grounded solely on the consent of its subjects, who decide to comply with its commands, voluntarily. As Laudani puts it, in La Boétie we see how it is the liberty and the tendency to resist oppression that precedes the formation of polities. In a sense, the possibility of disobedience is the presupposition of obedience. And when La Boétie writes 'resolve no longer to be slaves and you are free!'[48] he intends disobedience as already fully legitimated by human nature. By accepting limitations on their natural freedom to live under a condition of servitude, humans contradict their natural inclination; and when life under sovereign institutions, becomes unbearable, disobedience becomes a political act that makes it essential that human liberty be reaffirmed.

The disobedience that La Boétie advocated – Laudani claims – exemplifies a *destituent* form of conceiving political conflicts. Indeed, 'disobedience cannot, in fact, be explained as a direct clash with power but rather as the voluntary with-drawal of support from the sovereign's–tyrant's policy, in the explicit negation ... of its legitimacy'.[49] For this reason, he claims, destituent power could be interpreted as the return of the modern subject removed in the folds of the state's order as based on the obedience to the sovereign commands and the law. Destituent power, for Laudani, manifests itself as a 'conscious refusal to recognise the authority of who possess political power', as a 'voluntary subtraction of the support to the work of the sovereign/tyrant'.[50]

The destituent moment of modern politics, for Laudani, should not be thought in its autonomy; rather it should be weighed up in strict relation to constituent power. They are two instances of the same potential, moving around the modern ontology of the subject with its free will and moral autonomy, and creational-constituting potential. Destituent power precedes the constituent moment: it is the necessary negative presupposition of any attempt to transform reality, as expressed by the refusal to recognise authority or law as valid and sustainable. In other words: constituent power pre-supposes the moment of the negation of the present, and this is the destituent moment of politics. Such conception of the ontological foundation of politics tries to bridge the moments of the negation and affirmation, of destitution and constitution. And in fact, Laudani is somehow sceptical of those who subscribe, as Agamben does, to the radical opposition of constituent power and destituent potential.

Although logically sound, this strategy of conceiving the destituent moment of politics remains trapped, as it were, in the very discourse of constituent power. The moment of negation of the present – that Laudani calls destituent power – is an essential part of the very theory of constituent power. As Emmanuel Joseph Sieyès has already envisaged, constituent power is never exhausted in its institutionalisation but rests in a way as a shadow threatening the stability of the Nation, embedded in the very existence of the people (Nation) as a political subject.[51] In its creative essence, constituent power already includes both the moments of negation and that of creation. Calling the negative moment of the constituent/creational act 'destituent' does not help in understanding the destituent gesture in its positive singularity. A further problematic aspect of Laudani's concept of destituent power is its reliance on the metaphysical structure of modern subjectivity; that of the willing autonomous subject, whose affirmation is the ground and the end of the destituent act. Disobedience, as a practical materialisation of a destituent potential, is always the expression of the will of a conscious subject, which aims at re-establishing its somehow natural freedom. The destituent essence of the disobedience is, in this sense, a manifestation of the will of subtracting from an order in view of opening up the creation of a new situation. From this perspective, destitution must be realised according to the dictates of a subjective will.

Certainly, disobedience reflects what we have argued so far as characterising destituent potential. Disobedience is a political praxis that instead of aiming to seize power is materialised in a process of subtraction and withdrawal from the law's authority. In disobedience the norm is rendered destitute of its effectivity and performative mechanisms. But the challenge that the idea of destituent potential brings to modern politics is that of thinking a way of acting politically outside the traditional categorial/ontological determinations of western politics and ethics. To think of it in its autonomy, destituent potential must be separated from both constituent power and the metaphysics of the subject. For this reason, framing disobedience and destituent potential as a moment in the never-ending dialectic of constituent power, does not add much to our understanding of both constituent and destituent potential.

Without mentioning it explicitly, Agamben has presented a compelling paradigm of a destituent disobedience: that of Herman Melville's *Bartleby the Scrivener*.[52] Among the most popular, enigmatic and debated figures of modern/contemporary literature, Bartleby represents for Agamben the example of a political existence of the potential. As Jessica Whyte maintains, in the formula with which Melville's character resists and opposes the commands that his working position entails, the 'I would prefer not to', Agamben sees the opening of a 'liminal zone suspended between affirmation and negation, being and nonbeing, predicated on the renunciation of any will or reason to choose either option'; so much so that Bartleby seems to conduct 'an experiment in what can either be or not be, an experiment in potentiality'.[53]

The modern political canon, based on the image of a moral subject and politics as a praxis pointing towards the realisation of order, reduces potentiality to a mere presupposition hidden behind the master-concept of will, which determines and limits the realm of possibilities and that of necessity – what comes after is decided according to ethical coordinates of right and wrong, acceptance or refusal. Bartleby with his *I would prefer not to*, does not say that he *will* or that he *must* not do, but that he does not *prefer* to do. For Agamben, this represents an act of abandonment of the will – as that operator that can constrain the realm of possibility into the actuality of an event – or a suspension of any decision. 'Bartleby' Agamben writes 'calls into question precisely this supremacy of the will over potentiality' (P, 254); the obstinacy and folly of his 'I would prefer not to', makes acts alien to any willed decision, and his behaviour indeterminate: 'it is not that he does not want to copy or that he does not want to leave the office; he simply would prefer not to. The formula that he so obstinately repeats destroys all possibility of constructing a relation between being able and willing' (ibid., 255).

What makes Bartleby's acts so enigmatic is that he chooses not to choose: he 'does not consent, but neither does he simply refuse to do what is asked of him; nothing is farther from him than the heroic pathos of negation' (ibid., 256). Bartleby's action responds neither to the command of the law, nor to that of what he can do. And for this reason, the *I would prefer not to*, opens the space in which a being of pure potentiality can emerge out of a process of de-subjectification. According to the Western/Christian tradition the subject, modelled upon the image of God, is that entity which must and can act only according to its own will. The will, Agamben maintains, is that instrument that, by limiting and constraining what is potentially possible (the contingent), grants the passage to actuality: 'potential', he goes on 'can will, and a will that has willed must act according to its will .... human beings also can and must will, can and must responsibly check the unfathomable depths of their potential' (K, 58). The will is that dispositive that by limiting what one can potentially do, makes action directly referable to a single being, transforming it into a subject responsible capable of acting. Or, as Hanna Arendt suggested, the will fashions the self 'into an "enduring I" that directs all particular acts of volition. It creates the self's character' and embodies the *'principium individuationis,* the source of the person's specific identity'.[54] Placed at the core of culpability and virtue, will (good or bad) is what makes the negation and affirmation, refusal and acceptance, acts and decision of a subject. By choosing not to choose, Bartleby opposes the commands of the law and of his own will in a radical messianic act of suspension of the decision, which does not operate under the command of a superior law (moral or ethical), but points toward the subtraction of any command and any form of subjection.

The 'I would prefer not to', rests on a zero point of normativity: the negation of the order does not constitute the presupposition of a new one. As Slavoj Žižek puts it, Bartleby's
'refusal of the Master's order ... does not negate the predicate; rather he affirms a nonpredicate'; and this he goes on,
constitutes a passage from 'resistance or protestation, which
parasitises upon what it negates, to a politics which opens
up a new space outside the hegemonic position *and* its negation'.[55] For this reason, for Žižek, the *I would prefer not to* is not
something like an act of resistance towards the affirmation of
a new reality: if

> Bartleby's 'I would prefer not to' is interpreted as merely
> the first move of, as it were, clearing the table, of acquir-
> ing a distance toward the existing social universe; what
> is then needed is a move toward the painstaking work of
> constructing a new community – if we remain stuck at the
> Bartleby stage, we end up in a suicidal marginal position
> with no consequences ... however, this, precisely, is the
> conclusion to be avoided: in its political mode, Bartleby's
> 'I would prefer not to' is not the starting point of 'abstract
> negation' which should then be overcome in the patient
> positive work of the 'determinate negation' of the existing
> social universe, but a kind of arche, the underlying princi-
> ple that sustains the entire movement: far from 'overcom-
> ing' it, the subsequent work of construction, rather, gives
> body to it.[56]

Bartleby's non-compliance – his disobedience – is eminently
destituent: it does not leave room for the new to come; it
empties the commands of their operativity reducing them to
their mere inoperative literal enunciation.

~ * ~

We could think of the idea of destituent power or potential as
a conceptual recoil from the inexorable exhaustion of modern
political thought and practices; as an expression of refusal to
surrender to the catastrophe of the present, grown out of the
suspicion that there is something structurally wrong in the
way in which we have thought both political institutions and

revolutionary praxis. The thought of a destituent potential is crepuscular: it is a further signal of the twilight of the modern logic of sovereignty and constituent power – common to both the liberal and the left-revolutionary tradition – as an interpretative instrument to orient transformative politics. The destituent gesture points towards the neutralisation of the juridical, social and economic barriers that are limiting the full expression of human potentiality. As such it takes the form of a double coordinated movement: withdrawal from the constituted order, and the concomitant reappropriation of an autonomous capacity of self-determination. Insurrection and disobedience – as a practical materialisation of a destituent potential – converge in thinking the liberation from norms and institutions through desertion and disengagement, without necessarily founding a new order of rules.

Ivan Illich has defined the history of modern man as 'the history of the Promethean endeavour to forge institutions in order to corral each of the rampant ills [it is a] history of fading hope and raising expectations'.[57] Hope, he writes, 'means trusting faith in the goodness of nature, while expectation means reliance on results which are planned and controlled by man'.[58] Modern politics too is essentially Promethean. Revolutions, government as an *art*, constitutions, constituent power: the modern political vocabulary tells of the creational and transformative potential embedded in the human; of the very possibility of changing contingency (and nature) into a planned artificial administration of risks and turning 'hope into expectation'. For modern minds, the fact that, what has been done so far, has made our life into hell, barely even matters: reality is something that can be managed, created, and recreated at our own will, and the end of the world can the delayed (or managed) by using the same instruments that are fuelling its inexorable acceleration.

To the Promethean spirit of modernity, Illich opposes the ethos of the Epimethean man. In Greek mythology Epimetheus is Prometheus's 'dumb' brother. The two titans are often portrayed as representatives of mankind – the former unwise and injudicious (the etymology of Epimetheus is literally hindsight), the latter clever and ingenious. In Hesiod's narration, Epimetheus is the one who against his brother's advice decides to marry Pandora, the first woman created by the gods and sent to earth, with a very popular box, containing all ills and one good thing: hope. We know how it ended up: Pandora driven by curiosity opened the box letting all ills spread over the world and keeping hope inside. For Illich, Epimetheus embodies the ethical figure of 'embracing hope' against the expectation and failed promises of the Promethean faith in the technical and institutional management of contingency. Epimethean men are those who look suspiciously to the institution and services that have been created to cope with the ills spread all over the world; they welcome the immanence of their condition as the ground for establishing a renewed – fairer and more human – relationship with the other and with the world.

Destituent power is, in this sense, eminently Epimethean: it marks the closure, limit, and in a sense failure of the Promethean perspective, making possible the thought of a social and political life outside the institutional cages in which humans are trapped in their constant attempt to contain the ills that Pandora allowed to escape from her box.[59]

Notes

1. In summer 2013, Agamben delivered a lecture titled 'Vers une théorie de la puissance destituante' in Tarnac (France), as part of a conference titled 'Défaire l'Occident'. He then presented a different version of the text in November 2013 in Athens with the title 'From the State of Control to a Praxis of Destituent Power'. The texts of these two conferences were published in an article 'What is a Destituent Power?' and included in the volume *The Use of Bodies*.
2. On the politics of inoperativity, see: Prozorov (2014); Marmont, Primera (2020).
3. Pozorov (2014: 33).
4. 'Inoperativity' (*inoperosità* in Italian) is the translation of the French *désoeuvrement*, a term coined by Alexandre Kojève and later adopted and reformulated by Georges Bataille, Maurice Blanchot and Jean-Luc Nancy. Agamben adopted it to express his idea of a generic mode of potentiality as opposed to simple negativity or passivity. On the notion of inoperativity see: Salzani (2013); Zartaloudis (2011); Prozorov (2014).
5. Virno (2011 [1986]).

6. Agamben (2011 [1986]: 9).
7. Smith (2012–3; 2016).
8. As the theorist and activist of the Italian political movement of 'Autonomia', Franco 'bifo' Berardi argues in his first and probably most popular intervention in the revolutionary literature of the 1970s: 'refusal of work: this is an overarching strategy. No to the culture of work of Ulbricht, of Brandt, of Mao, Breznev or Nixon': Berardi (1970: 134).
9. Lewis, Short (1958: 560).
10. Benjamin (1978: 288).
11. Derrida (1992: 35). Derrida's term for 'law' is, of course, not the etymologically related 'loi', but 'droit'.
12. See Sorel (1999).
13. The Invisible Committee (2017: 78–9).
14. Ibid., 79.
15. Ibid.
16. Ibid., 80.
17. Agamben (2020c: 17).
18. Benjamin (2006: 305–6).
19. Agamben (2020c: 20).
20. Ibid.
21. See Tarì (2017: 18–9).
22. Colectivo Situaciones (2002/2011).
23. On the Paris urban revolt of 2005 see Amato et al. (2008).
24. The Invisible Committee (2015: 75).
25. Tari (2017: 20).
26. Colectivo Situationes (2011: 52).
27. Ibid.
28. The Invisible Committee (2015: 46–7).
29. Ibid., 49.
30. *Emporung* can be translated as 'revolt', 'rebellion' but also as 'indignation'. Henceforth, we will use the term 'insurrection' following the English translation of Stirner's work.
31. Stirner (1995: 279–80).
32. Jesi (2014: 52).
33. Ibid.
34. Newman (2016: 51).
35. Ibid., 54.
36. Ibid., 55.
37. Ibid., 56.
38. Bignall (2016: 64).
39. Berardi (2012: 68).
40. Colectivo Situaciones (2011: 195–6).
41. The Invisible Committee (2017: 85–5).

42. Ibid., 88.
43. See Laudani (2013; 2016).
44. Laudani (2013: 3).
45. Ibid., 2.
46. Ibid., 6.
47. La Boétie (2012).
48. Ibid., 8.
49. Laudani (2013: 37).
50. Laudani (2016: 25).
51. Sieyès (2003). Such an idea has been developed by Schmitt in *Dictatorship* (2014) and *Constitutional Theory* (2008: 271).
52. The figure of Bartleby has been the object of numerous critical readings. The potential political elements of the story have been under the scholarly spotlight for some time. See: Widmer (1969); Rogin (1985); Getman (2008).
53. Whyte (2009: 319).
54. Arendt (1978: 195).
55. Žižek (2006: 381).
56. Ibid., 382.
57. Illich (1971: 105).
58. Ibid.
59. Ibid., 109.

Three

Doing and Undoing Law

If we would master power we must face command openly and boldly, and search for means to deprive it of its sting.

Elias Canetti

Imperative

In the final chapter of *Opus Dei: An Archaeology of Duty*, Agamben writes that 'the imperative' is the constitutive 'verbal mode' of 'law and religion' (OD, 119). Both the rules of the law and the voice of God in monotheistic religions speak in the imperative – 'thou shalt not kill'. In linguistics and the philosophy of language, such verbal form is classified as a deontic modality, a category of speech that encompasses all those conditions of 'obligation or permission, emanating from an external source', from an 'authority such as rules or the law'.[1] Such utterances are also known as 'directives,' in that they direct people to do things.[2]

Imperatives, commands and rules are structured upon a binary framework, according to which an actual behaviour is expected as a result of an external cause. For the law, the imperative constitutes in a sense its linguistic form. Indeed, as Karl Olivecrona puts it, the imperative is an essential constitutive part of the law's normative power. As he claims, there are two principal components of legal norms (and of rules in general): the *ideational* (or *ideatum*) and the *imperative*. The former consists of the 'pattern of conduct represented in imagination and put forward in a text'[3] (the content of a norm). The latter, instead, denotes 'the impression that this action must or *shall* be performed' and 'the means used to convey this purpose'.[4] The verbal mode of the imperative is the linguistic form that such a purpose must take in order to become a norm: the formal expression of duty and obligation.

But what kind of objects are the law's imperatives? What figures of being do the commands of the law and its obligatory essence embody? In *Opus Dei*, and in the short essay *What is a Command?* included in the volume *Creation and Anarchy*, Agamben attempts to answer these questions. Underlying the imperative form, he argues, is an ontology that had a decisive influence on the way rules have been thought and represented in law and ethics. In 'the tradition of the West', Agamben maintains, there are 'two distinct and connected ontologies': an 'ontology of the command, proper to the juridical-religious sphere, which is expressed in the imperative and has a performative character; the second, proper to the philosophical-scientific tradition, which is expressed in the form of the indicative' (ibid., 120) and is concerned with what a thing *is*. The existential status of law's norms, and the sense of duty and obligation they express, must be understood as depending on a conception of being that Agamben defines as an *operative ontology* or *ontology of effectiveness* according to which being and praxis (to be and to do) overlap. According to this ontology, the being of a thing is constituted by its actual operation (its effect) and an entity must be 'actualised' and put in practice to gain such existence.

At the ontological level, Agamben maintains, 'being and substance are independent from the effects that they can produce'; on the contrary, for the ontology of effectiveness, being is 'indiscernible from its effects; it consists in them ..., and it is "functional" to them' (ibid., 63). But this, in a sense, represents a complication, if not a reshuffling, of Aristotle's ontological dispositive, since an entity in its actual existence [*energheia*] is no longer defined by a presence; rather it embodies an 'operativity' 'in which the very distinctions between potential and act, operation and work are indeterminate and lose their sense' (ibid., 64). For the ontology of effectiveness, being-in-act and being-in-potential are not separable: the being of a thing is reduced to its 'actuality' – intended as the effective realisation of its being. The operative ontology transforms being into a having-to-be [or having to take place]; and this explains, for Agamben, the existential conditions of those peculiar objects – such as duty and obligation – that we use in ethics and law. The normative apparatus that determines human life in forms finds its innermost logic in the ontology of command and operativity.

Office

In *Opus Dei*, Agamben retraces the roots of how the ideas of duty (office) gradually emerged as the dominant ethical and legal paradigm. Even though the many theological and philological interpretations sustaining this endeavour should not be dismissed, what is of the greatest interest from our perspective is Agamben's theorisation of an ontology of commands and imperatives, that is, at the same time, an ontology of law. In line with the postulates of his idea of a political-economic theology, he interrogates the ontological status of those entities which are usually expressed in the imperative through an archaeological investigation of the theological sphere and more precisely through an exegesis of the notion of *officium* (office): the term that refers to the liturgical praxis of the Church's ministers (priests). The doctrinal delineation of the sacramental-liturgical action of the priest, Agamben sustains, represents the paradigmatic *locus* in which something like an ontology of commands has been contemplated and eventually transmitted to ethics and law. Indeed, the concept of office (and duty), elucidates the operational link between life and forms of conduct and rules, between the *vis obligandi* embedded in commands and their performative effects on the plane of behaviour.

Commonly translated (at least since the seventeenth century) as 'duty', *officium* is that term that nominates the effective praxis of the liturgical life of the Church that, in the reciprocal terminological borrowing between theology, law and political thought, which characterises the dynamic of secularisation of Western political power, has eventually been transmitted to the sphere of the administration of the state. However, Agamben claims, the 'strong sense of moral and juridical obligation' that is usually conveyed by the term office (as a duty) 'is lacking in the Latin term' (ibid., 72). Much like a habit, the Latin *officium* refers to all forms of behaviour that are expected from individuals adhering to 'socially codified' statuses. It does not convey the ideas of an obligation, coercion or compulsion, to adhere to determinate rules and schemes of conduct; rather, it indicates what is socially acceptable from individuals belonging to a community structured on specific institutions. '*Officium*', Agamben writes, 'is what causes an individual to comport himself in a consistent way – as a prostitute if one is a prostitute, as a rascal if one is a rascal, but also as a consul if one is a consul and, later, as a bishop if one is a bishop' (ibid.).

As one reads in Cicero's first book of *De Officiis*, a crucial aspect of every theory of office concerns 'the practical rules by which daily life in all its bearings may be regulated'[5] and governed: or in other words the institution of communal life [*institutionem vitae communis*].[6] In the Roman world, office is akin to the *status* that an individual has in society; its existence and significance depends on the production of certain effects of obligation that for human beings are useful to conduct and to govern their lives and the lives of others. '"Conducting life [*vitam degere*]," "governing things [*rem gerere*]": this is the meaning of the "giving form to the use of life [*usum vitae conformare*]" and the "instituting the common life [*vitam instituere*]" that were in question in *officium*' (ibid. 74). It could be argued that an office is a form of life that emerged in the womb of society and becomes instituted as a model for the recognition and the fostering of social stability and control. Despite its undeniable connection with the sphere of duty, the term *officium*, Agamben stresses, does not entail the idea of a compulsory nature like that of commands or the norms of the law.

For Agamben, a decisive step in the constitutive evolution of the ontological grounding of the concept of office is represented by Ambrose's treaty on the ethic of priests – titled *De Officiis*.[7] As he suggests, the strategy adopted by the bishop of Milan consisted of 'transferring the concept of *officium* from the secular sphere of philosophy to that of the Christian Church' (ibid., 77), through a translation of the term *leitourgia* – that is the public function of the ministers – in *officium*. In Ambrose, 'office' is one of the elements of the liturgical action of the priest, which is constituted by the articulation of two elements: the *officium* of the priest (his *ministerium*) that is acting solely as instrumental cause and 'the divine intervention – the *effectus* – that completes it and renders it effective' (ibid., 80). The *effectus* designates the modality of the 'presence and operativity of Christ', which are the necessary elements for turning the instrumental action of the priest into a sacrament (ibid., 38). In the rite of the Holy Communion (the ritual representation of the sharing and delivery of Christ's body and blood), Christ's presence is made real, is made effective, actualised in the liturgical action. The mystery of the presence of Christ in the liturgy 'coincides neither with the presence of the historical Christ in flesh and bone (*sicut corpus in loco*) nor with his simple symbolic representation'; but the liturgy of the priest 'realises its effects' (ibid., 40), making the presence of Christ real and effective.

It is in this theoretical landscape that the traits of an operative ontology – or ontology of commands – emerged more explicitly. Central to this form of ontology is a specific conception of being that is ultimately dislocated into the spheres of actuality, praxis and operativity. If for the Aristotelean ontological dispositive, being is said in many ways – as in form or matter, as in potency or actuality – in the operative ontology, being becomes intelligible only through what it does, through its operativity. For Agamben, a symptom of this transformation is the appearance in early Christian literature of the translation of the Aristotelean *energeia*, with *efficacia* and *effectus*:[8] that is to say, 'the thing and the work considered inseparably in their effectiveness and in their function' (ibid., 46). For the ontology of commands, the substance of entities lies in their effectuality: that is, both in its actual realisation and in the operation of its actualisation. It follows that potentiality and actuality (as well as substance and form) conflate and enter a zone of indistinction; and the being of a thing is ultimately understood as its realisation (effect), on the model of Christ's presence as made real in the liturgical praxis of priests.

For the Church's doctrine, priesthood is defined as an office that confers on the person holding it the faculty of being *the* instrument of the sacramental action through which the presence of Christ is made effective. In the articulation of these two elements – the office of the priest and the divine intervention – the real biological and biographical dimension of the minister is somehow excluded and simply used as a sacramental instrument. The relationship between *effectus* and *officium* – between the agent-priest and the effective presence of Christ in the liturgy – seems therefore hinged upon a circular dialectic, in which the sacramental action defines and excludes the minister in his existential dimension. As Agamben writes, the sacramental action

> is divided into two elements, the first of which, *ministerium* (or *officium* in the strict sense), defines only the instrumental being and action of the priest ... The second, which actualizes and perfects the first, is divine in nature; moreover, it is, so to speak, inscribed and contained in the first, in such a way that the correct fulfilment of the priestly function necessarily and automatically implies the actualization of the *effectus* ... The divine *effectus* is determined by the human minister and the human minister by the divine *effectus*. Their effective unity is *officium-effectum*. *This means, however, that* officium *institutes a circular relation between being and praxis, by which the priest's being defines his praxis and his praxis, in turn, defines his being*. In *officium* ontology and praxis become undecidable: the priest has to be what he is and is what he has to be (ibid., 81).

The action of the priest (as much as the agency of magistrates, ministers or the imperator, and generally of figures holding an office) 'is not defined' by an external result (the work) – as if 'doing' or 'making' something – nor does it have its end in itself: *it is defined by its very exercise ... by assuming and fulfilling a function or an office*' (ibid.). Only when put in practice – that is in the moment of his concrete and actual exercise – can an office be such, and the officer be called as such. The office must be carried and effectuated by an agent, to gain what is usually called existence. In the delivery of a sacrament, the priest is an instrument through which Christ operates. For the priest, it is just enough to be an animated being for becoming the means of Christ's presence in the world.

What is at stake in liturgy and in the idea of the priest as a sacramental instrument is, for Agamben, the separation between action and its realisation 'from the subject who carries it out' (ibid., 24). The actual rite of the sacrament is a fragment of behaviour, the crystallisation of which is codified in an institution that determines existentially the life and function of the priest. And as 'happens in every institution', he writes, 'it is a matter of distinguishing the individual from the function he exercises, so as to secure the validity of the acts that he carries out in the name of the institution' (ibid., 21). The office of the priest, as a social figure in the Christian community is substantially independent of priests as individuals; however, without the priest as a subject-instrument, sacraments cannot gain existence.

The crux of Agamben's archaeology of duty is the uncovering of the structural ontological affinity between the act of carrying an office and the sphere of command (and of imperatives). As in the case of office, a command has a sense only when 'it takes as its object ... the action of another (who is assumed to have to obey, that is, to execute the command)' (ibid., 84). The imperative form of the command (the 'you shall') that defines the 'decree of the norm', to be such (that is to say to express a normative intention) has to be referred to 'the behaviour or action of an individual external to it' (ibid.). The (normative) imperative expresses the will that a certain behaviour must follow. Without the reference to the actualisation of specific behaviours and the pretence that such behaviours *must* follow the imperative statement, commands and norms more generally, cannot be distinguished by other particles and forms of language. Yet, as Agamben notes 'no substantial difference' exists 'between the action expressed on the constative level ("he walks") and the same action carried out in the execution of an order ("walk!")' (ibid.). What most characterises a command (or an order) is not solely the 'nature' of the act of commanding but 'also and above all the execution of the order' (ibid.) and its specific coercive nature, independently of the consequences and virtue of the action commanded.

The ontological status of the office and that of norms shows here their essential proximity: in both cases, the action of an agent is necessary to make them real. Only if actualised, can both the command and the office claim existence. 'Both the one who executes an order and the one who carries out a liturgical act', Agamben claims, 'neither simply *are* nor simply *act* but are determined in their being by their acting and vice versa. The official – like the officiant – is what he has to do, and he has to do what he is, namely a being of command' (ibid.). A law grasped in its potentiality – a non-actuality – would, in the vocabulary of jurisprudence, be ineffective. And this somehow confirms Wittgenstein's observation that the ultimate idea of a rule (and of rule-following) has to be derived from the actual existence of a rule – in the form of regularities and institutions, giving to the rules we follow their sense as rules. Duties, offices, commands and imperatives, then, are those objects whose ontological status makes their being dependent on their 'actual' taking place; that is, on their operational effect(s) on conduct and behaviour.

Ought and *Is*

The theological speculation over the office of the Church's ministers saw the emergence of a conception of duty as an action executed not because of its specific virtue, substantial goodness or natural inclinations, but solely because it is commanded – that is to say because it is a duty.[9] The ontology of command (of what has to be), for Agamben, complemented the conception of being that has been traditionally arrayed in Greek philosophy. In the Western tradition, he argues, there are two distinct, yet connected, ontologies: the first is the ontology of the *esti* – which underpins every understanding of what an entity *is* and defines and governs the ambit of philosophy and science; the second, the ontology of the *esto* – that describes the existential dimension of what *has to be* or *ought to be*, and concerns and explains the objects of the sphere of law and religion: commands, norms and imperatives. These two ontologies, he claims, 'incessantly divide and intersect, fight without respite and just as stubbornly crossbreed and join' (CA, 60), forming the pieces of bipolar machinery in which the pole of the 'is' is played dialectically against that of the 'ought'.

Based on the banal fact that imperatives, commands and in general norms, do not exist as objects in the world, jurists and moralists incessantly repeat that imperatives do not imply a *being* but only a *having to be*. When a command is proffered, its meaning cannot be derived from its eventual execution: the sense of the command lies in the fact that what is commanded *has to be* executed. Accordingly, an order, norm and imperative emanating from an authority, is 'perfect from the sole fact of being uttered'; whether it is 'disregarded does not in any way impugn its validity' (ibid.). The reality of an obligation is tangible solely in its effects, in the conscious or unconscious behaviour of agents, as part of the 'mental intention' of the subjects to which they are referred.

Such a conception of normativity has its most explicit and popular jurisprudential formulation in Hans Kelsen's legal philosophy. As Agamben argues, Kelsen's pure theory of law 'moves from an absolutisation without reserve of *sein* and *sollen*, being and having to be' (OD, 123); indeed, a pure science of law is possible only if legal norms are maintained in the place of the *sollen*, of the '*ought* to be'. A 'norm', Kelsen writes, 'is the meaning of an act by which a certain behaviour is commanded, permitted, or authorised', and is independent of the 'act of will whose meaning the norm is: the norm is an *ought*, but the act of will is an *is*'.[10] The consequence of such a postulate is the ontological separation of the sphere of the normativity of law from the very 'act' of enunciating and following rules. The *ought* is ontologically alien from the *is*; they cannot be either in a relationship of derivation or in a relation of implication. Kelsen writes:

> The difference between *is* and *ought* cannot be explained further. We are immediately aware of the difference. Nobody can deny the statement: 'something is' – that is, the statement by which an existent fact is described – is fundamentally different from the statement: 'something ought to be' – which is the statement by which a norm is described. Nobody can assert that from the statement that something is, follows a statement that something ought to be, or vice versa.[11]

In this sense, norms and the sphere of the real existence of human behaviour are displaced on different levels. Once it has expressed a will (i.e., through a legislative process), the linguistic enunciation of a norm enters the sphere of the *ought*, which is somehow self-referential: the *ought* depends on the *ought*, and does not claim to be an *is*. This distinction, as Ota Weinberger notices, is the same that which stands between the 'cognitive and the normative',[12] and has the functions of allowing the consideration of normativity as a self-standing sphere. Even if it corresponds to regularities in human behaviour, a norm cannot be derived from the actual social reality in which such regularities are usually grounded. What is considered as socially or behaviourally normal entails neither the necessity nor the obligation of being 'normal'. As long as the word norm, Kelsen claims,

> figures in the adjective 'normal', it is not in fact an 'ought' that is meant there, but an 'is'. A thing is 'normal' if it is what actually happens as a rule. So far as any 'ought' is also meant there, we are presupposing the validity of the norm that what tends to happen as a rule is also what ought to happen … To believe that, because a thing regularly happens in fact, it also ought to happen, is a fallacy. An 'ought' cannot logically be derived from an 'is'.[13]

Law's norms do not command subjects to behave in a specific established way, but only that they *have to* [*sollen*] behave in that specific way. For Kelsen, the law is indifferent to whether its dictates are followed. For the law, it is sufficient that in the case of a lapse of obedience a sanction must follow. A specific behaviour is stated legally, 'when and only when a legal norm posits the opposite course of conduct as the condition of an ordained sanction'.[14] In a pure theory of law, norms are directed not to their subject that must follow them, but to the functionary that must apply the sanctions in their name.

Nevertheless, the effort at constructing a pure system of law, Agamben sustains, is ultimately destined to failure; the 'two ontologies (being and having-to-be), while distinct, cannot be entirely separated, and they refer to and presuppose one another' (ibid., 124–5). The rule/sanction system is proof of this: 'to say that the norm that establishes the sanction affirms that the executioner *must* apply the penalty and not that he, in fact, applies it, takes away any value from the very idea of a sanction' (ibid., 125). It is the presence of a sanction (punishment) that marks the difference between a norm of law and a simple utterance. But in the rule/sanction system, the relationship between the sphere of normativity and behaviour is more complicated than what Kelsen suggests. The reference to a specific behaviour seems, in fact, always presupposed by the rule/sanction scheme. Weinberger summarises this aspect in this way:

> From the form of the sanction-norm 'If *A*, then *B* (the sanction) is to be', i.e., a hypothetical ought-sentence, the forbiddenness of *A* can be logically inferred when and only when it is known that *B* is posited as a *sanction*. This is the case when and only when the behaviour posited as condition of the obligatoriness of the sanction is assumed to be forbidden. In other words, the concept of a sanction contains an implicit reference to a behavioural norm, whose violation is the condition of the sanction. The behavioural norm must therefore be presupposed in any case.[15]

Legal norms are tied to the reality they aim at regulating via the presupposition of specific normality of behaviour, whose violation is the reason to apply the sanction. The sanction epitomises the fact that when a norm exists, it must positively affirm a specific segment of reality (what is deemed normal), ruling out and sanctioning its infringement. The commands of the law, thus, enforce and stabilise specific patterns of normal behaviour that are presupposed by the relative system of sanctions, which therefore remain somehow separated as 'norms' (what *ought* to be) from the actual behavioural plane.

Central to the very idea of a 'rule' is the codification and formulation of a specific pattern of behaviour, which – much like an office – becomes autonomous from the agents whose actions it is supposed to regulate. The normative world of institutions, rules and ultimately of the law, as Peter L. Berger and Thomas Luckmann suggested, involves a process of objectification and reification, according to which human institutions and the regularity of human phenomena are apprehended as separated from, and applied to, the realm of human life. Such dynamic of reification disguises norms and institutions as something 'other than a human product – such as facts of nature, results of cosmic laws, or manifestations of divine will',[16] gaining in this way the necessary symbolic authority to claim obedience and to have a decisive impact on reality. The law, as Emanuele Coccia puts it, is composed of many words and discourses that are socially effective, which have been isolated and separated in a specific space – the (sacred) space of the law, which safeguards its utterances physically, metaphysically and symbolically.[17]

Agamben's archaeology of duty exposes in a rather particular fashion the distinction and the functional connection between subjects and rules, norms and behaviour, words and reality. For this reasons Agamben could claim that the imperative, the form in which the law is expressed has a performative character. Even if ontologically irreconcilable, the plane of norms (*ought*) and the plane of the real need to be somehow tied; as long as commands call for their execution in order to be considered commands, the law – in order to gain its status as law – has to be logically made actual, effective.

Performativity

The law, Agamben writes in a compelling passage of *The Time that Remains*, 'could be defined as the realm in which all language tends to assume a performative value. To do things with words could even be considered as a residue in the language of a magical-juridical state of human existence, in which words and deeds, linguistic expression and real efficacy, coincide' (TTR, 132). The idea of law's performative value has proven to be particularly instructive to characterise the constructive link between law's language and reality; and indeed, Agamben returns repeatedly to this idea. The paradigm of the performative character of law could be enunciated as follows: as a linguistic practice, the law has the 'power' to create its own reference and objects in the reality it regulates. As such, the idea of performativity exposes 'the leap from language to reality that challenges every ban on the passage from ought to is',[18] which stands at the core of the very concept of normativity.

While pointing to the somehow genetic bond that law's normativity entertains with reality, the concept of an original performative essence of the law presupposes at the same time the hypothesis of a substantial distinction between the sphere of norms and commands and the world. Law's norms can have a real effect on reality as long as they are artefacts and not facts. What constitutes law's performative essence is the capacity to have tangible effects on reality through the constitution of a semiotic system, which presupposes and at the same time informs the realm of the factual.

The contiguity of the theory of performativity and law's practice has been brought to the fore by John L. Austin, who has initiated the linguistic/philosophical inquiry of performativity. In *How to do Things with Words*, he has argued that the 'widespread obsession that the utterances of the law ... *must* somehow be statements true or false, has prevented many lawyers from getting this whole matter much straighter', through the recognition of the essential performative character of legal utterances.[19] Austin's well-known hypothesis is that there are some linguistic elements, called *speech acts*, which are neither true nor false, but refer to a reality that their enunciation produces. When, for instance, we answer affirmatively to the ritual questions posed during the marriage service (I do), we do not merely act or describe what we are doing, we are producing something: the marriage between two acting subjects. The examples of speech acts are known: to declare; to promise; to swear; to apologise. When these words enter the discourse, the sentences uttered somehow produce the event they designate.

Crucially, speech acts necessitate certain conditions that, if not fulfilled, make them fail: only when uttered in precise circumstances can a speech act take place. Austin identified four necessary conditions granting the performative effect:

A1. There must exist an accepted conventional procedure having a certain conventional effect, that procedure to include the uttering of certain words by certain persons in certain circumstances, and further,

A2. the particular persons and circumstances in a given case must be appropriate for the invocation of the particular procedure invoked.

B1. The procedure must be executed by all participants correctly and

B2. completely.[20]

From this list of necessary conditions, we can see how a valid speech act is produced by the joint operation of two elements: one that might be called *procedural* – the rules that must be followed (accepted conventional procedure ... that must be executed correctly and completely); the second that could be defined as *authoritative* – which refers to those conditions related to the fact that a performative utterance can take place only if pronounced by the 'appropriate' agent.[21] When the necessary conditions are not fulfilled, Austin argues, we are in presence of certain *infelicities*, which make the performative act 'misfire' (not take place at all). For example, the celebration of a ceremony like a marriage without the necessary ritual-normative procedure, will make the marriage vow fail to bring about the intended effect and no marriage takes place. Likewise, it is in anyone's faculty to shout in public 'I declare a state of national emergency', but 'as it cannot be an act because the requisite authority is lacking, such an utterance is no more than words; it reduces itself to futile clamour, childishness, or lunacy'.[22]

The conditions that Austin distinguished as 'necessary' for a speech act are substantially of the same nature as the 'validating conditions' of contracts and covenants more generally.[23] The force of law's statements is dependent on the pronunciation (or validation) by the person whose status endows her with the necessary authority, as decreed by specific accepted rules and procedures. Here the concurrence of law's practice and the necessary conditions of the speech act is glaring: the sentence passed by a judge, to legislate, to stipulate a contract, etc. like a speech act, need the presence of both a procedural, formal-normative element and an authoritative, personal, a-nomic one to take effect. As Agamben argues in the closing of *State of Exception*, the juridical system in its manifold manifestation seems to be built on a

> double structure formed by two heterogeneous yet coordinated elements: one that is normative and juridical in the strict sense (which we can for convenience inscribe under the rubric *potestas*) and one that is anomic and meta-juridical (which we can call by the name *auctoritas*). The normative element needs the anomic element in order to be applied. (SE, 86)

The moment of the performative taking place opens a space in which the two elements – the procedural and the authoritative – composing the double structure of the juridical system enter a zone of indistinction, thus allowing the efficacy of law's words to gain effect. In other words, law's performativity permits the thought of a tangential point that connects the 'ought' and the 'is'; or in Agambenian terms, the crossing point of the two ontologies of the '*esto*' and that of the '*esti*' (CA, 60), making what *has to be* into *being*, and vice versa.

Force

What seems to be in question in law's performativity is the consideration of what is usually termed the 'force of law'. Such idiomatic expression, whose popularity is not affected by its evident and unresolved ambiguity, exposes the banal fact that the law pushes us to do things that we do not necessarily (or automatically) do – or want to do. Unlike other sources of normative powers, the law is equipped with instruments to 'force' compliance with its dictates, which are sustained by an aura of symbolic legitimacy. The system of sanctions that the law disposes of delimits its ambit of existence and ultimately its ontological status as something that *must be*. The force of law is what guarantees its essential performative character, giving reality to its authority as a series of commands that must produce effects on what it is called to rule. So much so that, Rudolph von Jhering claimed: the 'law without force is an empty name, a thing without reality, for it is the force, in realising the norms of law, which makes law what it is and ought to be'.[24]

As Jacques Derrida put it, embedded in the commonly used terminology of enforcement of the law, is the idea that 'there is no such thing as law (*droit*) that doesn't imply in itself, a priori, in the analytic structure of its concept, the possibility of being "enforced," applied by force'. Of course, there are legal norms 'that are not enforced, but – he goes on – there is no law without enforceability, and no applicability or enforceability of the law without force, whether this force be direct or indirect, physical or symbolic, exterior or interior, brutal or subtly discursive and hermeneutic, coercive or regulative'.[25]

This somehow innate requirement of enforceability, however, is grounded on the paradigmatic (and paradoxical) consciousness of the impotence of the letter of the law.

Let us now look for example at two passages taken from a standard introductory textbook on law enforcement and criminal law:

> Law is a body of rules for human conduct enforced by imposing penalties for their violation. Technically, laws are made and passed by the legislative branches of our federal, state, county and city governments. They are based on customs, traditions, mores and current need. Law implies both prescription (rule) and enforcement by authority.[26]

And,

> Without means of enforcement, the great body of federal, state, municipal and common law would be empty and meaningless ... All forms of society rely on authority and power. Authority is the right to direct and command. Power is the force by which others can be made to obey.[27]

All those institutional instruments through which law's force is manifested (in the form of a coercive force) give the law fullness and normative significance. They grant the passage from the *ought* to the *is*, making law's form (its formal enunciation as a command) and force to coincide. However, law's force cannot be deduced from its literal prescriptions but must rely on some external authoritative means. If emptied of any intelligible meaning, what remains of law's letters is, on the one hand, a pure imperative form, which commands nothing specific, demanding at the same time general (absolute) obedience, and on the other hand, a force exposed in its ultimate anomic essence. Indeed, Agamben points out, the formal/abstract status of law's operativity is that of being in force without significance: its requiring obedience independently by any specific content.[28]

Two decisive corollaries can be drawn from this aspect of law's normativity. First, the law *is* only when transgressed. The law is brought into its mundane presence, only in the form of a sanction, that is, only in the moment in which an agent takes of herself the task of invoking the law through a transgression of its commands. We are here faced with an evident dialectical paradox: the law manifests itself as force only through the negation of its commands. If the law is denied of the possibility of its negation – its taking place in the form of sanction – its existence is conflated in the substantial, transcendental impotence of its textual existence. Second, law's form and law's force are essentially irreducible to each other. In other words, the technical term force of law defines the ultimate separation of the *vis obligandi* of the norm, from its formal (impotent) utterance; so much so, that, as Agamben claims, it is perfectly plausible for specific decrees and measures that are not formally law (like the state of exception), to acquire its force (SE, 37–8).

Albeit ultimately dependent on each other, for the law force and form seem irreconcilable. And this, Agamben suggests, becomes particularly evident in the concept of law's application – that is when a particular fact is decided on by subsuming it under the directives of a given general rule. Such concept, he claims, has been 'put on a false track' (ibid., 39) by equating it to Kant's theory of determinant judgment, according to which the singular (particular) case is and must be considered as decidable in relation to a general known rule. The general rule here consists of nothing more than a principle encompassing a series of x cases, which in the moment of the judgment are subsumed logically under the generality of the norm. But as Agamben notes the application of a norm is not merely a logical operation, since it involves the passage from the logical/formal sphere to that of practice. Much like for language, he goes on

the relation between the general and the particular (and all the more so in the case of the application of a juridical norm), it is not only a logical subsumption that is at issue, but first and foremost the passage from a generic proposition endowed with a merely virtual reference to a concrete reference to a segment of reality (that is, nothing less than the question of the actual relation between language and world). This passage from *langue* to *parole,* or from the semiotic to the semantic, is not a logical operation at all; rather, it always entails a practical activity, that is, the assumption of *langue* by one or more speaking subjects and the implementation (ibid.)

'In the case of the juridical norm' the decision on the 'concrete case entails a trial that always involves a plurality of subjects and ultimately culminates in the pronunciation of a sentence, that is, an enunciation whose operative reference to reality is guaranteed by the institutional powers' (ibid., 39–40). The actual application of law's norm, though, is never included in the norm, but depends ultimately on something external: on the set of institutions and apparatuses appointed to fulfil such a task. It is the institutional edifice through which the law is administered, applied and enforced often through violent means that turns law's impotent utterances into authoritative commands. In short, law's operativity – that passage from the ought to the is – is produced through the articulation of a meaningful albeit impotent language and a meaningless anomic force administered through an institutional apparatus.

Violence

The law entertains a contentious relationship with the violent means of its enforcement. As Christoph Menke puts it, in so far as legal norms and sanctions are meant to halt violence and its reproduction, the law is essentially 'the opposite of violence'.[29] But the law, he goes on, is 'itself violence; legal decisions, too, use violence – external violence, which assails the body, as well as internal violence, which injures the soul'.[30] René Girard in *Violence and the Sacred* has explained such a paradox using the notion of vengeance. For a juridical system, punishment assumes the guise of a public vengeance, which 'succeeds in limiting and isolating its effects in accordance with social demands'.[31] Taken from the point of view of their logical structure, private and public revenge (in the form of the sanction), show no substantial distinctions: in both cases, it is a matter of combining violent deeds as a reaction to specific acts or events. Though the violence exercised by the law has the supposed peculiar faculty of interrupting the potentially infinite cycle of violence and counterviolence. The law – Girard writes – makes humans free 'from the terrible obligations of vengeance',[32] holding the means for 'stifling'[33] the spread of violence in society. The acquisition of a decisive role of limiting violence (and supposedly of pursuing justice) is, for the law, determined by the possibility of the implementation of yet another legal-unpunished violence. And this makes the relationship between law and violence, norm and sanction a mimetic one; where the negation of the norm is followed by a negation of something other – freedom, life, or the nullification of what is done contravening law's command.

The genetic link between law and violence stands out as one of the recurrent themes in Agamben's work.[34] Inspired by Benjamin's *Critique of Violence*, he has undertaken a genealogy of legal violence oriented toward the thinking of a renewed use of law freed from the curse of violence. Agamben's genealogical strategy was that of uncovering the contingency of the forms and functions of the violent means that have historically been implemented to demarcate the limits of law's authority and power. The volume *The Sacrament of Language: An Archaeology of the Oath*, represents a significant moment in this enterprise. Relying upon a series of classic documents (from Greek legal practices and philosophy to Cicero as well as more modern examples), Agamben here takes on an archaeological deconstruction of the practice of the oath, aimed at exposing what he has defined as the original 'experience of language' (SL, 53). What the sphere of religious, legal and political rituality to which the practice of the oath is related covered up is the specifically peculiar human phenomenon of the making up of a world out of language, or in other words, the creational potential implicit in every act of speech. As Émile Benveniste had claimed

> [The oath] is a particular modality of assertion, which supports, guarantees, and demonstrates, but does not found anything. Individual or collective, the oath exists only by virtue of that which it reinforces and renders solemn: a pact, an agreement, a declaration. It prepares for or concludes a speech act which alone possesses meaningful content, but it expresses nothing by itself. It is in truth an oral rite, often completed by a manual rite whose form is variable. Its function consists not in the affirmation that it produces, but in the relation that it institutes between the word pronounced and the potency invoked. [35]

As such, the rituality of the oath served to guarantee and reinforce the statement of a pact, an agreement, or a declaration; and it was not concerned with the 'semiotic or cognitive function of language', but with the 'assurance of its truthfulness and its actualisation' (ibid.). There are three fundamental elements of an oath: 'an affirmation, the invocation of the gods as witnesses, and a curse directed at perjury' (ibid., 31). At stake in the articulation of these elements is the actual correspondence between language and the world; the concretisation of what has each time been claimed and promised. The invocation of the gods as witnesses and the curse (because of perjury and the transgression of a promise) are the two elements that have been elaborated to guarantee the efficacy of the words pronounced in the oath.

In antiquity, Agamben notes, the curse – the application of which produced the 'putting outside the law' of the cursed[36] – played a pivotal role in the development of the legal practice as 'a practical auxiliary for the efficacy of law'[37] (ibid., 35). In the Greek laws of *Charondas*, for instance, the course accompanied the formulation of norms regarding the state's security and the self-standing of the city. It consisted of a specific form of punishment elaborated to sustain the validity and efficacy of law.[38] Based on a well-established historiography Agamben traces back to the experience of the curse in ancient Greece and Rome the matrix of what has been later developed as a legal sanction. He locates in the experience of the religious and juridical sphere of the oath the seeds of the emergence of legal violence as a fundamental element for law's effectivity. The curse he writes 'marks out the *locus* in which, at a later stage, the penal law will be established' giving sense to 'the incredible irrationality that characterises the history of punishment' (ibid., 38). In the sphere of the law, the curse (and the subsequent evolution of penal law) absolved in a sense the purpose of ensuring the actualisation of law's statements. As Agamben maintains, the force of law that sustains human societies and 'the idea of linguistic enunciations that stably obligate living beings, that can be observed and transgressed, derive from this attempt to nail down the originary performative force' of language, and represents, 'an epiphenomenon of the oath and of the malediction that accompanied it' (ibid., 70). As usual, Agamben here seeks help in Paul, more specifically in *Galatians* 3:10–13, when the Apostle speaks of a curse of the law [*katara tou nomou*]: 'cursed', we read here, 'is everyone who does not observe and obey all the things written in the book of the law'. Those who submit to the judgment of the law are under law's curse; and the fulfilment of law through messianic redemption cannot but pass through the deactivation and deposition of such curse.

For Agamben, in summary, the curse as an accessory element that has been historically elaborated to challenge perjury and to give law's utterances a force that human language cannot grant, represents a paradigmatic example for understanding the essential function of the system of sanctions and punishments that the law seems destined to lean on. Law's violence, as much as its ancestor, the curse, is meant to bridge the gap that separates and connects the sphere of linguistic enunciation (the norm) and the world. Anthropogenesis has left humans in the uneasy position of not being able to guarantee the correspondence between what they say, factual reality, and what they ultimately do. And the law with the violent means of its enforcement appears as a system of rites and institutions that aims at guaranteeing the performative actualisation of certain locutions that from time to time have been considered of particular importance, usually called norms or rules.

Agamben further develops his engagement with the law's violence in the volume *Karman. A Brief Treaty on Action, Guilt and Gesture*, and he does so through a close engagement with the legal concept of the sanction. In its canonical definition, a sanction 'is that part of the text of the law that contains the pronouncement of the punishment that strikes the transgressor' (K, 14). In other and admittedly simplistic words, the sanction constitutes the price to pay for having committed a guilty act, which, as expressed by the principle of culpability *nulla poena sine culpa* [there is no punishment without guilt],[39] designates the necessary presupposition for a sanction to be legitimate. However, such a foundational principle is not immune from logical difficulties. As Agamben put it, the fact that no punishment is applicable without fault, 'means that punishment can be inflicted only in consequence of a certain act, but the fault exists as such only in virtue of the punishment that sanctions it' (ibid., 13). The principle of cul-pability, for Agamben, should be reformulated as 'there is no guilt without punishment'. Such a trivial observation hides the crucial fact that guilt as such exists only as a product of a juridical order: outside of the law, all deeds and actions are radically innocent. The administration and delivery of sanc-tions delimit the ambit of guilt and crimes and is therefore the constitutive element of the law. Only by presupposing the negative element of the punishment can a norm be sustained positively; but in the end this means that the law consists ultimately of its sanctions.

Norms and sanctions appear here not as different elements or moments in the articulation of law's machinery: they operate somehow immanently in such a way that the norm acquires sense only when its negation becomes the object of a sanc-tion. The illicitness of an act, for Agamben, does not emanate from a 'quality immanent to the act' (ibid., 21) – that is, its not adhering to a given principle or norm (its wrongfulness) – but it is substantially the result of the predicament of a legal order, which renders that act sanctionable. As a result, a crime does not constitute a breaking of the law: 'in the formulation of the text of the norm the illicit appears as a condition and not as a negation of the law' (ibid.). But he goes on,

> It is not sufficient to say, however, that the law, by means of the sanction, produces crime. It is necessary to add that the sanction does not create only the illicit, but at the same time, by determining its own condition, above all affirms and produces itself as what must be. And since the sanction generally has the form of a coercive act, one can say ... that the law consists essentially in the production of a permitted violence, which is to say, in a justification of violence (ibid., 22).

From Agamben's perspective, the law is essentially a system of signs which permits the classification of certain acts as sanc-tionable, allowing specific agents to coerce others to comply with ordained behaviours under the threat of a punishment – which eventually assumes the guise of an unsanctioned (and unsanctionable) violence. The subject of law's imperative is existentially exposed to justified-legal violence, which to be such must remain unsanctionable – that is legal. What lies at the basis of any legal imputation and responsibility as the ultimate bearer of the operational link between law and violence, is bare life. Indeed, if the efficacy of law is obtained through the possibility of implementing justified-legal violence, as what ought to be, the law fulfils its ontological status only when the life it aims to command is abandoned to the possibility of being the object of unsanctionable violence.

As Agamben observes, the first appearance of 'bare life' – as the mere fact of living and as the main subject of legal imputations, penalties and violence – is included in the *Habeas Corpus Act 1679*. This piece of law, which has been regarded as foundational to modern Western democracies, contains the first explicit statement of the inclusion of the *zoē* as the main reference of the law. The writ reads as follows: 'We command that you have before us to show, at Westminster, that body X, by whatsoever name he may be called therein, which is held in your custody, as it is said, as well as the cause of the arrest and the detention'.[40] In the text that famously sanctioned the right of the individual to fair and justified imprisonment, Agamben sees the paradigmatic proof of the capture of the impersonal bodily life within the boundaries of the law as its primary subject. 'It is not the free man and his statutes and prerogatives', he claims, but the 'corpus that is the new subject of politics. And democracy is born precisely as the assertion and presentation of this "body": *habeas corpus ad subjiciendum*, you will have to have a body to show' (HS., 124). The act of showing the body of the imprisoned along with the reasons for its detention was intended as a form of guarantee of the same subject from any unlawful imprisonment. For the law determinant is the presence of a *corpus*, which represents the evidence and the locus of freedom and rights, and the punishment. 'The same legal procedure that was originally intended to assure the presence of the accused at the trial and, therefore, to keep the accused from avoiding judgment turns, in its new and definitive form, into grounds for the sheriff to detain and exhibit the body of the accused. *Corpus* is a two-faced being, the bearer both of subjection to sovereign power and of individual liberties' (ibid., 124–5). The law, thus, needs a 'body in order to be in force' (ibid., 124), and the proper subject of law, is consequently bare life: the human being with its naked, impersonal existence as exposed to legal unsanctionable violence. Bare life is the subject (as sub-jectum, as thrown at the bottom), the ultimate bearer of rights and penalties, the place in which protection, security, and the very possibility of being annihilated conflate and becomes indistinguishable.

Inoperative law

We can qualify Agamben's intervention in jurisprudence as belonging to that strand of positivist theory that envisages the law as a command sustained by a threat of violence and sanctions. Against the more 'optimist jurisprudence' that insists on the ideology of the rule of law and human rights, secondary rules and legal interpretation, which started to become hegemonic from the second half of the twentieth century, Agamben has revived and radicalised the idea of the law as an organised administration of coercion through violent means. In the end, as Frederick Schauer reiterated in the volume *The Force of Law*, 'coercion in law is so ubiquitous' that it 'may be the feature that, probabilistically even if not logically, distinguishes law from other norms, systems and numerous other mechanisms of social organisation'.[41] Only by turning a blind eye to the legal operation, is it possible to negate the violent nature of law's order: its being a 'field of pain and death'.[42]

Contrary to the traditional jurisprudential canon, which could be considered as ultimately oriented to a justification/legitimisation of law's violent means – either resorting to utilitarian arguments or by reference to a sort of 'natural' human tendency to inform social life juridically – Agamben's legal theory aimed at thinking the law in a radical new guise. With its messianic tone, his incursions into legal theory have constantly pointed to the idea of law's inoperativity (or destitution). In this sense, Agamben's jurisprudence is essentially a form of anti-jurisprudence.

Part of the constellation of thoughts moving around the idea of form-of-life, the idea of law's inoperativity encapsulates a process of overcoming of law as a command and violence. But what does it mean for the law to be made inoperative? What form will the law assume after its destitution? If, as we have seen so far, the law gains its effectivity only through the possibility of its enforcement – that is only when supported by legal violence – the destitution of law, its inoperativity, is obtained only through the severance of the genetic link between law's norm and force, between words and violence. But law's destitution is perhaps the hardest task. A non-coercive law, as a text that speaks but does not command, is from the point of view of Western legal tradition, something unthinkable: the night in which all laws become black.

Despite his bleak vision of the law's work, Agamben's writings are pervaded by a sense of law's futurability. Faced with the actual impossibility of turning legal violence for good, he invites us to consider a potential future in which the law is neither a justification for violence, nor the instrument through which human hierarchies and exclusions are formulated and enforced. 'One day', Agamben claims in one oft-cited passage of *State of Exception*, 'humanity will play with law just as children play with disused objects, not in order to restore them to their canonical use but to free them from it for good. What is found after the law is not a more proper and original use value that precedes the law but a new use that is born only after it' (SE, 63). The new use of the law, inaugurated by the deposition or destitution of law from its sacred authoritarian throne, is that which has severed the bond that ties the text of the law to violence, allows for the law to be simply lived or used and the life of humans to become not the form (or *bios*) of a subject proprietor but the form-of-life of a community of singularities.

Such an idea finds its clearest expression in *The Highest Poverty*. For Agamben, monastic rules, and Franciscanism in particular, illustrate a very articulated attempt at living a life outside of law's determination, according to an unenforceable rule that is lived through and not lived under. Agamben here refers to an episode of the life of Francis that from our point of view is particularly indicative: a companion once asked the saint why he did not intervene to correct and amend the decadence of the order, Francis answered firmly that: 'If I cannot convince them and correct their vices with preaching and example, I do not want to become a persecutor to pursue and frustrate them, like the power of this world [*nolo carnifex fieri ad percutiendum et flagellandum, sicut potestas huius seculi]'.*[43]

Although the image of law without sanctions somehow embodies the limit or the deadlock in which jurisprudence cannot but run aground, in the past such an idea was considered a real possibility. For Roman jurisprudence, Agamben claims, an unsanctionable norm was perfectly conceivable; and this is expressed by Ulpian's *Regulae*, in which laws fall into three categories:

> A law is perfect that forbids something to be done, and if it has been done rescinds it [*perfecta lex est, quae vetat aliquid fieri et si factum sit, rescindit*]. ... A law is imperfect that forbids something to be done, and if it has been done does not rescind it, and imposes no penalty upon him who breaks the law [*nec rescindit nec poenaminiungit ei qui contra legem fecit] ... A law is less than perfect [minus quam perfecta] that forbids something to be done, and if it is done, does not rescind it, but imposes a penalty upon him who violates the law [non rescindit, sed poenam iniungit ei qui contra legem fecit].* (K, 22–23)

Though the existence of rules without a sanction is not attested, Agamben writes, the acknowledgement of their possibility is of the utmost interest: 'it is significant that jurists, by situating them at the opposite extreme from perfect laws, felt the demand to conceive them as a limit-zone of the juridical sphere, yet still within it' (ibid., 23). The perfect law – that which can affirm the non-existence of its transgression – and the imperfect law, without sanction, constitute the limits of the space in which the totality of norms are placed. Here, what is 'striking', for Agamben 'is that the culture that transmitted to us the fundamental principles of law linked the sanction, if not to an imperfection, at least to a lesser perfection of the law' (ibid.).

As usual, Agamben hesitates to provide programmes or specific recipes for an inoperative law, other than those that can be allegorically deduced from some paradigmatic examples taken from the text of Western culture and legal tradition. It is worth looking here to the works of the philosopher

Daniel Loick, who – through a painstaking critique of sovereignty – has attempted at thinking of a non-coercive, non-violent law. In his book, *A Critique of Sovereignty*, Loick begins his stark criticism of the state's form and law's violence, by acknowledging the irony pervading the form that polities have historically adopted to shape their communal living: 'the *status civilis* continues to be determined by forms of behaviour that once characterized the *status naturalis* ...: while society believes it is freeing itself from nature's raw, wild modes of interaction, it unconsciously acquires those very same modes of interaction'.[44] With the creation of the state's apparatus, Western civilisation is believed to have abandoned the unregulated state of nature and war; while instead, it has openly legitimised the same violence through its institutionalisation and legalisation. 'The failure of the attempt to forgo violence-based forms of interaction [and] the scant success that politics has achieved in containing violence', Loick claims, invites us to reconsider the 'axiom that violence antecedent to the state can only be combated with more violence'.[45] And in this regard, a critique of sovereignty and its historical/institutional manifestation is paramount to demonstrating that the violence in society can only be obtained 'by fundamentally overcoming conventional forms of states rulership'.[46]

Taking on Benjamin's idea of a deposition [*Entsetzung*] of law, Loick thinks of a non-violent and non-coercive law through the decoupling of the law's operation and the sovereign principle. As he argues, the relationship between law and sovereignty has been traditionally considered according to three dominant paradigms: the law as the sovereign's command (i.e. in the role entrusted upon it by Jean Bodin, Thomas Hobbes and Jean-Jacques Rousseau); sovereignty as absolute power without law (as in Schmitt's decisionism); and sovereign power as substantially limited by the law (as in the liberal – Kantian – tradition). Alongside these three formulations, Loick places a fourth option: 'a fundamentally anti-sovereign, anarchist position (law without sovereignty that is Benjamin's position)'.[47] The law without sovereignty and violence is from this point of view a form of regulative/normative system that remains alien to the commands of a ruler. A non-violent form of law, he goes on, is well suited to a radically democratic society that refrains from the concept of sovereignty. Because it does not enforce its law with coercion, it takes on the character of a voluntary and therefore an-archic association. Law without coercion takes on the form of a communal agreement – with the persuasive resources of an agreement but without the violence of sanction to enforce it. It serves to coordinate collective action and the cooperation of the whole society, and therefore relieves people of excessive demands to make decisions in everyday life, establishing at least a weak stability of expectation.[48]

For Loick, a non-violent law is not only thinkable, but its existence is somehow historically attested. Judaism, he claims, represented one example of a legal tradition in which the law has been conceived as non-coercive. Throughout history, the halacha has been for Jewish communities a form of law, with an eminent juridical guise, that has shaped their form of life, laying down rules, forms of conduct and systems of dispute resolution, without recourse to state-sanctioned violence.[49] Such form of law has been essentially disjoined from any kind of sovereign or state power, lacking in this way a proper system of enforcement. The halacha has functioned as the 'constitutive' rule of Jewish communal life, without constituting power apparatuses. The example of halacha is apt for Loick's theorisation since it amounts to a sort of rehabilitation of law as a legitimate force in social life after it has suffered through a strong critique of its violent illegitimacy.[50]

While it is true that the Jewish law of the diaspora was not enforced by sovereign state or sovereign police, it is nevertheless equipped with some very clear forms of punishment[51] – the most popular of which is perhaps the *herem* [excommunication]. Nowadays in disuse, the *herem* has historically been implemented to disincentivise practices considered as against law or promoting heretical ideas. The halacha afforded the *Bit Din* – the rabbinic court entitled to adjudicate disputes based on Talmudic law and Jewish traditions – the power to implement a range of excommunicative punishments, from mild ostracism to full excommunication. And the history of European philosophy provides us with perhaps the most famous example of *herem*: that of

Spinoza. It is worth looking at length here at the text that sanctioned his excommunication:

> The Lords of the *ma 'amad*, having long known of the evil opinions and acts of Baruch de Spinoza, have endeavored by various means and promises, to turn him from his evil ways. But having failed to make him mend his wicked ways, and, on the contrary, daily receiving more and more serious information about the abominable heresies which he practiced and taught and about his monstrous deeds, and having for this numerous trustworthy witnesses who have deposed and born witness to this effect in the presence of the said Espinoza, they became convinced of the truth of this matter; and after all of this has been investigated in the presence of the honorable chachamim, they have decided, with their consent, that the said Espinoza should be excommunicated and expelled from the people of Israel. By decree of the angels and by the command of the holy men, we excommunicate, expel, curse and damn Baruch de Espinoza, with the consent of God, Blessed be He, and with the consent of the entire holy congregation, and in front of these holy scrolls with the 613 precepts which are written therein; cursing him with the excommunication with which Joshua banned Jericho and with the curse which Elisha cursed the boys and with all the castigations that are written in the Book of the Law. Cursed be he by day and cursed be he by night; cursed be he when he lies down and cursed be he when he rises up. Cursed be he when he goes out and cursed be he when he comes in. The Lord will not spare him, but then the anger of the Lord and his jealousy shall smoke against that man, and all the curses that are written in this book shall lie upon him, and the Lord shall blot out his name from under heaven. And the Lord shall separate him unto evil out of all the tribes of Israel, according to all the curses of the covenant that are written in this book of the law. But you that cleave unto the Lord your God are alive every one of you this day.[52]

The person sanctioned with the *herem* is declared *menuddeh* or defiled. Such a form of ban – or curse – 'was used to enforce the social, religious, and ethical conduct thought appropriate to a proper Jewish community, and to discourage deviancy not just in matters of liturgical practice but also in matters of everyday behavior and the expression of ideas'.[53]

Perhaps, what pushed Loick to interpret Jewish law as a form of non-coercive law is the identification of legal violence with modern sovereign violence – intended as that of the state's apparatus and the police. Certainly, this form of violence is the most visible of all the forms of violence directly or indirectly emanating from the law's very existence. However, there are other types of legal violence (structural and cultural) that are not less effective in sustaining law's order than a police force. From the vantage point chosen by Agamben, sovereign violence should be considered as an epiphenomenon – a historical accident – of the archetypal curse of the law that has accompanied the juridical sphere from time immemorial. The sovereign, Agamben maintains, 'is the point of indistinction between violence and law, the threshold on which violence passes over into law and law passes over into violence' (HS, 32): it is in this sense derivative from the articulation of law and violence. Decoupling law from sovereignty is a necessary, but not sufficient, step towards the thought of a non-coercive law. The political action that severs the supposed genetic link between law's word and violence, Agamben claims, opens the way to access an inoperative law, purified from violence, which appears as 'a word that does not bind, that neither commands nor prohibits anything, but says only itself' (SE, 88), that cannot but entertain a renewed relationship with life. Such an inoperative status of law could be contemplated only by questioning the very essence of commands and the mythological/ontological ground with which the Western tradition has conceived social life, language and imperatives.

~ * ~

For the Western mind the difficulty of conceiving a law without violence and an authoritative word that does not command, is rooted in the very archetypal legal forms and related foundational narratives that have shaped its political and juridical imagination. In some of the oldest examples of written law, such as the Hammurabi code, Mosaic law and the Law of the Twelve Tables in Rome – which surely had an impact on the development of law in the West – the principles of the *lex talionis* (an eye for an eye, a tooth for a tooth) and retributive justice play an important role. The *lex talionis* captures the general notion that those who harm another deserve equivalent harm in return: it is the offender's crime (rather than the injuries caused) that dictates the appropriate punishment. And as Agamben points out, in the *lex talionis* 'the juridical order does not originally present itself simply as sanctioning a transgressive fact but instead constitutes itself through the repetition of the same act without any sanction, that is, as an exceptional case' (HS, 26). And this, he goes on, represents something like an original inclusion in the law of the same violence it sanctions. Retributive justice, expressed by the *lex talionis*, has always had a bad reputation among jurists and philosophers, who generally dismissed it as a primitive form of justice, belonging to the dim origins of law's history of not-yet civilised humanity.[54] However, such a form of law has bequeathed to the Western imagination, both the logic structure of norms – according to which the infringement of law's commands must be followed by a sanction – and the fundamental jurisprudential principle of proportionality – according to which the punishment should be 'proportional' to the crime.[55] Indeed, as Herbert L. Hart once wrote, the notion that 'what the criminal has done should be done to him ... the killer should be killed, the violent assailant should be flogged' expresses the 'crudest form' of proportionality.[56]

Wherever you look, law's authority has always spoken (and continues to speak) the language of commands, coercion and punishments. It has built its aura of legitimacy on the supposed goodness of the order it produces out of fear and coercion, and by retributing justice somehow proportionally. It comes as no surprise that the failure of law's authority and efficacy has been constantly associated with violence, injustice, chaos and disorder. Paradigmatic in this regard is Thucydides' description of the plague in Athens, when the destitution of law's authority has been identified as the cause that unleashed the elementary instincts of citizens bringing the Athenian community to dissolution. The plague, Thucydides narrates, marked the beginning of increased lawlessness in the city. The people, facing the possibility of their imminent death did not 'persevere in what had once been thought the path of honour'; they felt 'less inhibited in the indulgence of pleasures previously concealed' and 'as a result they decided to look for satisfactions that were quick and pleasurable, reckoning that neither life nor wealth would last long'.[57] And, as 'long as no one expected to live long enough to be brought to justice and pay the penalty', they no longer felt bound by the law:[58] 'Neither the fear of the gods nor laws of men awed any man'.[59] Here the vanishing of law's capacity to instil awe in citizens, produced gradual dissolution of communal living; and as Hobbes captured it like no other in his *Leviathan*, it is the *awe* of laws and authority that is at the origin of the state: only if a power is treated with awe and revered can it coerce the conscience and behaviour of the multitude, granting in this way the order necessary for civil society to be in place. When the law speaks but does not command, when its punishments are not held in awe, what we are dealing with is the state of nature, the savage state that precedes society, politics and civilisation. And perhaps it is by looking to the "uncivilised" world that a non-coercive law could be envisaged as a real possibility.

The French anthropologist and ethnologist Pierre Clastres[60] has devoted his research to seeking a radical alternative to Western hierarchical and coercive society, by entering a constant and serious dialogue[61] with what are traditionally termed savage or primitive societies. With his fieldwork among the indigenous people of South America (mainly the Guayaki, Guaraní people, Yanomami and Chulupi),[62] Clastres' prime interest is that of de-substantialising the state, and the ethnocentric bias that oriented the West in conceiving statelessness in evolutionary terms as due to the lack of societal differentiation and specific economic coordinates. 'Primitive societies' is the name Clastres has given to the peoples he has encountered, to their essential alterity and multiplicity, which far from representing an immature stage of civilisation constitute the immanent exteriority of state's power: that alterity that can never be captured by Western political and economic apparatus without sanctioning its destruction. Primitive societies have been traditionally seen as societies without a state. For Clastres, this statement conceals a 'value judgment': statelessness means 'missing something – the state – that is essential to them, as it is to any other society: our own, for instance. Consequently, those societies are incomplete; they are not quite true societies – they are not civilized'.[63] Against this assumption, Clastres' work has been constantly oriented towards showing that primitive societies – devoid as they are of clear institutional apparatuses, often ignorant of writing, living at a subsistence level, with no state, law and religion – are such not due to a lack of elements that impede the emergence of a state, but because their very existence wards off, resists and averts that monster (the state) they supposedly do not understand.[64]

For Clastres, what most characterises primitive societies is the absence from their form of life of the function command-obedience that define the Western conception of power as coercion. As he claims, in *Society Against the State*, based on ethnological evidence, political power should be considered as a kind of universal, pertaining to the very human living in society. However, such power assumes two main forms: coercive and non-coercive. Coercive power, based on hierarchical authoritarian relationship is a particular non-universal form, whose concrete realisation appeared in some culture (the Western for instance). Primitive societies, on the contrary, are structured according to a non-coercive power, which is nonetheless *a* power but that is exercised in a non-hierarchical way and without resorting to coercive means. Neither social stratification, nor authority is present in non-coercive societies. And in Clastres' words, to the extent that such form of power cannot be attributed to any given source, and does not command anything, for primitive societies 'power, paradoxical by its nature, is venerated in its impotence'.[65]

The paradox of primitive impotent power finds its utmost expression in what Clastres as defined as 'duty to speak'. The power to speak, to dictate, to formulate commands and to set down the law, is what identifies the authority of the ruler: 'whether prince, despot, or commander-in-chief, the man of power is always not only the man who speaks, but the sole source of legitimate speech: an impoverished speech, a poor speech to be sure, but one rich in efficiency, for it goes by the name command and wants nothing save the obedience of the executant'.[66] Of course, this is true for coercive society, based

on social distinctions between ruler and ruled, lord and subjects, leaders and citizens; divisions that produce the necessary separation of 'power' and 'society', in which the former
is held and exercised by few, and at times against the latter.
In societies without a state, the relationship between speech
(and words) is inverted. Thus, 'in societies with a state speech
is power's *right*', Clastres writes, 'in societies without a state
speech is power's duty'.[67] In primitive societies chiefs do
not speak (neither command) because they are chiefs: on the
contrary, it is the society that commands the chief to speak.
But what the chief says is not to be listened to or obeyed.
The chief's speech is a ritualised act to which nobody pays
attention: 'almost without exception, the leader addresses
the group daily, at daybreak and dusk. Stretched out in his
hammock or seated next to his fire, he delivers the expected
discourse in a loud voice'; but 'as a matter of fact, there is no
gathering around the chief when he speaks, no hush falls,
everybody goes about their business as if nothing was hap-
pening. The word of the chief is not spoken in order to be
listened to'.[68] For non-coercive power, therefore, authority
speaks but does not command.

As Clastres argues, the responsibility of the chiefs was
mainly that of solving conflicts that might arise between
individuals and families and of restoring harmony without
using coercive means. And the success of the endeavour
is never guaranteed, for the chief's word carries no force
of law.[69] In the end, Clastres maintains, what makes the
chief a chief are his technical competences: his oratorical
talent, his expertise in hunting and his ability in waging
war. Obviously, for primitive societies a law-based communal order is inconceivable. The only normative device
that Clastres recognised as central to their life is what he
defined as primitive law, which is nothing more and nothing
less than the silent acceptance of being full members of the
community. Through initiation rites, the young members are
exposed to the only law whose memory is kept intact on
their body in the forms of marks, scars (or tattoos). This law
says: '*You are worth no more than anyone else; you are worth
no less than anyone else*, which is a principle that expresses
primitive society's refusal to run the risk of division, the risk
of a power separate from society itself, a power that would

escape its control'.[70] The mark on the body, on all bodies alike, declares: *You will not have the desire for power; you will not have the desire for submission.*[71]

Clastres' theories have not been immune from criticism. His assertory language, which opposes the standard academic canon for anthropology and ethnography, has been dubbed ahistorical, naïve, romantic and rhetorical; and his anthropological anarchism was at times received with contempt.[72] So why return to Clastres? And why should we look back to primitive people, if what concerns us is our life? Because, as Eduardo Viveiros de Castro brilliantly puts it, primitive society names 'the conceptual embodiments of the thesis that another world is possible: that there is life beyond capitalism, as there is society outside of the State'.[73] And this leads us to the bitter, yet somewhat hopeful conclusion that the destitution of law, the idea of a form of non-coercive regulation, must be thought only beyond and against our civilisation. The destitution of law is an act of de-civilisation.

Notes

1. The auxiliary verb 'shall', which is the common mode of expression of laws, is categorised in linguistics as 'commissive modality' – a sub-category of 'deontic modality' – which represents the condition that 'connotes the speaker's expressed commitment, as a promise or threat, to bring about the proposition expressed by the utterance'. See Palmer (2001: 10).
2. Searle (1983: 166).
3. Olivecrona (1964: 794).
4. Ibid.
5. Cicero (1928: 9).
6. Ibid., 8.
7. Ambrose (2001).
8. As Agamben notes, before finding its canonical translation as *potentia-actualitas*, the couple *dynamis-energeia* had been rendered by the Latin Fathers as *possibilitas-efficacia* (effectus).
9. Such modality of action, Agamben maintains, finds its most explicit and articulated expression in Immanuel Kant's ethics which, in its many formulations, does not indicate the good empirical substance of an action, but only the modality of how to act. Indeed, for Kant, duty is the necessity to

act according to pure respect for the [moral] law or in other words, it is an absolute subjugation to a void command [law]. See Kant (2002: 16).

10. Kelsen (1967: 5).
11. Ibid., 5–6.
12. Weinberger (1973: XV).
13. Kelsen (1973: 216–17).
14. Weinberger (1973: XIX).
15. Ibid., XXIII.
16. Berger and Luckmann (1966: 106).
17. Coccia (2015).
18. Croce (2015: 67).
19. Austin (1962: 19).
20. Ibid., 14–5.
21. See Fusco (2020: 17).
22. Benveniste (1971: 236).
23. See Scarry (2009: 29); Warrender (1957).
24. von Jhering (1913: 190).
25. Derrida (1992: 5–6).
26. Wrobleski and Hess (2006: 4).
27. Ibid., 61.
28. Šerpytytė (2019).
29. Menke (2018: 3).
30. Ibid.
31. Girard (2013: 24).
32. Ibid., 23.
33. Ibid., 24.
34. Since at least the early 1970s, with the publication of the essay *On the Limits of Violence*. See Agamben (2015).
35. Benveniste (1984), quoted in SL, 4.
36. Gernet (1984), quoted in SL, 35.
37. Ziebarth (1895), quoted in SL, 35.
38. Ziebarth has demonstrated, with ample documentation, the consubstantiality of the curse to Greek legislation. Its function was so essential that the sources speak of a veritable 'political curse', which always confirms the efficacy of the law. In the preamble to the laws of Charondas one thus reads: 'It is necessary to observe [*emmenein*] what has been proclaimed, but the one who transgresses is subjected to the political curse [*ara politike*] Ziebarth has traced the presence of the 'political' curse in the legal apparatuses of all the Greek cities, ... 'This means,' comments Ziebarth, 'that the entire constituted legal order, according to which the *demos* is sovereign, is sanctioned by means of a curse'.

Not only the oath, but also the curse – in this sense it is rightly called 'political' – functions as a genuine 'sacrament of power' (ibid., 37).

39. Also known as principle of culpability – formulated also as *Nullum crimen, nulla poena sine culpa*.

40. *Praecipimus tibi quod Corpus X in custodia vestra detentum, ut dicitur, una cum causa captionis et detentionis, quodcumque nomine idem X cemeatur in eadem, habeas coram nobis, apud Westminster, ad subjiciendum* (HS, 124).

41. Schauer (2015: 98).

42. Cover (1986).

43. Fracesco di Assisi (2004: 472–4).

44. Loick (2018: xv).

45. Ibid.

46. Ibid., xvii.

47. Ibid., 193.

48. Ibid., 216.

49. Loick (2018a: 102).

50. See Johansen (2020).

51. Within the framework of Jewish autonomy – that is the religious, social and cultural self-sufficiency that the Jewish communities enjoyed and enjoy within sovereign non-Jewish states – 'a great variety of penalties could be imposed on wrongdoers, including fines, imprisonment, *herem*, and – extremely rarely – capital punishment, according to judgment passed by a *bet din* under the ordinances of the community or a *hevrah*', see Elon (2007: 735–6).

52. Nadler (1999: 120).

53. Ibid., 127.

54. See, for example, Kelsen (1943).

55. VanDrunen (2008).

56. Hart (2008: 161).

57. Thucydides (2009: 99).

58. Ibid.

59. Thucydides (1959: 118).

60. Although a divisive figure, Clastres had a decisive influence on some significant French intellectuals such as Claude Lefort, Miguel Abensour and the young Marcel Gauchet. For a reconstruction of the Clastres' works and intellectual profile, see Moyn (2004) and Holman (2021).

61. Clastres (1979).

62. See Clastres (2000).

63. Clastres (1989: 189).

64. Deleuze and Guattari (1987: 357).

65. Clastres (1989: 47).
66. Ibid., 151.
67. Ibid., 153.
68. Ibid.
69. Ibid., 206.
70. Ibid., 186.
71. Ibid., 188.
72. See, for example: Geertz (2000); Moyn (2004); Graeber (2004).
73. Viveiros de Castro (2010: 15).

Four

Inoperative Being: Against Work

Production without possession, action without self-assertion, development without domination: this is its mysterious operation.

Lao Tzu

The idea of work

Any consideration of the nature of 'work' must begin with the preliminary and admittedly quite banal acknowledgement that its form and ideology are recent inventions. Only since early modernity, when capitalism with its correlated ethics and economic paradigms was established as a totalising socio-political system, has work – that is wage labour – been assigned the meaning and the moral value that we all know. In pre-modern societies, labour was not considered valuable in itself: generally, it was viewed as an activity that humans had to perform out of necessity, to satisfy certain natural needs.[1] With the transition to modernity, however, work became a dominant value, no longer 'defended on grounds of economic necessity and social duty' but 'widely understood as an individual moral practice and collective ethical obligation'.[2] Labour is surrounded by an aura of dignity, privilege, self-fulfilment and social recognition, which, considering the pain, boredom, alienation and precarity that most workers experience in their daily lives, turns out to be unsubstantiated void rhetoric. Moral arguments sustaining the idea of work, like a proper hegemonic ideology, shadows the reality of labour by abstracting it into the sphere of the ideal, embellishing it with the colours of ethical truths.

The ideology of work is grounded on the foundational narrative that portrays the human as made for and by its

119

own productive capacity.[3] Emerging in the nineteenth century, such a narrative defines the humanity of humans as an expression of their faculty to transform nature and to create an environment less hostile to survival.[4] Here, productive labour is part of an innate transformative exchange with nature, which is in a sense the constitutive metahistorical category of the secularised version of anthropogenesis. From this perspective, the work of the human becomes the origin of humanity itself: it is the production of a world,[5] from an immediate exchange with the environment, that gives a distinctive anthropological orientation to an otherwise general and unspecified form of living.

Placed on the threshold that separates and unites *humanitas* and *animalitas*,[6] the idea of natural productive capacity stands for the substance of human living. And work (or labour) as we all know it, is the historically institutionalised actualisation of such productive status. In Marxian terms, labour is the historically determined materialisation of labour-power [*arbeitskraft*]: that natural force which humans express through their physical ability and intellectual faculties.[7] Working, therefore, does not just have a meaning for itself, for the benefits that it brings about, but also for the fulfilment of humanity as such. And the *being* of humans is defined by a *poietic* practical-productive status, which assigns to the act of working a specific totalising ontological connotation.[8]

This foundational narrative has often been the target of Agamben's archaeological critique.[9] Indeed, the concept of inoperativity is drawn essentially in opposition to all those ideas deduced from the image of the human as a working-productive being. Inoperativity encapsulates the image of human worklessness as a real possibility, as a source for a strategic critique of labour. Today, questioning the idea of work as a dominant value, and as a kind of compulsive repetition structuring our form of life, is urgent not simply because – as Nietzsche once said – work represents 'the best policeman, that it keeps everyone in bounds and can mightily hinder the development of reason, covetousness, desire for independence'.[10] The challenge to society of work is, first of all, an attack on the social-schizophrenic input that couples the hegemonic intensification of work as the only means to realise one-self, and the reality of a world dominated by decades-long economic stagnation and growing automation of production with the consequent reduction and casualisation of labour.

Agamben's philosophy is certainly valuable as a critical stance against such a form of social schizophrenia. As Mathew Abbott claims, his works could be helpful as a theoretical resource for a 'renewed anti-work politics', despite the ontological tone and anti-normative character.[11] And the concept of form-of-life as an instantiation of an inoperative being logically implies a critique of the image of labour and work as a natural and moral necessity, and the idea of a way of living and acting towards the destitution of the social and economic structures based on the dynamics of exploitation of abstract labour, production and the process of valorisation.[12]

Doing-being-working

In *The Man Without Content*, Agamben attempts to retrace the ascendancy of work as a central value in the hierarchy of human practical life. He begins his argument by recognising how all humans' doing is commonly described as a 'praxis, that is [the] manifestation of a will that produces a concrete effect' (MWC, 68). Such an idea, he goes on, is so ingrained in our culture that we tend completely to neglect the fact that in the past 'doing' was conceived in radically different ways. The Greeks, Agamben writes, 'made a clear distinction' (ibid.) between *poiesis* and *praxis*. What distinguishes the two forms of doing is their purpose (*telos*). While the end of *praxis* is the action (doing) itself, *poiesis* instead refers to the 'experience of pro-duction into presence, the fact that something passed from nonbeing to being, from concealment into the full light of the work' (ibid., 68–9). Ultimately, the distinction between the two forms of doing lies in the presence or absence of something that persists or survives the action itself, that is: a product.

Although recognising its crucial function, Greek culture lacks a specific thematic consideration of work as a fundamental human activity. 'Doing' things to provide sustenance in antiquity was considered as equal to being driven by the force of necessity, which is something that does not pertain properly to human nature. Considered as belonging to the sphere of biological needs, the Greeks regarded work as part of bare biological existence, that is 'the cyclical processes of the human body, whose metabolism and whose energy depend on the basic products of labor' (ibid., 69); and for this reason, work was excluded from the existence of the free man and delegated to slaves.

In the unfolding of Western history, Agamben argues, the distinction between the three forms of doing – *poiesis* (production), *praxis* and *work* – had somehow gone lost. In the modern era, he goes on, the possibility of separating *poiesis* and *praxis*, production and action, has been absorbed in an encompassing idea of acting according to which the 'doing [of all humans] is determined as an activity producing a real effect … whose worth is appreciated with respect to the will that is expressed in it, that is, with respect to its freedom and creativity' (ibid.). Coherently with this process of convergence between *poiesis* and *praxis*, working, which occupied the 'lowest rank in the hierarchy of active life', could climb 'to the rank of central value and common denominator of every human activity' (ibid.). This happened, for Agamben, when Locke placed work as the ultimate source of the human right to property and when Adam Smith – and classic liberal economy – defined work as the source of all wealth and value.

For Agamben, such a conception of the human finds a crucial articulation in Marx. As we read in the *Economic and Philosophic Manuscripts of 1844*:

labour, life activity, productive life itself, appears to man in the first place merely as a means of satisfying a need – the need to maintain physical existence. Yet the productive life is the life of the species. It is life-engendering life. The whole character of a species – its species-character – is contained in the character of its life activity; and free, conscious activity is man's species-character. Life itself appears only as a means to life … In creating a *world of objects* by his practical activity, in his *work upon* inorganic nature, man proves himself a conscious species-being, i.e., as a being that treats the species as its own essential being, or that treats itself as a species-being. Admittedly animals also produce. They build themselves nests, dwellings, like the bees, beavers, ants, etc. But an animal only produces what it immediately needs for itself or its young. It produces one-sidedly, whilst man produces universally.[13]

Marx exposes such an idea even more explicitly in the *German Ideology* when he writes that human beings 'distinguish themselves from animals as soon as they begin to *produce* their means of subsistence, a step which is conditioned by their physical organisation. By producing their means of subsistence men are indirectly producing their material life'.[14] Here, the image of a productive vocation is elevated to an ontological status: humans are destined by their very nature to work and to produce their form of life. And this, for Agamben, constitutes a pre-established ethos or vocation that has permeated the Western modern conception of the human, so much so that 'the productive doing now everywhere determines the status of man on earth – man understood as the living being (animal) that works (laborans), and, in work, produces himself and ensures his dominion over the earth ... man today is the living being who produces and works' (ibid. 70–1). Consequently, all that humans do is conceived according to the idea of doing as producing something: works of art, poems, politics, state institutions and much more.

Agamben locates the archetypal foundation of being-human as grounded on a specific vocation or work, in Aristotle's *Nicomachean Ethics*, when the Stagirite raises the crucial question of the work [*opera*] of man:

> Just as for a flute player, a sculptor, or any artisan (*tekhnitē*), and, in general, for all those who have a certain kind of work (*ergon*) and an activity (*praxis*), the good (*to agathon*) and the 'well' (*to eu*) seem [to consist] in this work, so it should also be for man, if indeed there is for him something like a certain work (*ti ergon*). Or [must we say] that there is a certain work and an activity for the carpenter and the shoemaker, and for man there is none, that he is born with no work (*argos*)?[15]

In this passage, Agamben notes, *ergon* should be understood as 'labour' or 'work'. However, what is at issue here is not simply the definition of the concept of a human practice; rather, the work of man refers, in this context, to the very form of being-at-work: to the operation that defines the human *qua* human. The question of the *ergon* of men, in Aristotle, 'has a broader meaning, and involves the very possibility of identifying the *energeia*, the being-at-work of man as man, independently of and beyond the concrete social figures that he can assume' (WoM, 2). But if the 'essence' of the flute player, the sculptor, or more generally the artisan, is constituted by a specific correlated work (that of playing the flute, sculpting, etc.), for the human the establishment of a defining activity is a difficult task. Therefore, Agamben notes, Aristotle also takes into consideration the possibility of the human as *argos* that is defined by a being without works. But just after having advanced the hypothesis of an essential inoperativity of being-human, he discards it, and defines the *ergon* of the human as living 'a certain kind of life (*zōēn tina*) and that this is the being-at-work of the soul … in accordance with *logos*'.[16] The Aristotelean definition of the life of humans, Agamben points out, is somehow reached negatively, though a series of distinctions. What is proper to human life is not the mere fact of living – *zoe* – which is common to all forms of life (of plants and animals), but is an activity, or work, that consists of the 'actualization of the vital rational potentiality (and not, therefore, of the nutritive or sensitive potentiality)' (ibid., 5). All human ethics and politics are thus defined according to such conception of the human: and it is no surprise that the *polis* is ultimately structured based on the division and separation of the rational form of life and the nutritive mere biological life, confined in the *oikos*.

According to Agamben, the Aristotelean speculation has left 'Western politics [an] aporetic legacy': on the one hand it has bound 'the destiny of politics to a kind of work, which remains unassignable with respect to individual human activities'; and on the other hand it has left unexplored an alternative idea of the human, one which sees it as an inoperative being. And, Agamben claims, in leaving the question of the inoperativity of man unanswered, in Aristotle

the idea of an *argia*, of an essential inactivity [*inoperosita*] of man with respect to his concrete occupations and functions [*operazioni*] is unequivocally put forward … what is at issue in this question is the very nature of man, who appears as the living being that has no work, that is, the living being that has no specific nature and vocation. If he were to lack an *ergon* of his own, man would not even have an *energeia*, a being in act that could define his essence: he would be, that is, a being of pure potentiality, which no identity and no work could exhaust (ibid., 2).

In a sense, the whole of Agamben's political proposal is an invitation to take this second option seriously. Against the Western cultural canon, which has inherited a conception of acting that leans on the signatures of work, the major challenge is thinking towards a renewed inoperative ethos that takes the concepts of potential and form-of-life as its fundamental categories. The task for the coming politics is indeed that of elaborating an image of the human that is 'not defined by its relation to a praxis (*energeia*) or a work (*ergon*) but by a potential (*dynamis*) and by an inoperativity' (UoB, 247).

Of course, such a hypothesis is not an ephemeral one; it is an option that keeps on returning in various forms. Agamben refers for instance to Kazimir Malevich[17] and Paul Lafargue[18] (surely the list as we will see below is much longer), who, against the tradition that elevates labour to the activity through which humans realise themselves, have thought of inoperativity and life without work as the highest form of humanity. In so doing Agamben endows his idea of inoperativity with a decisive and anti-work tone. However, his understanding of inoperativity should not be considered as just a negation of labour. Any negative determination, he maintains, remains trapped and dependent on what it negates. To think of inoperativity positively, that is not as solely the negation of its supposed opposite, we should avoid reducing it to simple inactive life, idleness, or inertia – that is as not-work. To the extent that today to think of a distinction between *poiesis* and *praxis*, to do and to produce, is not possible anymore, Agamben invites us to consider an inoperative doing with no *ergon* or *telos*: something that we modern workers seem unable to conceive (CA, 26).

The labour of the moderns

In its historical determination as an abstract object that is sold in exchange for a salary, work is a form of exploitation of the human labour force that found its most explicit realisation in modern times, when the market and the commodity form became the primary reference of all human productivity. The classical world, Agamben points out, 'does not know the concept of labor' as separated by the *things* it produces, since 'productive activities are not conceived in relation to the unitary referent that the market is for us' (UoB, 15–19). All productive activities were defined by the final product (their *telos*) and never by the labour-process in its own autonomy.

Contrarily to modern societies in which the market has transformed different forms of labour into a commodity, reducing all human work to a general abstract category, 'in the sphere of ancient technique and economy, labor appears only in its concrete aspect. Every task is defined as in function of the product that it proposes to fabricate: the cobbler with respect to the shoe, the potter with respect to the pot'.[19] A further difference that separates modern work from that of the ancient world, is that while the former exists in relation to the 'public sphere' of the market, the latter is confined to the private dimension of the *oikos*, the organisation and hierarchy of which was 'determined by the necessities of subsistence and reproduction'.[20]

As Agamben maintains in *The Use of Bodies*, the traces of the social form of abstract labour – as an autonomous commodified activity – are already present in antiquity, more specifically in the Roman law institute of the 'usufruct' of the work of slaves. In Roman law, the usufruct was a personal servitude (*servitutes personarum*) defining the right that a person – the usufructuary – has in another's property. In its traditional definition, the usufructuary does not possess the legal title of the property: it possesses only the rights to use and to profit from the *fructi* of that property. In the case in which slaves are the object-property of usufruct, the usufructuary has the right to use and to make profit from their works (*operae*). And here, Agamben claims, we see the appearance of labour as akin to an abstract commodity that could be sold and alienated on the market for profit. Yan Thomas, the Roman law scholar to whom Agamben here refers, writes as follows:

> the fructuarius is entitled to a work that can be alienated for a price on the market: it can be rented out. In both cases, whether the slave is the object of a use or that of a usufruct, concretely speaking, he works. Only, the slave's activity, in everyday language his labour, does not have the same legal value in both cases. There are two possibilities: either the slave remains at the personal disposal of the *usuarius* in person. This is what I would call a service *'en nature'*. One could also call it 'use work', as one speaks of 'use value'. Or the slave's *operae*, separated from him, are a 'thing' sellable to a third party through the legal form of the contract. What the usufructuary receives, is only a pecuniary income. To the slave's 'use work' is added work that we could call commercial, as it has market value.[21]

In the institute of the usufruct, we see the emergence of work or labour as an abstract activity that can be purchased and sold on the market. The usufructuary does not have the right to alienate the property – to sell the body of the slave, or its use – but he has the right to make a profit by selling the work of the slave as a commodity. What is sold on the market is the slave's activity as such: its *fructus*. 'The separation of something like a labor activity is here possible', Agamben claims, 'only by separating the body as object of use from its activity as alienable and remunerable' (ibid., 16); and as Yan Thomas argues the worker-slave 'is split between two areas of law corresponding respectively to what he is as a body and what he represents as an income, an incorporeal asset'.[22] The (Roman) law has been capable of separating what is otherwise inseparable, a body from its activity, giving to the latter an autonomous existence with a quantifiable value, which is also independent of its actual product.

In the Roman law institute of the usufruct of slaves, we see the first emergence of the two natures or substances of work that characterise modern labour. In the modern, capitalist world, labour is always two-sided: it produces something (material or immaterial) and hence is concrete/real; at the same time, it is an expenditure of human labour-power that can be measured as pure duration, quantified and exchanged; and this kind of labour is substantially abstract. In its abstract form, work does not have a specific object that orients and gives meaning to its own existence: its scope is just to create a *social form* called value that can be quantified (usually in money) and sold on the market. The rise of abstract labour is strictly connected with the historical development of commercial exchange and the commodity form as the union of use-value and exchange-value; abstract labour is what establishes the (exchange) value side of the commodity. As such value (and abstract work) is not a natural datum but is a purely social form of considering objects. It is a projection of a historical/cultural fashion of quantifying and comparing objects, a fashion that is somehow perceived as already existing as preliminary to any productive activity. We are unconsciously oriented to think of production as pointing towards the creation of some value – quantified in money.[23] Some of what Marx has defined as commodity fetishism can be traced to this pre-history.

Abstract labour transcends the specificities of the single concrete productive acts: it is indeed a social construct that has taken the autonomous reality that we are all accustomed to, materialised through the commodity with which it is exchanged that is money. But this means that abstract labour entertains with its concrete productive side a rather peculiar relationship. When considered from the point of view of their exchange value, all the differences that the single products have in terms of use-value are reduced to a difference in their value and price. In its abstract version, labour becomes a commodity that as such is indifferent to the real properties of the concrete work and becomes an exchangeable thing. As objects having a price, commodities do not have physical/real differences, but only differences in price or value. In the market, the use-value is in a sense overshadowed: any produced good should have a concrete real side (in the case of the slave is the body) or should satisfy some needs; however, in the market, this concrete side is merely a support of the abstract value, made concrete in a quantum of money. And in mature capitalism, it is the abstract side of commodities and of work that determines the status of labour and consequently the worker. For the modern mind the only *telos* of work and production is value – the biggest quantity of value [read: money]. While use-value is demoted to a plain mediation, a mere passage for the multiplication of money.

With the emergence of capitalism and market society, work in its more abstract form becomes substantially an autotelic enterprise: the fetishist pride of the ever-growing implementation of labour-force, as separated from the satisfaction of concrete, subjective and social needs, materialises in a proper *ethos* of abstract labour – or in a specific form of life: that of the worker.[24] As Max Weber has noted:

> the *summum bonum* of this ethic, the earning of more and more money, combined with the strict avoidance of all spontaneous enjoyment of life, is above all completely devoid of any eudæmonistic, not to say hedonistic, admixture. It is thought of so purely as an end in itself, that from the point of view of the happiness of, or utility to, the single individual, it appears entirely transcendental and absolutely irrational. Man is dominated by the making of money, by acquisition as the ultimate purpose of his life. Economic acquisition is no longer subordinated to man as the means for the satisfaction of his material needs. This reversal of what we should call the natural relationship, so irrational from a naïve point of view, is evidently as definitely a leading principle of capitalism as it is foreign to all peoples not under capitalistic influence.[25]

What characterises the abstract form of labour in modern capitalist society is its being mired in the production of value – either as money or commodity. The *ergon* of the working man, and the *telos* of modern work, are reduced to the selling of labour-force in exchange for a quantum of money. This has been rendered possible only through a forcible separation of workers from means of subsistence and production. Abstract labour is that form of doing that rests on the fundamental severance from its objects and the necessary means and conditions for its actual taking place.[26]

The religious life of workers

In the short essay *Capitalism as Religion* – which borrows the title and some of the central claims from Benjamin's fragment written in 1921 and published only posthumously – Agamben sustains that capitalism, with its myths and rituals, assumed the guise of a religion. Capitalism, he writes, is not 'as in Weber, a secularization of the Protestant faith, but is itself essentially a religious phenomenon' (CA, 67) that has established money (as credit) as its main idol. Predictably, such an image of capitalism is accompanied by a dire diagnosis: as a form of religion, capitalism does not tend 'toward redemption but toward guilt, not toward hope but desperation, capitalism as a religion does not aim at the transformation of the world but at its destruction' (ibid.).

Benjamin's fragment – in the footsteps of which Agamben follows – delineates, despite the obscurity and density of a short text intended as a working note, some of the structural elements of the religion of capital. First, he claims, capitalism is a 'purely cultic religion, perhaps the most extreme that ever existed'.[27] The religious life of capitalism manifests itself in symbolisms and in the execution of rites that do not necessitate a legitimacy other than the cult of accumulation of money. There are no founding dogmas or any theology for such a religion, but a whole series of stereotyped liturgies and glorifying rituals – the ethic of abstract labour, exploitation, consumption, etc. – oriented by a form of utilitarianism that assumes a sacral connotation. Capitalism does not command us to have faith in a specified authority: it is enough that we all participate in its specific form of life.[28] The second element of the religion of capitalism, for Benjamin, is the permanence of the cult: 'there are no "weekdays". There is no day that is not a feast day, in the terrible sense that all its sacred pomp is unfolded before us; each day commands the utter fealty of each worshipper'.[29] For such a form of religion, the sacred and the profane collapse into a never-ending feast – or alternatively in never-ending work. Then, thirdly, 'Capitalism is probably the first instance of a cult that creates guilt, not atonement'.[30] By imposing its cult as a totalising domain that refers only to itself, and by denying any form of redemption, capitalism produces guilt and debt as a driving force.

To the extent that the only *telos* of work is the accumulation/ consumption of money, humans are perpetually trapped in a situation of scarcity or debt that forces them to sell their potential productive force to access the means to survive.

The commandments of the religion of capital are not the emanation of a sovereign-transcendental substance: they find their force immanently to the social order they regulate on the ground of the necessity common to most humans to work and consume. The form of life of capital is dominated by the rites and liturgies that we perform with devotion. Working, from this point of view, seems to assume the guise of a liturgical office that allows us to be actively part of the cult of capital, gaining not only access to the 'market of resources' necessary for our subsistence but also recognition as dignified individuals. 'Without Work, outside of Work, we are nothing': the workplace is the ultimate source of 'our happiness and self-respect – or, to say it in the new-age parlance of office culture, to "find ourselves" – as well as the love of what we do: is there any place where we can feel safer than when we are in our workplace, snug in the warm embrace of our office family?'[31]

For the religion of capitalism, as Benjamin has preconised, its cult and rituals are totalising experiences that involve human life in all its spheres. And work too seems to possess such a peculiar colonising power. While it is true that the worker, differently from the slave, sells its labour-power in given slots of time, it is nevertheless a fact that (especially in its more recent – post-Fordist – form) work seems to have invaded the whole of our daily life.[32] The mega-machine of capital, with its ethic of work and compulsive consumption, turns the capitalist cultic liturgies into a totalising experience. As Ivan Illich argued in the essay *Shadow Work*, industrial society saw the proliferation of forms of unpaid works that, far from being a bare addition to the life of workers, are a necessary complement to the very functioning of the economy. Differently from that form of unpaid work that has been labelled reproductive labour, shadow work refers to that

> unpaid work which an industrial society demands as a necessary complement to the production of goods and services. This kind of unpaid servitude does not contribute to

subsistence. Quite the contrary, equally with wage-labor, it ravages subsistence. I call this complement to wage-labor 'shadow-work'. It comprises what most housework women do in their homes and apartments, the activities connected with shopping, most of the homework of students cramming for exams, the toil expended commuting to and from the job. It includes the stress of forced consumption, the tedious and regimented surrender to therapists, compliance with bureaucrats, the preparation for work to which one is compelled, and many of the activities usually labelled 'family life'.[33]

The category of shadow work includes all those activities through which the consumer transforms a commodity into a usable good: it consists of all the time and effort necessary to add the value to a commodity, without which it would be unusable. Shadow work, is thus, an activity that people are coerced into doing when they try to satisfy a need through a commodity.

According to Illich, modern industrial society combined two modalities of work that correspond to two different forms/spheres of production. On the one hand, humans work autonomously towards the production of the means of their subsistence: this kind of work/production points to the creation of use-values in the context of the sphere that he called *vernacular* – which is the 'technical term used by Roman lawyers for the inverse of a commodity'.[34] On the other hand, we are constantly involved in working activities oriented towards the production of commodities for the sake of 'formal economy' and markets. If, as happened in modern industrial societies, the expansion of the production of commodities overcomes a certain limit-threshold, which makes the autonomous subsistence-oriented work/production phagocytised by commodity production, we assist in the proliferation of a plethora of shadow works – relating to all the non-paid work that the consumer must undertake to make usable the commodities bought on the market.

Shadow work, Illich claims, originated with the establishment of wage labour as the dominant form of productive activity: it is in this sense the necessary complement of the commodification of the world and the subsequent eclipse of use-value. 'In traditional cultures', he claims, 'shadow-work is marginal as wage-labour is often difficult to identify. In industrial societies, it is assumed as routine.'[35] In the industrial age, the process of valorisation was principally centred on the extraction of surplus value from workers' labour and on the consumption of commodities that workers were sold back 'so that they could replenish their bodily existence and sell their labour-power to the capitalist again the next day'.[36] The command of the ever-growing accumulation of capital demanded the qualitative and quantitative increase of production, with the consequent intensification and diversification of shadow works complementing waged labour so to make the industrial machine work properly. Commuting, for instance, is that kind of shadow work that coerces the worker to bring her labour-power to the workplace by car. But this kind of shadow work involves other forms of shadow work, inasmuch as a relevant portion of salaries are invested in the purchase and maintenance of all those instruments/commodities that allow workers to sell their labour-power. Education and the acquisition of knowledge, or human capital, are somehow unproductive activities, which in the commodified society of work have been transformed into shadow work functionally complementing the market of wage labour. With the growing number of commodities that have entered our life, the total volume of shadow work overcame that of waged labour, turning our own life into a perpetual workday. Indeed, the evolution of the technology of production reduced the quantity of labour-power necessary for production, while at the same time increasing productivity and the number of tools necessary for human living, with the consequent expansion of shadow work.

Paradoxically, the tendency of work to colonise all those spheres of our life that are not formally part of work time, which Illich has defined in relation to the industrial society, has become spectacularly more intense with the unfolding of post-Fordism and the eclipse of the factory as the epicentre of capital accumulation and the process of valorisation. While in industrial capitalism the separation between work (as the sphere of human life from which value was extracted), and the other unproductive sector of individual and social life was somehow identifiable, with the emergence of post-Fordism, the process of valorisation started to invest and subsume the whole of the life of individuals. This renewed form of accumulation considers the whole of the social field, in which subjects are controlled and governed *omnes et singulatim*, as a site of extraction of value, transforming the very vital substance of individuals into work: living and producing tend to become indistinguishable. In so far as life tends to be completely invested by acts of production and reproduction, social life itself becomes a productive machine. Immaterial labour, semio-capitalism, bio-cognitive capitalism, are all keywords nominating the shift in production/extraction of value typical of the post-Fordist modes of production, in which mind, language and creativity, have become the primary tools for the production of value.[37] For the latest phase of capitalism, the process of valorisation has enlarged the base of accumulation, putting to work the activity of education, care, reproduction, consumption, social relationships and free time;[38] and with the growing importance of social-media platforms and the exploitation of big data, the very psyche becomes a site of value extraction.

Yet, these evolutions brought about a radical change in the concept of work, making the separation between productive labour, cultural and artistic practices and leisure disappear: all human life is subsumed by capital and transformed directly or indirectly into productive activity.[39] As Daniel McLoughlin has pointed out, life under the post-Fordist spectacle resembles that of the monastery Agamben has analysed in *The Highest Poverty*: we live like monks in a governmental hierarchy, busily engaged in liturgical labour that occupies the totality of life, a work that both reproduces and acclaims the order to which we are subjected.[40] With the conflation of productive time with the very sphere of living, the idea of working-time as a measure of productivity and value vanishes. The liturgical labour of our life does not involve weekdays: for the permanent cult of the capital, in the post-Fordist time, the idea of work-value has left the place to a concept of 'value-life', where the whole of the living is the site of a process of value extraction.[41]

The end of work

Work in late capitalism is somehow trapped in an 'economic paradox'.[42] The glorification of the ethics of abstract labour – its obsessive (moralising) repetition and intensification – goes hand in hand with the narrative that portrays wage labour and human productivity as approaching their epochal end. The spectacular development of technology, the growing casualisation of work and cyclical-sacrificial economic devastation that in the last twenty years has invested the globe, occur as the ultimate signal of the definitive dethroning of work as the core practice and ultimate cypher of our form of life. Embroiled in such a paradox, the ideology of work combines contrasting messages, thereby becoming a delusional caricature of itself. This was already envisaged by Bertrand Russell a century ago when he wrote that: 'modern technique has made it possible to diminish enormously the amount of labour required to secure the necessaries of life for everyone',[43] however, 'we have chosen, instead, to have overwork for some and starvation for others. Hitherto we have continued to be as energetic as we were before there were machines; in this we have been foolish'.[44]

Part of the affective tonality of contemporary capitalism, the premonition of the *end of work*[45] is the logical reaction to the metamorphotic decline of the classic forms of industrial production, which has caused a radical change in labour conditions and gradually pushed the very idea of work (as material production) to the margin of our social imaginary. This further stage in the evolution of the relationship capital-labour is thought of as opening the gates of a new epoch in which the institution of waged labour is at risk of disappearing. Faced with the fact that technological advancements are making human material labour increasingly irrelevant to the purpose of production, our mood oscillates between the euphoria for the approach of a post-work/post-capitalist leisure society, and the depression of moving into the unknown territory in which the elimination of work could mean the misery of full unemployment. But whatever vision one might have of the future of labour, the fact is that the end of work is widely seen as representing an opportunity and attracting a growing consensus.

The idea that machines could liberate humans from the yoke of labour has been discussed for much longer than we might think. Its traces are already well articulated in Marx's *Grundrisse*, in those fragments in which he has engaged with the transformation of both work and value through the action or machines. Here Marx prefigured the gradual degradation and diminution of human work (living labour) thanks to the mechanisation of industrial production. The introduction of automatic machines in the production process, he claims, means that the worker 'only transmits and supervises and protects from damage the work of the machine and its action on the raw material'.[46] Workers, therefore, do not have proper control of the machine; their 'activity, limited to a mere abstraction, is determined and regulated on all sides by the movement of the machinery, not the other way round'; and the science behind the functioning that 'obliges the inanimate parts of the machine, through their construction, to work appropriately as an automaton, does not exist in the consciousness of the worker, but acts upon him through the machine as an alien force, as the power of the machine itself'.[47] Within the automated production system, the worker is integrated as 'prosthesis', which has no proper control over the machines but on the contrary is animated by them, making him a part of its mighty organism, a conscious organ subject to its virtuosity or alien power.[48] And the growing productivity that capital reaches 'by means of the transformation of the instrument of labour into the machine' is proportional to the diminution of necessary labour.[49] Marx here detects a contradictory tendency of capital, which by way of constant innovation and technological evolution, 'is instrumental in creating the means of social disposable time, and so in reducing working time for the whole of society to a minimum and thus making everyone's time free for their own development'.[50]

But what should be done with a life liberated from work? What should the meaning and content of free time become? These are some of the questions that have oriented the rather unorthodox research of André Gorz, an author who has had a decisive influence in defining the contours of the end-of-work theory. Gorz starts by acknowledging the somehow inevitable consequences of the leaps in productivity afforded by the technological development of the means of production, and the related question of what a post-work society should look like. 'Advances in technology', he claims, 'pose the question of the meaning and content of free time: better still, of the nature of a civilisation and a society in which there is far more free time than working time and in which economic rationality ceases to govern everyone's time'.[51] For Gorz, a return to the Fordist societal model is not a viable option. Quite to the contrary, the current technological-economic system is an invitation to think an exodus from the centrality of wage labour and a new model of society in which the time freed from work is sustained economically and transformed into a time for the realisation of human potential. Of course, this path is not free from risks and cannot be deterministically produced: 'the development of the productive forces – he maintains – may, of itself, reduce the amount of labour that is necessary; it cannot, of itself, create the conditions which will make this liberation of time a liberation for all'.[52] The challenge is indeed that of a 'programmed, staged reduction in working hours, without loss of real income, in conjunction with a set of accompanying policies which will allow this liberated time to become time for free self-realization for everyone'.[53]

Gorz proposes an emancipatory politics of time, which should aim at taking control of the processes of technological advancement 'already under way and orientate them in a direction which corresponds to their own inclinations':[54] 'a politically co-ordinated reduction of working hours, to take place on a society-wide scale'[55] coupled with a citizen's basic income. Providing people with an unconditioned universal basic income is a necessary presupposition for the development of a non-economically oriented form of life. A basic income is an instrument that could take life out of economic rationality. For Gorz, a basic income could help to foster social practices outside the sphere of profit and valorisation, opening the space for social care and gratuitous gestures and relationships; to give a renewed form to all those dimensions of the human that economic rationality has perverted.[56]

The latest and perhaps more spectacular addendum to the theory of the end of work is that provided by the 'accelerationist' hypothesis. As Nick Srnicek and Alex Williams explicitly claimed in their *Manifesto for an Accelerationist Politics*, the constitution of a post-capitalist/post-work society should pass through the unleashing of the 'latent productive forces' that the current development of technology in late capitalism provide. For accelerationism, the only way of realising a post-capitalist world is to 'accelerate' some latent processes embedded in global capitalism (those pertaining to the development of technologies, communication, means of production, etc.) to liberate their potential to the point of using them in an egalitarian/libertarian and communist way. Against what Srnicek and Williams call folk-politics, that is 'the constellation of ideas and intuitions within the contemporary left that informs the common-sense ways of organising, acting and thinking politics' aiming to 'bring politics down to the human scale by emphasising temporal spatial and conceptual immediacy,[57] denouncing the dominion of capital abstraction and technological grip over human life – such as the Occupy movement, the Zapatistas, Tiqqun, the Invisible Committee, etc. – accelerationism poses itself as a grand-scale Promethean politics of maximal mastery over society and its environment that purports to embrace the potential implicit in technological progress to liberate humanity from the catastrophe of capitalism. For accelerationism 'there is no more – and so there never will have been – an "outside" of capitalism, an exterior that would be anterior to it, a wilderness beyond its history', and as a result the only way of exiting it, is to create a way out from the inside, by steering the machine (of capital and the state) to self-destruction that eventually will open a new world.[58]

Central to such a narrative is the question of work: an accelerationist politics 'must seek to combat the centrality of work to contemporary life' avoiding the 'tendency to place value upon work, concrete labour and craft work' all expressions of folk-politics. For the advancement towards a post-capitalist world liberated from work, Srnicek and Williams argue that four minimal demands must be realised: '1. Full automation; 2. The reduction of the working week 3. The provision of a basic income 4. The diminishment of the work ethic'. These proposals ideally form a programme for a 'new hegemonic formation', opposed to both the neoliberal and the social-democratic options. The accelerationists' proposal hinges upon the idea that technology, although not neutral, can be repurposed in an emancipatory form. Every technological innovation carries a political meaning and re-orients human life: 'technology expands into the smallest nano-scales' so much so that 'no aspect of our lives remains untouched by technology, and indeed, many would argue that humanity is intrinsically technological'.[59] Contrary to the anti-technological primitivism permeating part of left-folk politics that purports to destroy our living environment so to liberate our life from the techno-capitalist dominion, accelerationism recognises that the potential embedded in technology should be controlled and used to create a counter-hegemonic emancipatory project:

> If technology designed to reduce skilled labour permits domination by a managerial class, it also opens up spaces for job-sharing and the reduction of work. If technology that reduces production costs reduces the percentage of people employed, it also reduces the need for people to work. If a technology that centralises decision-making over infrastructures facilitates private control, it also pro-vides a nodal point for collective decision-making. These technologies embody both potentials at the same time, and the task of repurposing is simply one of how to alter the balance between them. One goal of any future-orientated left could be to outline these broad parameters of adju-dication, and to pursue further research and analysis in determining how specific technologies can be repurposed and mobilised towards a postcapitalist project.[60]

Of course, such a proposal is not immune from criti-cism.[61] One does not have to resuscitate the Heideggerian ontological/apocalyptic vision to understand that the rela-tionship between humanity and technology is that of (inter) dependence, while at the same time the technological sphere and the growing complexity of the knowledge behind it, are becoming an autonomous sphere, the control of which is at best the gift of a few.

What is more, the technological development that we have observed in the last few decades seems to have had the oppo-site effect. As David Graeber argued, while it is plausible that technology is potentially capable of making work disappear – and making flying cars – this has not yet happened, and it does not look likely to happen in the immediate future. On the contrary, he goes on, 'technology has been marshalled, if anything, to figure out ways to make us all work more': rather than seeing a reduction in working hours, we have sadly assisted to the proliferation of jobs that are 'effectively pointless. Huge swathes of people, in Europe and North America in particular, spend their entire working lives performing tasks they secretly believe do not really need to be performed'.[62] Graeber argues that instead of working less and letting our life be eased by technology, we have chosen to go in the opposite direction: the growing productivity that technology affords us has pushed us to create a plethora of useless unproductive jobs which cause more harm than good. What he calls 'bullshit jobs'.

Perhaps, the ethic of abstract labour is so ingrained in our minds, that it is inconceivable for us to think about getting access to the means for survival without passing through the pain of work. The thesis of the end of work, through the acceleration of some latent potentiality embedded in the already-present processes internal to capital, here encounters the external limit of cultural and metaphysical forms shaping the abstract world of human practices and values. And unless one has an unshakeable faith in historical materialism or determinism, the route towards a post-work society should pass through the elaboration of new paradigms, words and ontologies.

Inoperative work

If in Agamben a certain anti-work attitude is present, it cannot but oppose the hypothesis of the liberation from work through technological means, as predicated by the accelerationists. Although his idea of a coming politics has been interpreted as a form of accelerationism,[63] Agamben's theoretical proximity with Tiqqun and the Tarnac 9 experience, and his disillusioned vision of technology make him firmly part of what Srnicek and Williams have named folk-politics. Inoperative politics is 'fundamentally anti-teleological':[64] it purports the abandonment of that sort of determinism that

thinks the future as determined starting from a given vocation (or work) of the human, towards the conceptualisation
of a radical break and destitution of our form of life. The task
for the coming politics is not to accelerate the end of what
is somehow already ending (i.e., work as production) but
to think of a form of inoperative practice beyond the operative coordinates of the modern conception of the human-as-
working-being. And the critique of work implicit in such a
proposal entails the idea of a non-work practice that is not a
negation of work (as idleness), but the liberation of human
practical life from the signatures that have oriented it as productive in essence.

Inoperativity, Agamben points out in *The Use of Bodies*,
must be thought in strict relation to the Marxian concept of
'form of production': 'it is certainly true', he goes on, 'that, as
Marx suggested, the forms of production of an epoch contrib-
ute in a decisive way to determine its social relationship and
culture', however, 'in relation to every form of production, it
is possible to individuate a "form of inoperativity" that, while
being held in close relationship with it, is not determined
by it but on the contrary renders its works inoperative and
permits a new use of them' (UoB, 94). From the point of view
of Marx's historical materialism, capitalism is manifested in a
class society that through the institutions of private property
(in the means of production) and the necessary complement
of abstract labour, allow the appropriation of value created
by workers producing commodities and services in exchange
for a wage.[65] Following Agamben's argument, inoperative
work should be considered as that kind of praxis that is
obtained through the destitution of the constituting conditions of labour under the capitalist mode of production.

Agamben's anti-normative philosophy does not (and
cannot) provide us with a recipe for a post-work society.
However, we can try to find a point of development in his
conception of inoperativity that could help us delineate an
anti-work political proposal. Let us look to the concept of the
feast, which for Agamben represents a paradigmatic example
of inoperativity. The feast, he writes,

is not defined by what is not done in it but instead by
the fact that what is done – which in itself is not unlike

what is accomplished every day – becomes undone, rendered inoperative, liberated and suspended from its "economy," from the reasons and aims that define it during the weekdays (and not doing, in this sense, is only an extreme case of this suspension). If one eats, it is not done for the sake of being fed; if one gets dressed, it is not done for the sake of being covered up or taking shelter from the cold; if one wakes up, it is not done for the sake of working; if one walks, it is not done for the sake of going someplace; if one speaks, it is not done for the sake of communicating information; if one exchanges objects, it is not done for the sake of selling or buying. Every feast involves this element of suspension and begins primarily by rendering inoperative the works of men. In the Sicilian feast of the dead described by Pitre, the dead (or an old woman called *Srrina,* from strena, a Latin name for the gifts exchanged during the festivities of the beginning of the year) steal goods from tailors, merchants, and bakers to then bestow them on children (something similar to this happens in all feasts that involve gifts, like Halloween, where the dead are impersonated by children). Presents, gifts, and toys are objects with use and exchange value that are rendered inoperative, wrested from their economy. In every carnivalesque feast, such as the Roman saturnalia, existing social relations are suspended or inverted: not only do slaves command their masters, but sovereignty is placed in the hands of a mock-king (*saturnalicius princeps*) who takes the place of the legitimate king. In this way the feast reveals itself to be first and foremost a deactivation of existing values and powers (N, 110–11).

The element of suspension that is involved in the feast, and that characterises the very concept of inoperativity, consists in the uncoupling of the actions that we perform in our everyday life from their effectuality and economy, in the deactivation and destitution of the existing values and powers. Inoperativity defines the status of a purposeless action: the praxis with no *telos* of a generic being with no commanded *ergon.* 'What is essential' in inoperativity, Agamben writes 'is a dimension of praxis in which simple, quotidian human activities are neither negated nor abolished but suspended and rendered inoperative in order to be exhibited, as such, in a festive manner' (ibid., 126). Throughout history, such a festive dimension of our everyday life has been constantly captured and reified in rules, norms and institutions, and rendered as the obligatory categorial matrixes of our form of life. In this regard, inoperativity sharply captures the process of liberation of that gratuitous festivity embedded potentially in all human practices. And this implies perhaps the hardest of the tasks: the destitution of the abstract institutions that have been created and recreated seldom (if not always) independently of the singular will to form and command our life and the perceptions we have of it.

From this perspective inoperative work assumes the paradoxical form of work devoid of its actual values and powers – or, in other words, going outside and against the current metaphysical (read: abstract) category of labour. As we have seen earlier, the *telos* of modern work is nothing other than the production of value (eventually quantified in money). Labour, as we know it, is a commodity among others to be sold on the market. Therefore, inoperative work (or praxis) is a form of *doing* that cannot be alienated into a commodity. As Marx has argued the dual character of the commodity – the union of a use-value and exchange-value – is reflected in labour so that the concrete aspect of working activities corresponds to the use-value of the commodity, while at the same time in its abstract form labour is constituted as exchange value.

In one of his earlier engagements with Marx, Agamben writes that 'the doubling of the product of work, which presents us now with one face now with another, without making both visible in the same instant', what is known as the fetishism of commodity 'presents more than a simply terminological analogy with the fetishes that are objects of perversion. The superimposition of the use-value corresponds, in fetishism, to the superimposition of a particular symbolic value on the normal use of the object'.[66] Commodification adds to the commodified thing a value that exists only virtually as a reflection of a social imaginary, which nevertheless appears to us as real, making the object entering into the enchanted-spectacular world of commodities. But 'the transfiguration of the commodity into enchanted object', for Agamben, 'is the sign that the exchange value is already beginning to eclipse the use-value of the commodity'.[67]

Modern labour, as a commodity, is trapped in the same form of enchantment: it withdraws from the specific concrete aspect of its product and becomes an abstract yet real object that we somehow possess and exchange, independently of our real productive practices. What is specific about abstract labour is not the fact that humans make and create things or that they carry out social tasks. What characterises most labour in modernity is its being a form of doing material-ised into an isolated sphere (that of work), as separated from the actual concrete dimension of the life of humans, which somehow lives on its own. From this point of view, inop-erative praxis is that form of doing which has cut ties with labour: a form of practical life liberated from the fetishist enchanting power of commodity and value. It is a purpose-less form of doing that resists reification and alienation and remains immanent to the living practical dimension of the life of the individual. To borrow John Holloway's neat expres-sion, inoperative praxis is *doing against labour*.[68]

~ * ~

Under the decisive influence of Guy Debord's *Society of Spectacle*, Agamben sees life under a capitalist regime as dominated by a total form of commodification, which has hollowed out any form of use-value through the expropria-tion of everything from immediate fruition – from resources to the very potential acts of our practical life. When Toni Negri polemically argued that Agamben's thought leads us to the reaffirmation of use-value,[69] he was somehow right. To the extent that the only form of value and production is essentially reduced to exchanged value, to the commodity form or money, inoperativity could be seen as a re-evaluation of use-value against abstract labour and the process of val-orisation. For Negri, this stance is 'singularly unproductive'; 'the task that humanity has to embrace is', he goes on, 'that of manipulating the existent to construct a new world ... [I]f there are only exchange values, it is with them that we must reconstruct the world':

We do not know where we shall arrive, but we know that we can only move in a world of commodities, of reified things and bodies – to submit them to production and to invent the common through production. It is only in production that life and existence intersect, and it is only through it that this relationship can and must be continually revolutionised.[70]

The strategy Negri outlines here is the opposite of that which can be drawn out of Agamben's concept of inoperativity. A post-work/post-capitalist society, for Agamben, cannot be the product or the actualisation of a project, but the deactivation/destitution of the empty forms of our life, to open them up to a new use bringing them back from the separated enchanted realm – that of law and commodity – to the immanence of our concrete living. Moreover, as Jessica Whyte has pointed out, 'Agamben's work is animated not by a return to use value but by the possibility of what he terms a "new use" – that is a nonutilitarian relation to the world'[71] based on getting away with value[72] as the foundational category of capitalist commodification. But this, as Robert Kurz affirmed, adopting a language Agamben most likely would not dislike, necessarily entails a break with the basic ontological categories of capitalism. 'Concepts such as labour, money, and market', he maintains, 'represent the petrified determination of modern capitalist ontology'.[73] Ontological categories, for Kurz, should not be conceived as transhistorical or as defining a given/natural category of the human; rather they are something historically contingent that determined 'a form of society or mode of production and a mode of living'.[74] And the break with modern capitalist ontology is nothing other than vehemently declaring 'as barbaric the core of the capitalist machine' and to get rid of 'abstract labour and its inner structure of discipline and reified human administration that is generally misunderstood as civilization'.[75]

Notes

1. Until the emergence of capitalism, work was considered as a necessary evil to access resources to survive, and it was despised inasmuch as it resulted in exhaustion. The Bible,

for instance, defined labour as a sort of curse imposed on humanity. The word labour – in the modern sense – is not present in ancient languages, and this is evident from the etymology of such a term. The French *travailler*, derives from the Latin (vulgar) *tripaliare*, that is to torture with the *tripalium*, an instrument that was used to punish slaves. The Latin *labor* – that is the root of the Italian *lavoro* and the English labour – originally meant 'load' and was synonymous with pain, suffering and fatigue, Jappe (2019: 188–9). On work in antiquity see Finley (1973).

2. Weeks (2001: 11).
3. Mendes (1980).
4. Such a narrative emerged out of a process of the secularisation of the conception of the human, according to which far from being God's creation humans are conceived as a highly evolved animal having the peculiar faculty of transforming and creating their own environment (and their own life). Starting perhaps with Herder, the idea of humans as creator of their nature, life and destiny plays an important role in Marx's philosophy of history, finding its utmost elaboration in the philosophical anthropology of Gehlen (1988; 2016) and Plessner (1970).
5. In *The Fundamental Concepts of Metaphysics: World, Finitude, Solitude*, Heidegger argued that 'As we said, man is not merely a part of the world but is also master and servant of the world in the sense of "having" world. Man has world. But then what about the other beings which, like man, are also part of the world: the animals and plants, the material things like the stone, for example? Are they merely parts of the world, as distinct from man who in addition has world? Or does the animal too have world, and if so, in what way? In the same way as man, or in some other way? And how would we grasp this otherness? And what about the stone? However crudely, certain distinctions immediately manifest themselves here. We can formulate these distinctions in the following three theses: [l.] the stone (material object) is worldless; [2.] the animal is poor in world; [3.] man is world-forming [weltbildend]': Heidegger (1995: 177).
6. Nizza (2020: 57).
7. In Chapter VII of *Capital*, Marx distinguished labour-power from labour using the categories of potentiality and actuality: 'labour-power in use is labour itself. The purchaser of labour-power consumes it by setting the seller of it to work. By working, the latter becomes actually, what before he only

was potentially, labour-power in action, a labourer' Marx (1990: 153). Here again we see how the 'use' of the simple capacity of labour is labour itself, as not something alienated from the worker. Indeed, in the free use of one's capacity to work, work is only in potential. For Marx, only by selling such capacity in the form of a commodity, can a person actually become a labourer. Work, therefore, for Marx, is the historical actualisation of a faculty – which according to a traditional Aristotelean conception falls into the realm of the potential.

8. Fleming (2015: 5).
9. The critique of the image of the human as a working being has been a constant occurrence in Agamben's works since at least *The Man Without Content*.
10. Nietzsche (1997: 105).
11. Abbott (2016: 42).
12. Ibid.
13. Marx (1975: 276).
14. Marx (1976: 31).
15. Aristotle 1097b, 22 ff. as quoted in WoM, 1.
16. Aristotle 1098a 7, as quoted in WoM, 1.
17. Malevich (1921).
18. Lafargue (2012 [1883]).
19. Vernant and Vidal-Naquet (1988: 28).
20. Gorz (1989: 15).
21. Thomas (2021 [1988], 286–7).
22. Ibid., 280.
23. Jappe (2013: 19–20).
24. See Kurz (1991: Chapter 1).
25. Weber (1995: 18).
26. Bonefeld (2011).
27. Benjamin (1996: 288).
28. Salzani (2013a: 14).
29. Benjamin (1996: 289).
30. Ibid.
31. Campagna (2013: 12).
32. As Theodor Adorno has argued, in a renowned essay, what we all know as free time (or spare time), like that moment in which life is temporarily liberated from the yoke of labour, is nothing other than 'a continuation of the forms of profit-oriented social life. Just as the term showbusiness is today taken utterly seriously, the irony in the expression "leisure industry" has now been quite forgotten. It is widely known but no less true therefore that specific leisure activities like

tourism and camping revolve around and are organised for the sake of profit. At the same time the difference between work and free time has been branded as a norm in the minds of people, at both the conscious and the unconscious level. Because, in accordance with the predominant work ethic, time free of work should be utilized for the recreation of expended labour power, then work-less time, precisely because it is a mere appendage of work, is severed from the latter with puritanical zeal': Adorno (2001: 189).

33. Illich (1980: 8).
34. Ibid., 31.
35. Ibid., 8.
36. McLoughlin (2016: 103).
37. Berardi (2009: 21–2).
38. Fumagalli (2017: 57).
39. Ibid.
40. McLoughlin (2016: 108).
41. Fumagalli (2017).
42. Campagna (2013: 11).
43. Russell (2004: 11).
44. Ibid., 11.
45. *The End of Work* is the title of a famous book by Jeremy Rifkin (1995). The widely debated thesis of the book is that technological development and innovation will boost worldwide unemployment, which will be countered via state intervention and the growth of the third sector.
46. Marx (1980: 142).
47. Ibid., 142.
48. Mackay and Avanessian (2014: 9).
49. Marx (1980: 144).
50. Ibid., 153.
51. Gorz (1989: 4).
52. Ibid., 185.
53. Ibid.
54. Ibid.
55. Frayne (2015: 36).
56. Gorz (2020).
57. Srnicek Williams (2015: 9). The list of the experiences that they classify as folk politics is quite long: the Occupy movement, Spain's 15M, student occupations, Tiqqun and the Invisible Committee, the Zapatistas, 'contemporary anarchist tinged politics', political localism, the slow food movement, ethical consumerism, the 100-miles diet, local

currencies, 'veneration of small-scale communities or local businesses', and 'general assemblies and direct democracy'.
58. Viveiros de Castro and Danowski (2017: 51).
59. Ibid., 145.
60. Ibid., 152.
61. See Noys (2014).
62. Graeber (2018:9).
63. Whyte (2013).
64. Primera (2019: 129).
65. Foley and Duménil (2016).
66. Agamben (1993: 37).
67. Ibid., 38.
68. Holloway (2010: 157).
69. Negri (2007: 124).
70. Ibid.
71. Whyte (2013: 133).
72. As Moishe Postone wrote, 'humanity can fully awaken from its somnambulistic state only by abolishing value. This abolition would entail abolishing the necessity for productivity to be constantly increased …, and would allow for a different structure of labor, a higher degree of control by people over their lives, and a more consciously controlled relationship with the natural environment.' Postone (1993: 383).
73. Kurz (2005: 357–8).
74. Ibid.
75. Ibid., 365.

Five

On Use, Law and the Common

Property and law are born and must die together.
Before the laws, there was no property:
take away the laws, all property ceases.

Jeremy Bentham

Separation

In his essay *In Praise of Profanation*, Agamben writes that the religious essence of capitalism pushes to the extreme the 'tendency' peculiar to all religious phenomena to separate 'everything, every place, every human activity in order to divide it from itself' (Pr, 81), in this way precluding their free use. Religion – he goes on – is that sphere of human social life characterised by the constant removal of 'things, places, animals, or people from common use [to] transfer them to a separate sphere' (ibid., 74): that of the sacred. The procedure (or act) that regulates and marks the passage from the sphere of the profane order to that of the sacred – from the human to the divine – is the sacrifice. Separation appears to Agamben as part of the defining features of religion; and conversely, every separation contains a kind of religious essence.

Such a tendency is somehow expressed in the very etymology of the word 'religion' that, Agamben remarks, does not derive from the Latin *religare* (to bind), but from *relegare*, which is a term that 'indicates the stance of scrupulousness and attention that must be adopted in relations with the gods, the uneasy hesitation … before forms and formulae – that must be observed in order to respect the separation between the sacred and the profane' (ibid., 74–5). Religion, therefore, is not the sphere in which the human and the divine encounter one another; but the place in which they find their maximal-existential separation. Sacred things, all those objects sacrificed that belong to the gods are removed from the free common use and the commerce of men. And their restitution to the sphere of the human, their becoming (again) open to free use pass through an act somehow equal and contrary to the sacrifice: profanation.

In a commodified world like the one in which we live, where our life is mediated and informed by the spectacle of value and the marker, the religion of capital, Agamben maintains, realises a 'pure form of separation, to the point that there is nothing left to separate' (ibid., 81): a total consecration/ separation that seems to reabsorb and neutralise any potential profanation. 'In the commodity', he writes,

> separation inheres in the very form of the object, which splits into use-value and exchange value and is transformed into an ungraspable fetish. The same is true for everything that is done, produced, or experienced, even the human body, even sexuality, even language. They are now divided from themselves and placed in a separate sphere that no longer defines any substantial division and where all use becomes and remains impossible. This sphere is consumption … What cannot be used is, as such, given over to consumption or to spectacular exhibition. This means that it has become impossible to profane (or at least that it requires special procedures). If to profane means to return to common use that which has been removed to the sphere of the sacred, the capitalist religion in its extreme phase aims at creating something absolutely unprofanable (ibid., 81–2).

With a gesture typical of his philosophical style, Agamben here appropriates and reformulates some well-established assumptions about the nature of capitalist accumulation and the process of commodification. The logic of capital – hinging as it does upon processes of accumulation and commodification – is that of the constant enclosure that seeks to 'forcibly separate people from whatever access to social wealth they have which is not mediated by competitive markets and money as capital'.[1] Capitalism separates humans from free access and use of resources making them available only as a commodity in the market. From this follows the essential inability to *use* the world – the things it is composed of and, ultimately, our self.

The first vivid account of how capitalism as a social and economic system arose out of a process of appropriation and separation, is offered by Marx's first volume of *Capital*, in what he has called primitive accumulation. Along with the eviction of peasants through the privatisation of land and the transformation of common property rights into private property, primitive accumulation also involved the imposition of abstract labour as the dominant form of work and the suppression of alternative traditional forms of production, the generalised appropriation of assets and natural resources, and the total monetisation of exchange and the creation of the credit system – all supported by the nascent nation-states, which using violent means created the legal background for the promotion of these processes. But all the elements that Marx described as defining primitive accumulation, as David Harvey claims, 'have remained powerfully present within capitalism's historical geography'.They have given rise to 'new mechanisms of accumulation by dispossession'[2] that have subtracted from the free fruition of anything, from genetic materials to cultural forms, intellectual creativity, and the production of knowledge more generally. Accumulation, dispossession, and separation, rather than defining a preliminary stage of human history towards the imposition of capitalism as a form of life, represents something like the very kernel, the logic of capital formation of the social.

The justification of the logic of appropriation and separation embedded in the religion of capitalism has been central to political philosophy since the inception of modernity – from Locke's theory of private property to the French Declaration of the Rights of Man and the Citizen. Perhaps there is no better explanation of the moral ground of the logic of separation than that of the *Tragedy of the Commons*, a term invented by Garrett Hardin in 1968.[3] Hardin's thesis is as clear as it is controversial: when faced with shared scarce resources, people caring only for their selfish desires will end up consuming and destroying what is held in common. Hardin's attempt to justify such a thesis is not based on experimental evidence and ignores the history and practice of both the enclosure and the commons. Despite having the guise of a thought experiment, such an idea had a wide resonance. Of course, reality tells us a different story. The fairy tale of the tragedy of the commons stands with the reality of the *tragedy of the non-common*:[4] the commodification of the whole world and the destruction of nature in all its forms that produce and fuel the socio-environmental global catastrophe that we are witnessing day after day.

To common

It is no surprise, though, that against capitalist realism the question of the *common* in the last few decades saw a revival, especially among those deeply discontented with the current *weltanschauung*. The common – that regime in which the access to resources and its administration is direct, collective and not for profit, that remains for communities of all the world an actual form of organisation – has become the banner under which a significant number of anti-capitalist movements are carrying out their struggles. Implicit in the idea of the common as a political instrument, is the allusion and proposal of a transformation of the whole institutional asset; the breaking into the interstices that separate the public and the private to create a renewed form of the public sphere outside the border of the state and capital. In this sense, Pierre Dardot and Christian Laval write, 'the term common does not so much refer to the *resurgence* of the eternal Communist Ideal but designates the *emergence* of a new way of challenging capitalism and imagining its transcendence'.[5] Therefore, the idea of common does not simply express the exigency of amending the evident flaws of capitalism and the legal-political framework of its dominance; rather it purports a radical change in the system of norms and the ethical value of possessive individualism.

But what exactly is the common? And what are common goods? The literature on the subject is vast, and it is not the purpose of this chapter to give an exhaustive overview of the relevant discussions.[6] A good starting point to answer those questions is Massimo De Angelis' definition of the common goods as 'use value for a plurality'.[7] Goods held in common, he claims, have a twofold character: 'they are goods in the sense of being social objects of value, use value, objects (whether tangible or not) that satisfy given socially determined needs', which require 'a plurality claiming and sustaining the ownership of the common good'.[8] In emphasising the aspect of use value and of plural ownership, such an understanding of the commons encapsulates the idea of a social system essentially alien to the logic of capital, which if developed through a sufficiently robust force and organisation could open up space for a post-capitalist form of life. And the focus on the common as a renewed form of social and political practice makes such a concept an operative one. Indeed, as Linebaugh argues 'the common is an activity ... it might be better to keep the word as a verb, an activity, rather than as a noun, a substantive'.[9]

Commoning or communisation[10] has become a stable element in the practical horizon of emancipatory strategies through the subtraction of resources and spaces from the reach of the state's power and capital accumulation. As a renewed configuration of humans' relationships with themselves and the world, the common cannot but put into question the instrument that has traditionally been used to regulate such relationships: the law. The commons are not strictly speaking enemies of individual property, but of the excesses due to their unlimited accumulation. And at the same time, they are not hostile to the government: they try to put a limit on the excesses of power, through decisions directly taken by communities of those who use the commons. As such, the process of commoning does not necessarily entail the abandonment of the instruments offered by legal culture and practice; rather it promotes a change in the rules of the current social system turning the law into an instrument to favour the common, instead of remaining as it is the means fostering, with its legitimate monopoly of violence, private property and capital accumulation. From such a perspective, the creation of the common does not envisage a radical break with the juridical order. On the contrary, it could nestle in the law, transforming the legal system to serve the purposes of the common.[11] Embedded in this (more reformist) strategy[12] there is a conception of the law as an instrument that can be appropriated, traversed and used in a wide-ranging project of transformation of reality.[13]

The notion of the 'common' is a recurring trope in Agamben's oeuvre. In works like *The Coming Community* and *Means Without End*, the term has been used to define the possibility of thinking a renewed form of political community outside the identitarian logic of the nation-state and against the growing tendency to separate and expropriate that is embedded in the very existence of capitalism as a social and economic system. As we read in *Means Without Ends*:

> above and beyond the concepts of appropriation and expropriation, we need to think, rather, the possibility and the modalities of a free use. Praxis and political reflection are operating today exclusively within the dialectic of proper and improper – a dialectic in which either the improper extends its own rule everywhere, thanks to an unrestrainable will to falsification and consumption (as it happens in industrialized democracies), or the proper demands the exclusion of any impropriety (as it happens in integralist and totalitarian states). If instead we define the common (or, as others suggest, the same) as a point of indifference between the proper and the improper – that is, as something that can never be grasped in terms of either expropriation or appropriation but that can be grasped, rather, only as use – the essential political problem then becomes: 'How does one use a common?' (MWE, 117).

These thoughts found a decisive development in the later efforts especially in the *Highest Poverty* and *The Use of Bodies*, where he has more extensively elaborated concepts like use, poverty and the common, defined through the idea of the inappropriable. For Agamben, the theorisation of the free use of the common as that space of indifference between expropriation and appropriation, between the proper and the improper constitutes one of the central problems with which a coming politics cannot avoid dealing. As we will see in the following pages, Agamben's conceptualisation of the common[14] and the inappropriable features the common as what cannot be produced legally, opposing in this way all those efforts to consider commoning as an institute or an as collective property, that could be realised and sustained through legal means.

The inappropriable

The chapter in the *Use of Bodies* titled 'The Inappropriable' – which includes with some variations the text of a lecture Agamben delivered at the Architecture Academy of Mendrisio (Switzerland)[15] – is a decisive moment for Agamben's speculation over the concepts of *use* and *common*. Agamben starts by retracing the conclusion of the volume *The Highest Poverty*. The possibility of the use of things for living as separate from legal property rights was the central strategy that the Franciscans adopted in their polemics against the Vatican hierarchies, in order to justify their poverty in legal terms. The form-of-life of the friars minor is lived through an outright renunciation of property; and the use is the dimension that is established through this act of renunciation. As we have seen, this attempt was destined to succumb to the attack of the curia. For Agamben, what is of interest in this fragment of history is not whether the Franciscan definitions of poverty and use 'could have been more or less rigorously argued'; it is rather that the Franciscans were not able to forge a concept of use and poverty in their own right, as not founded on an act of renunciation – that is, in the last analysis, on the will of a subject – but, so to speak, on the very nature of things' (UoB, 80). And this is what Agamben aimed to do with the elaboration of the concept of the *inappropriable*.

Agamben begins his theorisation of the inappropriable by reading Benjamin's fragment *Notes to a Study on the Category of Justice*, in which the categories of justice and inappropriability appear as closely linked to each other. It is worth looking at it at some length here:

Every good, limited by structures of time and space, has a possessive character trait that is an expression of its ability to pass away. Possession that is trapped by the same finitude, however, is unjust. For this reason, there is no system of possession, regardless of its type, that leads to justice. This, however, lies in the conditions of a good that cannot be possessed – a good through which all goods become propertyless. In the concept of society, one seeks to give a good to a proprietor that is able to transcend its possessive character. For this reason, every socialist or communist theory falls short of its goal, as the right of every individual extends to every good. If individual A has a need z, which can be satisfied by good x, and, for this reason, it is believed just that a good y, which is the same as x, should be given to individual B to placate the same needs – this is incorrect. There is, namely, the entirely abstract right of the subject to every good on principle, a right that is not based on needs but rather on justice and whose last inclination will not possibly concern the right to possession of the individual but a right to goods of the good. Justice is the striving to turn the world into the highest good. These thoughts lead to the supposition that justice is not a virtue like other virtues (humility, neighborly love, loyalty, courage), but rather constitutes a new ethical category, one that should probably no longer be called a category of virtue but a category of virtue in relationship to other categories. Justice appears not to be based upon the good will of the subject but forms the state of the world. Justice refers to the ethical category of the existing, virtue the ethical category of the demanded. While virtue can be demanded, justice, in the end, can only be the state of the world or the state of God.[16]

In this fragment, justice is presented not as a distribution of goods or resources accruing to the needs of the individual. The subjective demand of good, for Benjamin, must not be considered as emerging from specific needs, but as grounded on justice, which he writes is something that cannot be appropriated. Justice is not a right of the person; it is a generic right to the good that is manifested in a state of the world. It is, Agamben writes, a category that is not inflected in obligations, but refers to existence as such (UoB., 81). And in so far that justice, he goes on, coincides 'with the condition of a good that cannot be appropriated, to make of the world the supreme good can only mean: to experience it as absolutely inappropriable' (ibid.). Drawing on Benjamin's fragment – which for Agamben is radically Franciscan – poverty (as a condition of being propertyless) 'is not found on a decision of the subject but corresponds to a state of the world' (ibid.), on that form-of-life that is simply lived. If for the Franciscan theorists use is what is established through a renunciation of ownership, Agamben points out, 'the perspective is necessarily reversed and use appears as *the relation to an inappropriable*, as the only possible relation to that supreme state of the world in which, as it is just, it can be in no way appropriated' (ibid.).

Defined as a relation to an inappropriable, the concept of use here finds a positive determination, which does not require the negative dialectical element of 'renunciation'. And from this point of view, the very concept of poverty professed by the Franciscans assumes a renewed formulation (and a broader meaning). Indeed, Agamben writes in *Creation and Anarchy*: 'to be poor means to use, and to use does not mean simply to utilize something, but to maintain oneself in relation with an inappropriable' (CA, 38). For this reason, poverty is truly expropriative not so much because it demands renunciation (of property), but because it is what comes out through an immediate relation with inappropriable things. This, Agamben writes, is 'what Francis's *vivere sine proprio* means: not so much or not only an act of renouncing juridical ownership but a form-of-life that, in so far as it maintains itself in relation with an inappropriable, is always already constitutively outside the law and can never appropriate anything to itself' (ibid.). To the extent that law and property (in the form of power to appropriate) entertain – as in the quote from Bentham which forms the exergue of this chapter – a genetic and genealogic bond, the inappropriable by its own definitions stands out as an element resisting the legal form. The inappropriable delimits a zone of indifference where the machine of (property) law cannot allocate the proper and the appropriable anymore.

Agamben's delineation of the concept of inappropriable in *The Use of Bodies* ends with a brief discussion of the issues of intimacy and privacy which is particularly instructive from our perspective. He writes:

> We can call 'intimacy' the use-of-oneself as relation with an inappropriable. Whether it is a matter of bodily life in all its aspects ([...] urinating, sleeping, defecating, sexual pleasure, nudity, etc., to be) or of the special presence-absence to ourselves that we live in moments of solitude, that of which we have an experience in intimacy is our being held in relation with an inappropriable zone of

non-consciousness. Here familiarity with self reaches an intensity all the more extreme and jealous insofar as it is in no way translated into anything that we could master (UoB, 91–2).

The use-of-oneself that is the content of intimacy defines in a way the most proper of our individual life; it refers to all gestures, habits, styles, tics, but also our body and language, with which we automatically and unconsciously experience ourselves, but of which we do not possess a structured mastery. For Agamben, intimacy is that sphere of our private and bodily life that accompanies us and our existence as a clandestine 'inseparable from us to the extent that, as a stowaway, it furtively shares existence with us' (ibid., xx). Life, private life, is what we experience as a 'faceless' tedious companion, as something divided and separated and 'yet always articulated and held together in a machine, whether it be medical or philosophico-theological or biopolitical' (ibid.). Intimacy as the use-of-oneself in its aporetic scission and inseparability that sustains the statute of life in our culture is also the name of the meaningless common that founds and defines the proper of the human life. Against the standard meaning of the term, here intimacy does not correspond to the proper of a subject; on the contrary, it is what humans existentially share: the inappropriable of ourselves is what we share as common, which therefore cannot but be defined through its inappropriability. It is the impersonal – participated in by anyone, since belonging to anybody – underlying any subjectivity, which through the mediation of the different apparatuses and signatures in which power is expressed, is made into the proper and property of every individual.

This 'opaque sphere of non-awareness' (ibid., 92) that Agamben calls intimacy is what modern law has tried to capture and regulate through the category of privacy. The modern subject, he claims, is defined 'by means of his faculty (which can take the form of a true and proper right) to regulate access to his intimacy' (ibid.). What seems to be in question in the very definition of privacy, is the very constitution of the self: 'intimacy is a circular apparatus, by means of which, by selectively regulating access to the self, the individual constitutes himself as the pre-supposition and proprietor of his own privacy' (ibid.). In a sense, the law of privacy reifies and transforms our intimacy (our free use-of-oneself) into an object that must belong to the person, which (much like a property) has the right to decide over its access. By establishing what parts of our intimacy can be considered as a property, the law leaves with the same gestures all the other parts freely accessible and at its disposal, showing once more its biopolitical nature. But in the last two decades, we have become aware that, either because of a war on terror or an epidemic, such right to privacy as property is not immune from sacrifice on the altar of security. For the law, the inappropriable of life turned into property somehow remains a field of appropriation and regulation. 'Against this attempt to appropriate the inappropriable to oneself, by means of right or force, in order to constitute it as an *arcanum* of sovereignty – Agamben argues – it is necessary to remember that intimacy can preserve its political meaning only on condition that it remains inappropriable. *What is common is never a property but only the inappropriable'* (ibid., 93). The free use-of-oneself could be thought of as constituting the self in autonomy, as long as it remains inappropriable: only if it resists becoming a property, that is to say only if it stands out as the common or as a form-of-life.

The inappropriable here is conceived as an element that calls into question the law as grounded on the possibility of an appropriation. Apart from a few exceptional cases, modern legal systems traditionally regulate property by distinguishing between public and private, as an attribute of physical or juridical persons. And what stands outside this dichotomy remains somehow appropriable, either by individuals or by the state. Since its inception, modernity saw the crushing of the common in the chokehold of private property and the state's property (public). And in the last century, with the neoliberal race to unrestrained privatisation, the separation of private and public has in a sense got lost. Ultimately, public property has assumed the form of a collective private property at the disposal of the ruling classes and private interests.[17] From this perspective, the inappropriable, as what resists appropriation (and expropriation) is placed in the zone of indistinction between the proper and the improper, between the public and the private. And its access or constitution is possible only through the destitution of the possibility always present in and regulated by the law to determine and enforce appropriation.

The institution of the common

Let us now look back, once again, to Agamben's interpretation of the delusional Franciscan attempt at defining their life *legally* in common outside of law's determination. What the Franciscan theorists relentlessly argued against the attacks of the curia is that the highest poverty professed and lived through a renunciation of any form of property, is justified – legally – on a *de facto* use of things as opposed to the legally determined rights to use. Bonagratia of Bergamo clearly illustrates this principle analogically: 'in the same way in which the horse has a *de facto* use but no property rights over the oats that it eats, the religious who has abdicated all property has the simple *de facto* use [*usum simplicem facti*] of bread, wine, and clothes'.[18] For Agamben, the vindication of a *usus facti,* as opposed to *usus iuris,* revealed itself 'to be a double-edged sword, which had opened the path to the decisive attack carried out by John XXII precisely in the name of the law' (HP, 137). In the bull *Ad conditorem canonum,* the Pope sanctioned the essential impossibility of separating use and property with a subtle legal argument: in the consumable things essential to the sustenance of the friars minor – such as food and drink, clothes, etc. – a clear-cut separation of ownership and use is impossible. In so far as the factual use of such things coincides with their destruction (*abusus*), such a form of use does not exist in nature and consequently cannot be possessed.

By legally justifying their extra-legal life, the Franciscans in a way underestimated the operational power of the law. As Agamben maintains, by distinguishing a *de facto* use and use of rights (in the form of property) they certainly had the merit of exposing the nature of property in law (and the nature of law *tout court*) as a psychological reality based on the intention to possess, and as the product of law's operations. However, in opposing the factual use to a right to use, they fell prey to the very machine of law they tried to escape. The law, Agamben points out, functions by dividing facts and law, instituting between them a zone of indistinction, through which the fact (i.e., the law's outside) is captured, categorised, and included in the law. To capture what stands outside of its ambit is indeed the primary operation of the law. As for property law, for example, possession is a matter of fact, which involves certain typical legal consequences. By the same token, in Roman law the things unowned were defined as *res nullius*; but 'since the first one who collects or captures them becomes ipso facto their owner, they are only the presupposition of the act of appropriation that sanctions their ownership' (ibid., 139). To claim facts against the law is therefore playing the law's game since facts can be procedurally made into rights – as the brocard says, *ex facto oritur ius*. Within the realm of law the common – what is not owned and that is therefore left open to the free use of all – seems a field of conquest: the mere presupposition of the very existence of private property and all the rights and facts that derive from it. In summary, the institution/constitution of the common – as inappropriable – appears in law's eyes a very fragile enterprise. The inappropriable is in some sense the unsaid of the law (while being an indispensable element of the law): it is that which cannot be conceived as having a proper legal form, which is at the same time the presupposition of all legal forms of property.

An example of the inappropriable-instituted could be found in the Roman law category of the *res nullius in bonis*. As Yan Thomas in the essay *La valeur des choses* sustains, the legal definition of the things [*res*] that could potentially constitute the substance of private patrimony, was obtained negatively by removing and separating certain objects that originally belonged to the sphere of the appropriable [*res nullius*] making them inappropriable through a legal operation that assigned them to the gods or the city. In Roman law to make things 'appropriable', Thomas writes, 'it is necessary that certain things are excluded from the area of appropriation and exchange, and then assigned to the Gods or the city'; these sacred removed and separated things, are classified as 'things belonging to a property that does not belong to anybody (*res nullius in bonis*)', whose alienation and commerce is prohibited.[19] And the delimitation of the ambit of sacred inappropriable objects effectively rendered all the other things open to appropriation and commerce. Therefore, for Roman law, the public space is divided into two spheres: one at the disposal of the state which includes objects that could be sold and made appropriable, such as public land, and another space, which includes all that is for public use – such as squares, theatres, markets, gantries, roads, rivers, water systems, etc. – whose unavailability was absolute. The inappropriability and inalienability that defines such things [*res nullius in bonis*] were not deduced by their natural characteristics or because of a specific use-value or utility, but it was obtained through law's operation.

As Dardot and Laval argue, the Roman designation of *res nullius in bonis* is perhaps 'the closest historical precedent' of the institution of the common: 'anything that falls under this designation is not at the free disposal of the state, because such objects or resources are not susceptible to appropriation'.[20] While the soundness of this historical paradigm for the idea of a collective use is for them beyond doubt, the crucial issue to address is *how* to make it real without the risk of recreating the same forms of power that the institution of the common tries to overcome: 'Can we dissociate the act of designating or institutionalizing the common from its collective use without reintroducing relations of mastery?'[21]

Dardot and Laval's book *Common: On Revolution in the 21st Century* is a very long and articulate answer to this question. The programmatic purpose of their effort is unequivocally expressed early in their text when they claim that '*The common is not a good* ... [but] a political principle through which we are able to build the commons, maintain the commons, and sustain the commons. It is, as such, a political principle that defines a new system of struggles on a global scale'.[22] Here the common does not pertain to the very nature of things, but is something that is established through a praxis (whose outcome cannot be appropriated but remains somehow immanent to the common of a collective). 'Our preliminary concern', they claim, 'is to determine what kinds of practices are able to invent rules of use that are themselves capable of becoming customs over time'.[23] For Dardot and Laval the common does not have a subject that can potentially claim its property or authorship, 'as a form of collective practice – the common – produces its own kind of subject, it stands to reason that this subject is not the subject *of* the common since it did not pre-exist the very practice that produces'.[24] As such, the common does not simply exclude private property: it excludes property as a category.

Pertaining to the sphere of human praxis, the common and what is held as inappropriable, for Dardot and Laval, must be considered in relation to an institutional framework. In other words, the common must be instituted practically, through what they call an instituent praxis that is the 'conscious activity of the institution'.To institute, they maintain, 'consists above all in the act of establishing legal rules [which] is neither to create rules ex nihilo nor to formalize or consecrate post factum rules that already exist but which are not recognized in law'. [25] Instituent praxis, thus, essentially aims to create new conditions, and new subjectivities through a process of self-transformation undertaken immanently in and through the institutions forming the imaginary underpinning social practices of a community.

As Dardot and Laval maintain the instituent praxis should not be confused with the exercise of constituent power, since it 'does not have the majesty of a solemn foundation act, and it does not need a subject that pre-dates it'[26] and because it represents an 'activity that begins from the already instituted' and proceeds by 'establishing new rules that retrospectively endow this inherited past with new meanings'.[27] The instituent praxis reshapes the already instituted to create new rules of law for the institution/administration of the common. Although the insistence with which Dardot and Laval sustained the alterity of instituent praxis with respect to constituent power, their theory appears in the end still to be embroiled to the constituent principle. As Agamben argued, the very idea of praxis, as an autonomous sphere of doing, as opposed to *poiesis* and production, has somehow got lost, so that for the Western mind all doing – from politics to art and labour – is meant as an act of producing/creating that pertains to a willing subject. And this is something that Dardot and Laval admit when they submit that the 'instituent praxis is a *self-production of a collective subject in and through the continuous co-production of the rules of law'*.[28]

However, unless one considers instituent praxis in terms of spontaneism[29] – which Dardot and Laval carefully avoid doing – every praxis and doing requires an acting/creating subject (collective, individual, delegated, etc.), whose definition as in-the-making or already made makes little difference. In other words, any creative praxis is essentially constituent in so as far it requires by its own definition an agent, who acts within given historical/material conditions to bring into actuality that which is potentially possible. Furthermore, to claim that the autonomous-instituent moment is conditioned by the very historical substance and materiality of the *in-situ* institution, does not settle the alterity of a praxis to any constituent power. In the end, as Schmitt has argued, the constituent moment involves the conscious decision of a subject (the people), who decides in favour of the formalisation of something that is already substantiated: the very existence of the people as a material institutional fact.[30]

From our point of view, what represents the most interesting and critical aspect of their theory of the common is the reliance on law and legal language as a technique to bring into reality and to sustain the common. This reliance is featured by the two authors. The instituent praxis is a co-production of *rules of law* that should lead to the institution of the common as an encompassing form of social life. Therefore, they cannot but argue that the 'common is a political construct' which 'is not "anarchist" in the sense of the simple negation of power or the contradictory refusal of all authority'.[31] In short, to institute the common as inappropriable means to 'prohibit its appropriation in order to more effectively appropriate it'.[32] But by what means should the law of the common and the prohibitions and obligations sustaining it be enforced? What instruments are at the disposal of the 'gendarme who keeps an eye on things and intervenes'[33] to enforce such prohibition? The genetic bond with violence that grants the efficacy of the law, its norms, obligations and prohibitions, is something that Dardot and Laval left as an unsaid behind the curtain of the supposed goodness of the instituent praxis as self-government. In the end, what seems to be at stake in this attempt at thinking the institution of the common is a radically democratic version of the *res nullius in bonis*, in which the institution and administration of the inappropriable are delegated to collective self-government. Nonetheless, this does not eliminate the fundamental question of law's violence and the relation of mastery that is logically implied in it. If the insanities of the twentieth century left us a lesson, it is that the violence that the law makes legal and legitimate needs to be considered in all its dimensions including that of generalising and normalising the recourse to violence. For the law, as Cornelius Castoriadis claimed about the ontology of creation, it 'leaves room, in the most abstract way, for the possibility of the instauration of an autonomous society as well as for the reality of Stalinism and Nazism'.[34]

The use of the law

Up to this point, we have seen how the common as inappropriable entertains a contrasting relationship with the law. From the Roman law expression *res nullius in bonis* to the various form of communal access to resources (the commons), historically the access to common goods appeared essentially as a normative enterprise. In the end, it is through laws and norms (either customary or expressly juridical) that communities have traditionally organised themselves and their access to resources. However, the history of the emergence of the modern state saw the total crushing of the practice of communal sharing through the forcible application of the dichotomy of private/public law as a standard mode of administration of the access and use of things. For the modern mind, formed as it is on possessive individualism free use has become unthinkable.

Established under the banner of the concentration of powers and authority, the modern state was envisaged as a tool to respond to the need for security that the medieval feudal system was no longer able to afford. The modern state works by coupling the claim of the monopoly on the legitimate use of force and the creation of an administrative-bureaucratic structure for governing the population. Sovereignty is the juridical concept with which the two elements have been framed in unity. In this all-modern process, the law has been transformed and compressed into an absolutist/authoritarian guise as the voice of sovereign almighty power. The logic of the formal unique and hierarchical law, decided officially and administered bureaucratically from top to bottom, operates to limit violence and to grant security through the implementation of another violence, which was legal and unpunishable. In so doing the modern mind has operated a kind of sanctuarisation of the law itself: it operated its enclosure inside the sacred administrative boundaries of the state, formulating an equivalence between legality and state's power.

By acknowledging this process, in his *Common Goods: A Manifesto*, Ugo Mattei argues that to revive the idea of the common it is necessary to 'reject on the one hand the equation between law and the state, and that of law and the repression of conflicts, and on the other hand to turn down the artificial barrier that separates law from politics and ethics, which have transformed law into a technology known only to professionals and inaccessible to lay people'.[35] In other words, the access to the common should pass through the commoning of the law, which 'restores the centrality of the person, granting it full access to all goods (law included)'.[36] For Mattei, thinking the law as common necessitates a proper form of the cultural revolution: the overcoming of the ontological and epistemic conditions that have formed the modern mind, the very separation between subject and object, human and nature that the Cartesian tradition posed as the ground of the philosophy of *to have*. Modernity institutionalised into the machine of law and the state the idea of the human as separated from nature, making the latter into something absolutely appropriable and manageable. The image of the human that the modern law is enforcing is that of possessive individualism, which in Macpherson's words is a conception of the individual as essentially the proprietor of his person, who owes nothing to society, which is nothing other than a 'calculated device for the protection' of the right to property.[37] The modern juridical culture evolved out of this image, and it has never been able to elaborate alternative ideas other than those subsumed under the categories of the rule of law: the illusion that we could be ruled by norms and not by men, the purpose of which is the protection of our property. The idea of the common, Mattei claims, being substantially alien to the ontological structures of the modern mind, rejects the logic of 'having': it is an 'ecologic-qualitative' category, which resists property in all its forms. And to the extent that rights can be possessed (I have rights), the common cannot have the form of a right.[38]

What form could the law as a common take? Or in other words, what is the meaning and function of the law made inappropriable and only used? If we take Agamben's propositions seriously, we must conclude that law-as-common resists any form of appropriation and remains alien to the prerogative of any authoritative subjectivity (the state, the sovereign, the caste of individuals that compose the judiciary, lawyers and so forth). Law-as-common is a type of law that can only be used. However, this implies a total transfiguration of legal practice, the destitution or profanation of law's authority and its restitution to a renewed free and common use. In the concluding section of *State of Exception*, Agamben writes that 'the question of a possible use of law' could be meaningfully raised only in relation to the space that is opened through the severance of the 'nexus between violence and law' (SE, 88). Only by separating the words of the law from the instrumental violence that has been historically implemented to grant their performative capturing of life, does it become possible to think a (new) use of the law. A law that is only used is in a sense liberated by its forcible obligatory character, destituted of its sacred transcendental essence and used without being enforced. Use, Agamben claims, 'consists in freeing a behaviour from its genetic inscription within a given sphere ... the freed behavior still reproduces and mimics the forms of the activity from which it has been emancipated, but by emptying them of their sense and of any obligatory relationship to an end' (Pr, 85). The use of the law (as common and inappropriable) does not ideally change the letter of the law, but in mimicking its traditional form, liberates it from its telos, its force and violence. 'We will then have before us a "pure law" ... a word that does not bind, that neither commands nor prohibits' (SE, 88).

We arrive here at the same question with which we ended Chapter 3: what form does the law assume when the violent institutional machine sustaining its application has been profaned? An answer to this question, although paradigmatic (which is to say anything but definitive), can be found in *The Highest Poverty*, where Agamben refers to the emergence of texts called *consuetudines* in Augustinian, Benedictine and Cistercian monasteries. The interpretation of these texts, Agamben writes, on the surface simply describe the monk's habitual restrictions, often in the first person as complements or completions of the rules is misleading. In reality it is a matter of a restoration of the rules to their originary nature as transcriptions of the monks' *conversatio* or way of life. The rule that, while arising out of habit and custom, had been progressively constituted as a Divine Office and liturgy returns now to presenting itself in the humble garb of use and life. The Consuetudines, that is to say, are to be read in the context of the process that, beginning in the thirteenth century, shifts the center of gravity of spirituality from the level of rule and doctrine to that of life and forma vivendi. But it is significant that form of life is attested in these writings only in the form of consuetudo, as if the actions of the monk acquired their own sense only by being constituted as use (HP, 141).

The form of law in common, that law that is only used and not enforced, is that which pertains to the custom or habit. But, Agamben maintains, the habit is 'the form in which potential exists and is given reality as such' (ibid., 59); it is a *'form-of-life and not the knowledge or faculty of a subject'* (UoB, 62). The law as a habit, therefore, maintains in its actual existence the character of pure possibility: it remains in relation to its potentiality not to pass into act – not to express its innate performativity. The habitual law operates immanently to the sphere of living; it does not boil down to a command in need of obedience but confuses itself with the daily gestures, uses and custom that to the extent that they do not belong to anyone are participated in by all.

~ * ~

In *Anthropology from a Pragmatic Point of View*, with a language still firmly confident in the plausibility of universal concepts, Kant defined that state of things in which law and freedom are not enforced as anarchy:

Freedom and law (by which freedom is limited) are the two pivots around which civil legislation turns. – But in order for law to be effective and not an empty recommendation, a middle term ... must be added; namely force, which, when connected with freedom, secures success for these principles. – Now one can conceive of four combinations of force with freedom and law:

A. Law and freedom without force (anarchy).
B. Law and force without freedom (despotism).
C. Force without freedom and law (barbarism).
D. Force with freedom and law (republic).[39]

Of course, for Kant only the last option amounts to a proper civil constitution. This is not the right place for a proper analysis of Kant's naïve optimism. It is enough to note that he was writing before the unfolding of the history of modern liberal/democratic states. If anything, the lesson that the last couple of centuries has taught us is that option D is far from being a civil constitution and by use of the state of exception can include and become both B and C. What is more interesting in such a classification is that option A (*anarchy*) – law and freedom are decoupled from force (and violence) – is the one that has never been experienced in Western history (of course, one could question also if D has ever 'existed' – but let us try to give some credit to the hegemonic fantasy of the Western mind). Faced with the catastrophe of the present, the time has come for us to start taking option A into serious consideration.

Notes

1. De Angelis (2007: 144).
2. Harvey (2004, 74).
3. Hardin (1968).
4. Dardot and Laval (2019).
5. Ibid., 5.
6. Decisive in raising the question of the common in the context of emancipatory politics is the work of the Noble Prize Elinor Ostrom. See Ostrom (1990; 2002). On the commons from an historical perspective, see Linebaugh (2007). For a more philosophical and political-oriented discussion of the common, see: Federici (2011); Negri, Hardt (2009); De Angelis, Harvie (2013); De Angelis (2017); Dardot, Laval (2019).
7. De Angelis (2017: 29).

8. Ibid., 30.
9. Linebaugh (2007: 279).
10. See Noys (2012).
11. Capra and Mattei (2017).
12. Starting from ministerial commission on the reform of common goods, presided over by Stefano Rodotà and from the social struggle against the widespread privatisation of public utilities, such an approach is rather popular in Italy. See: Rodotà (2018); Capra and Mattei (2011; 2017); Lucarelli (2013); Chignola (2012).
13. Chignola (2012: 8).
14. On Agamben's concept of the common see: Watkin (2014); Boano (2017); Primera (2019).
15. Included in the volume *Creation and Anarchy*.
16. Benjamin wrote this fragment in 1916 [Notizen zu einer Arbeit über die Kategorie der Gerechtigkeit]. I refer here to the English translation by Eric Levy Jacobson included in Jacobson (2003: 166–9).
17. Dardot and Laval (2019).
18. Bonagratia (1929: 511), quoted in HP, 110.
19. Thomas (2002: 1432) – author's translation.
20. Dardot and Laval (2019: 180).
21. Ibid., 180–1.
22. Ibid., 28.
23. Ibid., 277.
24. Ibid., 181.
25. Ibid., 301.
26. Ibid., 302.
27. Ibid., 304.
28. Ibid., 305.
29. Which is a hypothesis that should be considered seriously.
30. The proximity of Dardot and Laval's ideas to the constituent tradition is also evident in the vocabulary in which they are expressed – government, deliberative activity, governance, revolution, democracy, are all key terms in their effort at thinking a world to come. From their perspective, the common is the principle, the *archè* that should begin and command the revolution for the twenty-first century, which should produce a form of self-government of the common based on a shared deliberative activity on the model of radical democracy. But if the task for a new emancipatory politics is also to change the social imaginary of communities all over the world, should we not start by changing its very structure, that is the language in which it is expressed?

31. Dardot and Laval (2019: 313).
32. Ibid., 407.
33. Althusser (2014: 68).
34. Castoriadis (1997: 362).
35. Mattei (2011: 60).
36. Ibid.
37. Macpherson (1962: 3).
38. Mattei (2011: 61).
39. Kant (2006: 166).

Six

From the Anarchy of Power to the Anarchy of Being

> Asking why this body is affected by this form-of-life rather than another is as meaningless as asking why there is something rather than nothing. Such a question betrays only a rejection, and sometimes a fear, of undergoing contingency. And, a fortiori, a refusal even to acknowledge it.
>
> *Tiqqun*

An-archē

In the essay *What is a Command?* Agamben writes: 'Anarchy has always seemed more interesting to me than democracy' (CA, 54). As revealing as not programmatic, this comment is one of the rare moments in which Agamben exposes a rather explicit political affinity. The recurring stark critique of sovereignty, his lack of faith in law and the juridical, his contempt for capitalism and commodification, and the elevation of use and poverty as paradigms of a more ethical form-of-life, make Agamben's political theorisations firmly aligned to anarchist-libertarian thought. Yet it is true, as Simone Bignall notes, that 'Agamben makes scant reference to thinkers in the anarchist tradition'.[1] Indeed, in the concluding section of *The Use of Bodies*, he seems to approve Reiner Schürmann's critique of classic anarchism, according to which, what the patron saint Proudhon and Bakunin did, 'was to displace the origin, to substitute the "rational" power, principium, for the power of authority, princeps – as metaphysical an operation as has ever been. They sought to replace one focal point with another'.[2]

Agamben's critique of the traditional form of anarchism was in a sense already affirmed in the introduction to the volume *Homo Sacer*, where he sustained that 'the weakness of anarchist and Marxian critiques of the state was precisely to have not caught sight of this structure [the exception] and thus to have quickly left the *arcanum imperii* [of sovereignty] aside, as if it had no substance outside of the simulacra and the ideologies invoked to justify it' (HS, 12). So, for Agamben, the failure of anarchism consisted in theorising to get rid of political authority and the state, invoking another kind of authority, that of morality and society, substituting a command with another command. But he nevertheless also claimed that 'if there is something that I would like to entrust to your reflection, it is precisely the problem of anarchy' (CA, 77). So, what does Agamben mean by anarchy? And how do Agamben's political ontology and his theory of destituent potential fit with the idea of anarchy and anarchism?[3]

Agamben confronts the problem of anarchy along two convergent argumentative lines. Moving away from the established political meaning of the term, he has on the one hand, theorised anarchy as the utmost essence of power, and on the other problematised it, in the context of a renewed conception of the ontological relationship between essence and existence, between being and practice, that stands as a founding element of the concept of form-of-life in ontological terms. These two streams of thought are strictly related: the latter can be viewed of as a real possibility only by means of exposing and grasping the former.

Let us now start by looking at two passages respectively from *The Use of Bodies* and the essay *Capitalism as Religion*:

> Benjamin wrote once that there is nothing more anarchic than the bourgeois order. In the same sense, Pasolini has one of the officials of Salò say that the true anarchy is that of power. If this is true, then one can understand why the thought that seeks to think anarchy – as negation of 'origin' and 'command,' principium and princeps – remains imprisoned in endless aporias and contradictions. Because power is constituted through the inclusive exclusion (exceptio) of anarchy, the only possibility of thinking a true anarchy coincides with the lucid exposition of the anarchy internal to power. Anarchy is what becomes thinkable only at the point where we grasp and render destitute the anarchy of power (UoB, 275).

And,

> against the anarchy of power, I do not intend to invoke a
> return to a solid foundation in being: even if we ever pos-
> sessed such a foundation, we have certainly lost it or have
> forgotten how to access it. I believe, however, that a clear
> comprehension of the profound anarchy of the societies in
> which we live is the only correct way to pose the problem
> of power and, at the same time, that of true anarchy.
> Anarchy is what becomes possible only when we grasp the
> anarchy of power (CA, 77).

Anarchy – the anarchy Agamben endorses – must be considered in line with the very etymology of the term as an-archy,
that is negation/destitution of the *archè*, intended as the
'origin' and 'command'. As we have seen earlier, Agamben
defines the logic of the exception – according to which something is separated, excluded and rearticulated as the *archè*:
that presuppositional mechanism that throughout history
has been revealed as constantly informing the architectures
of powers. But the *archè* 'is not to be understood in any way
as a given locatable in a chronology', rather, 'it is an operative force within history' (ST, 110). Like the Big Bang 'which
continue[s] to send toward us its fossil radiation', and 'like
the child of psychoanalysis exerting an active force within
the psychic life of the adult' (ibid.), the *archè* constitutes an
ineffable force shaping the understanding of the concrete
historical experience.[4] Accordingly, the *polis* is founded on
the scission of life in a *zoē* (animal life) and *bios* (a politically
qualified life – a form of life); the human is defined through
the exclusion-inclusion of animality; and law through the
exclusion-inclusion of state of anomy and violence (UoB,
264-265). Agamben claims that the apparatuses through
which power is manifested have always operated through
the inclusive exclusion of their negation: of anarchy and
anomy; therefore 'of anarchy we understand only the war
of all against all, of anomy we see only chaos and the state
of exception' (WDP, 72). Both dimensions, though, can be
accessed only at the price of leaving behind the complicated
sleight of hand that consists in negating the target of one's
argument to the point of excluding it, while at the same

moment furtively re-cycling this exclusion within the argument in order to provide it with an even more irresistible structure.

To the extent that the mechanism of the exception is constantly informed and commanded by the ontological dispositive of the scission of being (that which articulates essence and existence – potentiality and act) that underlies any ontological difference, its destitution necessarily implies a kind of ontological break (or revolution). It is necessary, Agamben writes to 'replace the ontology of substance with an ontology of how' (ibid., 73), that is, with a modal ontology. Such a form of ontology makes it possible to go 'beyond the ontological difference that has dominated the Western conception of being' making it possible to 'rethink from the start the problem of the relation between potentiality and act' (ibid.). For the modal ontology – as we will see more extensively later in the chapter – the modification of being, does not entail a passage from potentiality to act, but happens on a terrain in which the potential and the actual, form and substance, remain immanent to each other. The ontology of modes does not think the coming into being of an entity as commanded by substances, identities or differences: the mode is immediately different and identical to any substance. It is in a sense *anarchic* since it does not require a faculty, a principle, or a command to think the event of being.

We might say, though, that the true anarchy that Agamben speaks about is that which rises out of the destitution of the ontological ground on which stand the apparatuses of power, shaping and orienting our form of life, and its replacement with a modal ontology that allows us to think beyond the traditional western conception of being. In this way, Agamben tries to think toward the deposition of the somehow absolute authority of the *archè* of power, to open a space in which being and life could be freed from laws, commands and principles, and therefore experienced in their immanent potentiality and freedom. The destitution of the anarchy of power leaves as a fundamental residue what could be defined as the anarchy of being, as the existential status of a form-of-life.

Bipolar machine

The Kingdom and the Glory is the study in which Agamben's idea of the anarchy of power finds its most explicit formulation. The question it addresses is why power in the West has assumed the form of a government. Making use of political theology as a method, Agamben's hypothesis is that 'the economic-governmental vocation of contemporary democracies is not something that has happened accidentally but is a constitutive part of the theological legacy of which they are the depositaries' (KG, 143). The investigation of the theological premises of such 'governmental vocation', which dates to the early Church Fathers, allows Agamben to extend and in a sense correct Foucault's genealogy according to which governmentality is essentially a modern phenomenon that emerged out of a radical break with the traditional paradigms of power centred on law and the principle of sovereignty. For Foucault, the rise of governmental rationality marked the passage from the old-sovereign power configured as the 'right to *take* life or to *let* live', to the modern bio-power 'to *foster* life or *disallow* it to the point of death'.[5] From this point of view, sovereignty is characterised negatively as primarily oriented to the possibility of the 'delivery' of death; its formal manifestation is the juridical order framed upon the structures of the legal rule and concomitant punishments. For the paradigm of sovereignty, life is merely what remains when power stands still, when the sword of the law remains in the scabbard. Governmentality, on the contrary, entails a positive capture of life into the calculation of politics, for which the living substance (in its biological, social and cultural dimensions) becomes the object of power, and life's administered flourishing, the purpose of political care.

In *The Kingdom and the Glory*, Agamben sustains, with and contra Foucault, that the sovereign power and biopolitics are two distinct paradigms of power that mould the two poles of a bipolar mechanism, the centre of which is empty – or anarchic. Within Agamben's research path, theology represents the place in which the models were elaborated. From Christian theology, he writes, derive two 'political paradigms, antinomical but functionally related to one another': political theology, 'which founds the transcendence of sovereign power on the single God', and the 'economic theology', which replaces this transcendence with the idea of an *oikonomia*, conceived as an immanent ordering-domestic and not political in a strict-sense of both divine and human life' (ibid., 1). The first paradigm marked the path toward political philosophy and the theory of sovereign power; on the contrary, 'modern biopolitics up to the current triumph of economy and government over every other aspect of social life' (ibid.) derive from the second paradigm. The two paradigms correspond to two different configurations of power, which are strictly related, so that the economic (immanent) administration and government of 'men and things', is the execution of something that is disposed and ordained sovereignly.

Agamben's archaeological investigation brings into focus the role that the notion of *oikonomia* played in the genesis of the theological doctrine of the Trinity. The term *oikonomia*, which in its original Greek meaning defined the managerial administration of the household, has been used in the context of early Christian theological speculations to safeguard monotheism from the re-emergence of a plurality of divine figures, as a means of preventing the fracture in the ontological unity of God in the three central figures of the father, son and Holy Spirit. Without any substantial semantic alteration, the term *oikonomia* became the operator that allowed the conciliation of the Trinity with divine unity. The monarch-like God is one in its substance, but his administration [*oikonomia*] of the world is manifested as a trinity. In this way, 'the divine being', Agamben claims, 'is not split, since the triplicity of which the Fathers speak is located on the level of the *oikonomia*' and not on the level of being, or substance.

For all the considerable historical success of this strategy of escaping the split of God's essence into the three figures, Agamben notes that the 'caesura' that has been avoided on the level of being 're-emerges' as a 'fracture between God and his action, between ontology and praxis' (ibid., 53). Dividing the 'substance or the divine nature from its economy', he goes on, 'amounts to instituting within God a separation between being and acting, substance and praxis' (ibid.). The scission does not concern divine being, but divine action. Since Trinity is an economic, administrative matter, the economic praxis through which God 'governs the world is, as a matter of fact, entirely different from his being, and cannot be inferred from it' (ibid, 54). Thus, being radically different from his substance (essence), God's economic government is alienated from God's being, and does not find its foundation in it. God's government, as Agamben suggests, is in this sense without any foundation: it is anarchic. Indeed, anarchy is 'what government must presuppose and assume as the origin from which it derives' (ibid., 64). And the word *oikonomia* refers to this an-archy.

In theological terms, the fractures between ontology and praxis – as unfolding in the doctrine of the creation *ex nihilo* of the world, through a free divine act without actual foundation – implies the logical differentiation between the transcendent pole of sovereign power and the government as its immanent actualisation. The two poles, although irreconcilable, are functionally interconnected in a governmental machine. Sovereignty is divided; but it is also – in a specific way – opposed to government. This opposition places sovereignty as the legitimating element of government (the concrete actualisation of power), and government as designating the very concrete existence of sovereignty. If 'Kingdom and … Government are separated in God by a clear opposition', Agamben claims, 'then no government of the world is actually possible'; there would be, 'on the one hand, an impotent sovereignty and, on the other, the infinite and chaotic series of particular (and violent) acts of providence. The government is possible only if the Kingdom and the Government are correlated in a bipolar machine' (ibid., 114), the centre of which is empty. The modern state, to the extent that it presents itself through the structural 'distinction between legislative or sovereign power and executive or governmental power' (ibid., 142) has perfectly inherited the double structure of the bipolar-governmental machine.

Formed by elements that are connected but not ontologically grounded in their relationship, the administration of power in the West assumes anarchy as its ultimate foundation. For Agamben, the groundlessness of governmental praxis stands here as the necessary condition of the economic government of men and things. The fracture that separates sovereignty and government 'insofar as it makes the praxis free and "anarchic" opens in fact, at the same time, the possibility and necessity of its government' (ibid., 66). Such anarchic inheritance determines the entire economic dispositive of Western governmentality, from the separation of powers to the invisible hand of the economy. Anarchy – as that form of free praxis that is not founded on determined being – constitutes the *archè* of government: that foundational element that must be constantly captured and excluded to make the machine work. 'Anarchy – Agamben writes – is what government must presuppose and assume as the origin from which it derives and, at the same time, as the destination toward which it is traveling' (ibid., 64).

For Agamben, the governmental machine appears as built on a void, which makes its powers essentially un-founded on any stable figure of being. Anarchy, as that form of praxis – as that form of life – that, freed from any ontological ground and vocation, is what any form of government – either authoritarian or democratic – both presupposes and excludes, but in which it also finds its foundation. In this sense, government exists as that form of anarchic apparatus that thwarts and conceals the ungovernable potential anarchy of life. However, by being un-grounded and anarchic, earthly powers are constantly seeking to reaffirm their legitimacy, either by violence and security mechanisms, or by the consent of their subjects. Agamben calls this consent 'glory'. Divine transcendence, the general will, the people, government by consent, are all strategies that in the history of political thought have concealed the constitutive anarchy of power, thus legitimising the exclusion of the anarchy of being and life.

Modal ontology

The scattered sections in which Agamben has exposed his idea of inoperativity as a political category, have found a systematisation – albeit non-programmatic – in *The Use of Bodies*. Here he has established that the cutting of the ties that bind life with the apparatus of sovereign power necessitates a substantial revision of the ontological categories grounding it. Thinking of politics and ethics freed from the principle of sovereignty becomes possible only by replacing the Aristotelean ontological dispositive with a new ontology of potentiality, which Agamben called 'modal ontology'.

Expressed differently, the deactivation of the *archè* of power – of the logic of the exception – i.e., both the liberation of the anarchy of being and the constitution of a form-of-life, necessitates a radical reframing of the fundamental onto-logical scission between essence and existence, potentiality, and act.

For Agamben, as we have seen earlier, Aristotle has bequeathed to the Western tradition a form of interrogat-ing the being of entities (things as well as humans) start-ing always from a fundamental separation and articulation of two elements, so that the identity of a being is the apo-retic construction of something that *is* and something that *is not* (but is, instead, only presupposed). For the ontological dispositive, Agamben maintains, 'being has been divided into an inessential existent and an inexistent essence' (UoB, 125). Aristotle has in a sense tied the traditional ontology of substance to a dialectical mechanism according to which the being of entities – their identity and singularity – must be understood through the necessary relationship between irreconcilable parts. Essence and existence, potentiality and act, form and matter, are the coordinates within which being is said in many ways. Yet, their individuated coincidence remains somehow difficult to establish. And attempting to define the nature and form of the ontological difference, phi-losophy has serially incurred into inconclusive distinctions and theorisation. Overall, this series will form the history-of-being, and ontology as we know it.

Perhaps, the hurdle on which the ontological disposi-tive has run aground, showing its fundamental limits, is no other than the definition of the singular existence of a body in its own identity as different from all others, with which in certain cases it shares the same nature. The question, known as *principium individuationis* [principle of individuation], considered through coordinates of the Aristotelean disposi-tive, becomes rather enigmatic: 'if one thinks the relation between essence and singular existence on the model of the Aristotelian relation between potential and act, possible and actual', Agamben writes, 'individuation remains problem-atic. What drives the possible to produce itself in ecceity, to actually realize itself in act in this or that singularity?' (ibid., 157). In dividing essence and existence – potentiality and act – the ontological dispositive can think the singularity of an existing entity, in the end, only as composed of two separated elements, and more importantly, it cannot answer the question of the passage to act – or to existence otherwise than by referring back to the separation itself or to a third element: 'In the potential/act apparatus' Agamben claims,

> Aristotle holds together two irreconcilable elements: the contingent – what can be or not be – and the necessary – what cannot not be. According to the mechanism of relation that we have defined, he thinks potential as existing in itself, in the form of a potential-not-to or impotential (*adynamia*), and act as ontologically superior and prior to potential. The paradox – and at the same time, the strength – of the apparatus is that, if one takes it literally, potential can never pass over into the act and the act always already anticipates its own possibility. For this reason Aristotle must think potential as a hexis, a 'habit,' something that one 'has,' and the passage to the act as an act of will (ibid., 276).

For the ontology of substance, the essence 'human nature' and the fact that a specific human exists in its individuality and identity, are not the same thing; essence expresses what a thing is, it is in a sense the ground from which the various attributes of a thing are said. The existentive being – or existence – is not its essence, but the individual reality of the thing with its attributes and modes. The essence of an x-human that exists and the essence of an x-human that does not exist, are absolutely the same: humanness/humanity/human nature. The x-human existing is instead totally different from its essence, which nevertheless is something that must be presupposed to be identified as such. Existence as the individuation of a being according to a substance or essence is the substance of essence in act; and its identity is somehow composed and formed by property, accidents and attributes that makes a substance into actuality. And it is this passage from essence and existence (the taking place – the coming into actuality) that the ontological dispositive, Agamben argues, is incapable of explaining satisfactorily. No matter how the terms of such a division are defined or articulated (essence/existence; potentiality/act; form/matter/ being/ beings), what is decisive for Agamben, is that in Western culture, being, as much as life – but also the *polis* and the anarchic link between sovereign power and government – are always conceived starting from the ontological difference. And it is to overcome and to destitute such ontological-biopolitical dispositive that he conjured up the idea of a modal ontology. 'It is necessary – Agamben claims – to replace the ontology of substance', the ontology of the *is* 'with an ontol-ogy of how. The decisive problem is no longer "what" I am, but "how" I am what I am' (WDP, 73).

In *The Use of Bodies*, after having traced a brief genealogy of the concept of 'mode' as emerged in early and late scholasti-cism, Agamben identifies in Spinoza the elements proper to modal ontology. Spinoza's radical ontology is formulated, for Agamben, in the proposition 'there is nothing besides substance and modes' [*praeter substantias et modos nihil existit*].[6] Although framed in the same language and based on a similar fundamental distinction as that of the ontology of substance, the relationship substance/modes, Agamben maintains, allows the difficulties that the ontological differ-ence has constantly brought about to be overcome.

Spinoza conceives the relationship between modes and substance in a peculiar, and to a certain extent technical, way: 'by mode I mean affections of a substance or that which is in another thing through which it is also conceived',[7] but 'modes cannot be or be conceived without substance',[8] they are modification of the substance. By distinguishing modes and substance, Spinoza seems to replicate the traditional essence/existence dichotomy: 'the essence of a human being is constituted by specific modifications of the attributes of God. For the being of substance does not belong to the essence of a human being. Therefore, the essence of human being ... is an affection or mode which expresses the nature of God in a specific and determinate way'.[9] Here the human is a mode, and it is, therefore, a modification of a substance – God; but, at the same time, the being of a substance does not belong to the human. Observed from the traditional ontology of sub-stance we are here faced with the same fundamental scission, according to which essence (the substance) and existence are ontologically irreconcilable.

However, Agamben notes, there is one concept that Spinoza has developed, which offers a key to reconsider the substance/modes relation outside the coordinates of the traditional ontology: immanent cause. In *Ethics* Proposition XVIII and the following proof, Spinoza writes that 'God is the immanent and not the transitive cause of all things ... All things that are, are in God and must be conceived through God and therefore God is the cause of the things that are in him ... Then, there can be no substance besides God nothing which is in itself outside of God; ... Therefore God is the immanent and not the transitive cause of all things. Q.E.D'.[10] Crucially, the immanent cause, for Agamben, defines 'an action in which agent and patient coincide, which is to say, fall together', in which the substance 'constitutes itself as existing' (UoB, 165). But, he goes on,

> in order to think the substance/modes relationship, it is necessary to have at our disposal an ontology in the middle voice, in which the agent (God, or substance) in effectuating the modes in reality affects and modifies only itself. Modal ontology can be understood only as a medial ontology, and Spinozan pantheism, if it is a question of pantheism, is not an inert identity (substance = mode) but a process in which God affects, modifies, and expresses Godself (ibid.).

The relation between substance and modes is not that of identity or difference: the concept of immanent cause defines the active movement in which the substance expresses itself in the modes, becoming in a sense nothing other than the modes [there is nothing besides substance and modes]. The modal ontology that Agamben has in mind radicalises the idea of an immanent cause, in so far as it thinks being as something that 'uses-itself, that is to say, it constitutes, expresses, and loves itself in the affection that it receives from its own modifications' (ibid.).

Agamben finds a further useful element for the delineation of a modal ontology in Leibniz' concept of demand [*exigere*], which is defined as 'an attribute of the possibility: *omne possibile exigit existere* (everything possible demands to exist)'. What an object or a body demands is existence: the possible demands to become real – the potential to pass into act and essence demands existence. 'Existence – Agamben writes – is not a *quid,* a something other with respect to essence of possibility; it is only a demand contained in essence' (ibid., 168). The concept of demand, by seemingly collapsing existence and essence, to be grasped in all its implication, necessitates a revision of the traditional ontology of substance; something that for Agamben, Leibniz did not do. Indeed, he attributed 'demand' to the sphere of the potential and essence, making of existence the objectification of the demand. Leibniz, thus remained in a sense embroiled in the ontological dispositive of scission of being.

Agamben tries to radicalise the concept of demand, developing it in a direction that Leibniz tried to avoid. 'What is a possibility that contains a demand? And how are we to think existence if it is nothing other than a demand?' (ibid.,168) Agamben affirms:

> An essence that becomes a demand is no longer a simple possibility or potential but something else … Not only are possibility and essence transformed by demand; act and essence as well, invested with demand, lose their fixity and, contracting themselves on potential, demand to be possible, demand their own potential. *If existence becomes a demand for possibility, then possibility becomes a demand for existence.* Leibniz's posing of the problem of demand is here reversed: the possible does not demand to exist, but rather, it is the real that demands its own possibility. Being itself, declined in the middle voice, is a demand, which neutralizes and renders inoperative both essence and existence, both potential and act. These latter are only the figures that demand assumes if considered from the point of view of traditional ontology (ibid., 170).

From the point of view of modal ontology, demand pertains to the sphere of existence: it is not the possible that demands to exist: it is the real – the existence – that demands its own possibility. Individuated objects – in their existent reality – are modalities of being *demanding* their possibility to exist, simply, as modes.

Immanent cause and demand are two concepts that Agamben appropriates as a part of the vocabulary of a modal ontology, to think beyond the ontological difference. For the ontology of modes, 'being does not pre-exist the modes but constitutes itself in being modified, is nothing other than its modification'; and if 'demand and not substance is the central concept of ontology, one can then say that being is a demand of the modes just as the modes are a demand of being, on the condition that we specify that demand here is neither a logical entailment nor a moral imperative' (ibid., 170). In the singular existence of things and humans, the mode is not an expression of a substance, nor even a mere fact; is an 'infinite series of modal oscillation, by means of which substance always constitutes and expresses itself' (ibid., 172). And in so far as being is never prescribed as the actualisation of substance – or as an inevitable logical consequence or imperative – but is a perpetual immanent modification, modal ontology thinks existence as anarchic: as the unprincipled expression of its own modification. Gilles Deleuze argued that the world of the ontology of immanence is essentially anti-hierarchical, that is a species of anarchy: the anarchy of beings in Being.[11] The destitution of the ontological-biopolitical dispositive that is pivotal in Agamben's idea of a modal ontology, allows to think being in its *essential* anarchy, something that comes to exist with no commanding vocation or substance but only as an integrated series of oscillating modalities.

Insofar it centres on the question of how-beings-are, modal ontology assumes without mediation an evident ethical (and political) connotation. 'The concept of mode', Agamben writes, is a 'threshold of indifference between ontology and ethics. Just as in ethics character (ethos) expresses the irreducible being-thus of an individual, so also in ontology, what is in question in mode is the "as" of being, the mode in which substance is its modifications' (ibid., 174). The modifications of being are its existential ethos, i.e. 'its being irreparably consigned to its own modes of being' (ibid.). The modal ethics that Agamben thinks towards is not prescriptive: it is fundamentally anarchic. By coinciding with its modes, the singular modal existence is that which does not presuppose a substance, or vocation, or orientation, other than what its modes are. The modal ethics is that which pertains to a form-of-life:

to that life that is only its own forms, which are never obligatory patterns but first and foremost simple possibilities. As Agamben affirms 'the modification of being is not an operation in which something passes from potentiality to act, and realizes and exhausts itself in this' (WDP, 73); rather it is the process according to which the actual form of a being remains tied to its own potential.

The use of life

The image of the human that transpires from Agamben's modal ontology is intrinsically chaotic. A life that is only oscillating-modes and not the actualisation of an essence through intervening attributes and accidents, is a life that has lost a stable ontological foundation and ultimately a firm legibility. In a sense, modal ontology is the one that better explains the conception of life as lacking preordained vocation (or *ergon*) and living essential in the *mode* of the potential that Agamben has defined as the innermost character of the human. Neither any 'specific biological vocation' nor 'whatever necessity' (CC, 3), law, custom or institution, mark out the substance of the human. The real of life is a perpetual metamorphotic creation of modes, whose unpredictability is limited and informed by abstract categories and signatures: the elements through which power is manifested and administered. Institutions, the rules of the law, moral imperative, are forms through which life's modes are governed and rendered legible – through the correlate capturing and hollowing of the essential anarchy of being-human.

When Agamben writes that 'the constitution of a form-of-life fully coincides ... with the destitution of the social and biological conditions into which it finds itself thrown' he is not proposing to return to any more original 'authentic form of life' (UoB, 277), that has been somehow lost in time. Although belonging often (if not always) to a remote past, the paradigmatic figures through which he has thought inoperativity and destituent potential, must be taken for what they are: as examples, rules that can never be prescriptively formulated but that are nevertheless useful to think prefiguratively of our future. Agamben's coming politics does not entail the implementation, creation or re-creation of anything. There are no other forms of life to be established. Rather the task is to make use of what we already are: to become the modes of our life. 'A form-of-life is – he claims – that which ceaselessly deposes the social conditions in which it finds itself to live, without negating them, but simply by using them' (ibid., 274) and making use (of life) here names that practice that destitutes the world as we know it. From this point of view, the concept of use could be considered as the practical side of the modal ontology/ethics. 'Use', Agamben claims, 'is constitutively an inoperative praxis, which can happen only on the basis of a deactivation of the Aristotelean apparatus potential/act' (ibid., 93); and the process of self-constitution of being through its own modification is the same medial process that characterises use as an ethical and political praxis. But what does it mean to use? And how can use as a praxis assume an ethical and political meaning?

The modern conception of the verb 'use', Agamben points out, is covered with a fundamental utilitarian connotation – the value of something of use (its use value) lies, in the end, in its usefulness. However, the term use in the more remote past had quite a different meaning. The Greek *chresthai* and the Latin *uti* [to use] do not signify 'utilisation of something', but have the specific form of not having a meaning in themselves. Indeed, they derive their meaning 'from the term that follows it'. So that *chresthai logoi*, lit. 'to use language' = to speak; *chresthai symphorai*, lit. 'to use misfortune' = to be unhappy; *uti honore*, lit. 'to use an office' = to hold a position *uti lingua*, lit. 'to use the tongue' = to speak (ibid., 24–5). Grammarians classify the verb *chrestai* as a middle voice: neither active nor passive, but the two falling together. Such verbal modalities imply a peculiar conception of the acting subject: 'whereas in the active, verbs denote a process that is realized starting from the subject and beyond him', middle voice verbs express a process that is all internal to the subject. Against the modern conception of use, which always involves the idea of a subject-using-an-object, in the middle voice verbs, 'the subject that completes the action, for the very completing it, does not act transitively on the object, but first and foremost implies and affects itself in the process'; this process therefore denotes a 'singular topology, in which the subject does not stand above the action, but is itself the place of its occurrence' (WDP, 68).

In the relation of use, therefore, subject and object become somehow indistinguishable: the agent of the use constitutes itself in the act of using, becoming paradoxically the subject/object of the use. To use [*chresthai*], Agamben writes,

> *Expresses the relation that one has with oneself, the affection that one receives insofar as one is in relation with a determinate being.* The one who *synphorai chretai* has an experience of himself as unhappy, constitutes and shows himself as unhappy; the one who *utitur honore* puts himself to the test and defines himself insofar as he holds an office; the one who *nosthoi chretai* has an experience of himself insofar as he is affected by the desire for a return. *Somatos chresthai*, 'to use the body,' will then mean *the affection that one receives insofar as one is in relation with one or more bodies.* Ethical – and political – is the subject who is constituted in this use, the subject who testifies of the affection that he receives insofar as he is in relation with a body (UoB, 28–9).

Against its modern/utilitarian conception, Agamben advances a more ethical and political idea of 'use'. Such a concept is immediately practical and ethical, since it is through use that the subject models itself in relation to the affections that it receives in the moment of entering in relation with one or more bodies. 'To enter into a relation of use with something – Agamben writes – I must be affected by it, constitute myself as one who makes use of it. Human being and world are, in use, in a relationship of absolute and reciprocal immanence' (ibid., 30). Here the metaphysical articulation between subject and object is rendered inoperative: in the praxis of use subject and object enter into a zone of indifference. But exactly because in the use the constitution of the subject in its relation with other bodies is at stake, it assumes an eminent ethical and political weight.

In as much as it originates through a relation of use with the social, biological and juridical forms in which we normally live, a form-of-life does not assume the guise of a subject proprietor of its forms, nor even that of a subject *of* its many different forms. It represents that form of living that is nothing other than its anarchic mutable forms. The use of life liberates the human existential dimension from any prescriptive vocation, command or principle [*archè*]. To be in a relation of use with the forms of our life means to constitute ourselves through the forms, and not to be constituted *by* the form. Here, however, it must be stressed that to use one's life does not have to be conceived in terms of passivity or inertia. Use, Agamben claims, is in an inoperative praxis that could come to pass only through and after the destitution of the ontological-biopolitical apparatuses that make our life intelligible and governable. In this sense, we can make ourselves in a form-of-life only through an active-subtraction, destitution, or profanation of the architecture of power: only by trying to orient our practical life – the use that we are destined to make of life – as to make ourselves truly ungovernable.

We have seen throughout how Agamben has considered a form-of-life as a properly human life that emerges through the destitution of the institutional conditions (juridical, social, biological, etc.) in which it finds itself thrown. The destitution of life and the establishment of a relation of use with it, does not pass through a destruction or abolition of the forms in and through which we live. Inoperativity – like destitution – is deposition, deactivation and conservation of what we already are. In this sense, a form-of-life comes into being out of a relation of use with destituted forms. But what kind of use could we make of what is deposed and preserved?

The world of humans – those animals without a specific biological vocation – is an immense accumulation of things, norms and customs: those elements that we label culture and define as opposed to nature. The use of one's life is therefore mediated by semantic coordinates, that could be formulated as rules. Any form of life is experienced as part of a semiotic/semantic order, orienting – in most cases unconsciously – the way in which we use our life. The use-of-oneself, is a habitual praxis that remains in a strict relation with 'a zone of non-consciousness, which is not something like a mystical fog in which the subject loses itself, but the habitual dwelling in which the living begin, before every subjectivation, is perfectly at ease' (ibid., 63–4). This zone of non-consciousness is not removed or inaccessible, on the contrary it rests in a constant relation with our living: 'using-oneself means maintaining oneself in relation with a zone of non-consciousness, keeping it intimate and close just as habit is intimate to use' (ibid., 64). In the gestures of our everyday life, we are unconsciously acting through uses, customs, and institutions, and in so doing we are not commanded or coerced. The sphere of the habitual is, therefore, not the property of a subject, but the impersonal substratum of any process of subjectivation: it represents the moment in which the un-conscious rules shaping the gestures of our everyday life are never separable from our very practical living; the moment in which the constituted (ourselves) and the constituent (the un-conscious zone) fall together into absolute immanence.

In the book *L'Idea di Mondo*,[12] Paolo Virno advances an interesting distinction between the *rules* [*regole*] through which we are making use of our life, and the *norms* of the law: the 'rule is one with the use, innervates it, it cannot exist outside the use' – it remains so to say immanent to the use of life – while the 'legal norm is separated from the use, and postulates the very suspension of the use'[13] and in a sense tries to stabilise the very use of our life. The varied and never prescribed uses of our existence, for Virno, are therefore alien to the legal form, and seldom radically oppose it. In a sense, the stake of all social and political conflict is the affirmation of specific modalities of using life, and for this reason, the law's imperatives and norms are constantly involved in the capture and elimination of the rules and uses of life that are threatening its stability.[14] From this point of view, a form-of-life is that ethical and political praxis that perpetually deposes social and juridical conditions and norms, bringing them to the level of the rule as habit: where they become part of the lived experience of a use of life. What is rendered inoperative in a form-of-life becomes a 'use' and a 'habit', a non-coercive rule whose renewed usability emerges out of its being liberated from any *vis obligandi* and made into an essential, anarchic – that is without an authoritative origin – command.

~ * ~

The true anarchy that Agamben identifies as coinciding with the lucid exposition, grasping and destitution of the anarchy of power, is the ultimate locus in which inoperativity and form-of-life become thinkable as real possibilities. The anarchy that the ontological-biopolitical dispositive constantly captures is what must be liberated to expose the true anarchy of being – as inoperativity, indifference and use. The modal ontology is what allows the contemplation of the point in which the poles of the ontological dispositive conflate and become indistinguishable. Only by actively opening a space of indifference where essence and existence, potentiality and act, life and form, coincide, can a form-of-life constitute itself. The vital inoperative praxis that defines the status of a life as inseparable from its form is in itself anarchic – that is not dependent on any given substance, vocation or ends. As Agamben has insistently argued, the radical change in the ontological relations and the constitution of a form-of-life are not the outcome of an event – not even of a creational act. Inoperativity is already present in what we are – the task is to liberate it through a destituent gesture: what will come after is not a reconstitution of the foundation of being, but simply a way out.

This chapter began by asking if and in what ways inoperativity and a political ontology of destituent potential fit within the tradition of anarchism. On the one hand, Agamben distances himself from classic anarchism, and on the other hand he has placed anarchy at the centre of his speculation. Considering what we have argued so far, Agamben's political proposals show an evident affinity with what has come to be known as post-anarchism:[15] that stream of contemporary libertarian thought that tries to merge some elements of classic anarchism with post-structuralist philosophy, to rejuvenate the anarchist paradigm. Although Agamben's works are not easily classifiable, the presence of common theoretical elements and the fact that his theories have influenced post-anarchist authors makes this potential affiliation plausible and worth examining.

With his idiosyncratic style, Hakim Bey in his *Post-Anarchism Anarchy* – which represents the very first occurrence of the term post-anarchism – acknowledged the growing irrelevance of anarchism for the radically diverse social body of Western contemporary societies: 'Between tragic Past & impossible Future', he claims, 'anarchism seems to lack a Present … if the movement is to grow rather that shrink, a lot of deadwood will have to be jettisoned & some risky ideas embraced'.[16] For Bey, to leave the path of obsolescence,

'Anarchism must wean itself away from evangelical materialism & banal 2-dimensional 19th century scientism [and] experiment with new tactics to replace the outdated baggage of Leftism'.[17] In this sense, post-anarchism intends to provide anarchist thought with new interpretative instruments, to comprehend and to contrast the current forms of domination, through a critique of the very foundations (epistemological and ontological) of classic anarchism. It tries, in a sense, to encroach on the metaphysical territory on which it has been historically grounded.

The classics of anarchism considered human subjects in an essentialist way, based on the image inherited by Enlightenment humanism, as naturally moral and rational, with an innate tendency to sociality and co-operation, which the state's power thwarts and corrupts. The revolution against power is therefore the act of rational agents forming an ethical social body whose purpose is the establishment of an anarchic order in which social harmony could thrive. Post-anarchy questions precisely this narrative; indeed, it thinks politics that begin with anarchy rather than thinking it as the ultimate goal of a process; it starts 'from the non-acceptability of power, a position which opens up a space of contingency and freedom rather than following a set pattern of anarchism'.[18] As such, post-anarchy does not present itself as ideologically shaped. On the contrary it is grounded on a specific ontological anarchy, which considers beings and actions as always potentially contingent and not oriented by specific substances or *teloi*. Post-anarchist politics is then concerned with tactics, rather than strategies; it favours valuing the means – the *how* – instead of the ends of political practices, and in a sense opposes the traditional idea of revolution as well as the classic anarchist uprising of the social body against power.

Against the image of the rational self-centred 'Man of Enlightenment humanism'[19] and the concepts of class, post-anarchism conceives the agent of change as a form of radical subjectivity that does not conform to fixed identities, vocations, or a 'constant, stable set of properties'.[20] Saul Newman, the author who has most systematically developed the concept of post-anarchism, has defined post-anarchist subjects as those who 'carve out a terrain of life and a form of existence which is ungovernable to the extent that is opaque to power' and is essentially devoid any 'predetermined identity, pattern or *telos*'.[21] Modelled upon Agamben's concept of *whatever singularity*, the post-anarchist subject is a form of 'ontologically anarchic existence', in the sense that it is not defined by any identity vocation or biological destiny. Prefigured by Hakim Bey, ontological anarchy is perhaps the main hallmark of post-anarchism.[22] As Newman claims, ontological anarchy names the 'gesture of de-grounding, removing questioning the absolute authority of the *archè*; it is in a sense a 'form of ontological anti-authoritarianism', that liberates 'the action from its *telos*, from the rule of ends, from strategic rationality which always sought to determine it'.[23] From the post-anarchist perspective, anarchy is therefore no longer an end to be reached through a programme of action; rather it manifests itself in an ethical and political act of withdrawal and indifference to power. Although the parallel with Agamben's political theory is evident here, we should not (and cannot) conclude that Agamben is *stricto sensu* an anarchist. Yet, the presence of certain distinctive common elements, and the fact that his works have been a source of inspiration for the elaboration of post-anarchism, make him proximate to the post-anarchist horizon.

Notes

1. Bignall (2016: 49).
2. Schürmann (1986: 6). See UoB, 276.
3. Agamben's engagement with the concept of anarchy and with the anarchist tradition is an ambiguous one. As we have seen, on the one hand he has opposed traditional anarchism, on the other hand 'anarchy' remains a recurring trope in his work. Critical contributions on Agamben, anarchism and anarchy are not very plentiful. Along with the already quoted Bignall (2016), it is worth mentioning Kniss (2018) and Rauch (2020). Agamben has also played an important role in Saul Newman's development of a post-anarchist theory. See Newman (2016).
4. As William Watkin puts it: 'The *archè* represents a moment of arising of specific discursive formation – not the origin of the formation but the moment when a certain set of paradigms operate in signatory fashion to make it possible to

compose a set of named discourse based on what it allows to be said': Watkin (2013: 45).

5. Foucault (1998: 138).
6. Spinoza (2018: 14).
7. Ibid., 3.
8. Ibid., 4.
9. Ibid., 51.
10. Ibid., 21.
11. Deleuze (1978–1981). The original French reads: 'Ce monde de l'immanence ontologique est un monde essentiellement anti-hiérarchique ... C'est la pensée anti-hiérarchique. À la limite, c'est une espèce d'anarchie. Il y a une anarchie des étants dans l'être'.
12. Virno (2015: 126).
13. Ibid.
14. Ibid.
15. Post-anarchism defines a form of political theory that tries to merge the anarchist tradition with post-structuralist philosophy. The label post-anarchy has been coined by Hakim Bay. However, the first organic intervention in post-anarchist thought is Todd May's *The Political Philosophy of Poststructuralist Anarchism* (1994). The theory of post-anarchism found an organic elaboration in Saul Newman's works (2001; 2011; 2016). On the development of post-anarchism, see Rousselle, Evren (2011). Agamben's proximity to post-anarchism has been briefly mentioned by Fabbri (2011).
16. Bey ([1987] 2001: 69).
17. Ibid., 70.
18. Newman (2016: 15).
19. Newman (2011: 141).
20. Ibid.
21. Newman (2016: 18).
22. Bey (1991; 1994).
23. Newman (2016: 10).

Conclusions: Six Theses on Form-of-life

One thing that this book has carefully tried to avoid is to enquire into Agamben's political thought as a unitary or unified theory. Surely, it needs just a quick glimpse at his books to realise how his works are composed of a multitude of fragments, which are not assimilable to a clear epistemological whole, but go to form a constellation of theoretical points. Inoperativity, anarchy, use, potentiality, destituent potential are somehow dispersed elements that this book has considered in their operational linkage to the concept of form-of-life. At this point, as a form of epilogue – which does not aim to set out the last word on the matter – let us summarise in the form of breakable postulates the core arguments advanced in this book.

~ * ~

1. *Hodos.* In so far as the ontological-biopolitical dispositive operates by separating and re-articulating political (qualified) life (and its social and juridical forms) from bare life, a form-of-life is the third element that cannot be reduced to bare life but remains at the same time immanent – in a relation of use – to the forces that attempt to constitute it through this biopolitical separation. Form-of-life is the 'way out': the *hodos* leading to the interruption of the tragedy of our present through an endless profanation of privileged conventions.

2. **Superpolitical apolitical.** By disrupting the logic of the exception that fuels the operation of the ontological-biopolitical machine, a form-of-life acquires without mediation a radical political meaning, which marks the

pathway towards a post-statist politics. When the separation and re-articulation of biological-natural life and a qualified life, that is when bare life cannot be (re)produced, when rules and life fall together immanently into a zone of indistinction, the state with its laws and subjects exposed to obligations and sanctioned violence wanes. A form-of-life becomes eminently political by severing its ties with the *polis*: it is in this sense superpolitical and apolitical.

3. **Undoing the law's command.** A form-of-life emerges out of the destitution of juridical apparatuses that aim to capture the form-of-life that we potentially are in identities through violence. That is, a form-of-life is what one experiences at the moment in which law's functioning is rendered inoperative by the praxis of decoupling law's letter and judgment from the violent means that have been projected to guarantee its legitimacy and grant its unerring efficacy. A form-of-life designates a way of living in which the law's imperatives are no longer the command of an authority, but the coincidence of political and juridical forms of being with the simple gestures and habits of our everyday living in their contingency, fluidity and potentiality.

4. **Destituent praxis.** In a form-of-life, constitution coincides with destitution and vice-versa. Yet the politics of destituent potential and inoperativity is not passivity or idleness. On the contrary, destituent politics is a series of distinctive practices of withdrawal, desertion, (destituent) insurrection and disobedience, whose ultimate purpose is not the creation or institution of new rules or a new qualification of life, but the liberation of something that is kept only potentially present in what we are. It is the liberation of the life of form-making, in a sense, whereby the potentiality of form-making coincides with living and is already present in what we are, as its how we are. As a result, such destituent praxis is a logic that stands opposite to that of constituent power. While the constituent act aims at grounding an order (of rules, institutions, signs, things, etc.) through actualising something

that is held until then as merely possible, the destituent act reminds its form and its life of its own always-present potential inoperativity. In this sense, a destituent praxis deprives power of its foundation and legitimation in the form of a means to an end, as a process and progress of actualising predetermined potentials, by exposing their contingency and arbitrariness.

5. **The destitution of the subject.** The concept of form-of-life thinks life as a generic form without a subject: indeed, it constitutes itself through the deposition of the subject. A form-of-life is not an expression of substance with a given identity and properties (accidents); it is an instance of de-subjectivation, which leads to the affirmation of the 'whatever' against the 'individuated'. A form-of-life is that life in which the impersonal and the subjective become indiscernible but are nevertheless distinguished through specific modes, gestures, habits and potentiality. It expresses the 'how I am what I am'. A form-of-life does not obey or transgress any vocation or work; it does not realise a principle or a command: it is immediately a form, a mode, a habit and use of life. It is a non-subjected stream of modes, free to assume or depose any form as its own. A form-of-life is a singularity, a de-substantialised being; a body affected by its own modes and gestures, whose generic being places it potentially in contact with all others.

6. **Ontological anarchy.** A form of life is an instantiation of the anarchy of being as expressed in a modal ontology. In so far as it constitutes itself through its modes, a form-of-life is not the expression of an essence or a substance; it lacks an *ergon* and pre-given orientation, other than the modes with which it makes use of its own forms. Living in a form-of-life means experiencing a true anarchy: the indeterminacy and contingency of being that the apparatuses of power strive to capture and exclude. By liberating life from the guiding authority of foundational principles, a form-of-life is a proper experience of freedom as a means rather than an end, of the innermost potentiality that frees all practices from any determined *telos* (including that of conceiving freedom as a telos).

Bibliography

Abbott, M. (2016), 'Glory, Spectacle and Inoperativity: Agamben's Praxis of Theoria' in D. McLoughlin (eds) *Agamben and Radical Politics*. Edinburgh: Edinburgh University Press. 49–70.

Adorno, T. (2001), *The Culture Industry: Selected Essays on Mass Culture*, J.M. Bernstein (eds). London: Routledge.

Adorno T. and Sohn-Rethel A. (1991), *Briefwechsel 1936–1969*, C. Gödde (eds), Munich: edition text + kritik.

Agamben, G. (1993), *Stanzas: Word and Phantasm in Western Culture*, trans. R. Martinez. Minneapolis, MN: University of Minnesota Press.

Agamben, G. (1993), *The Coming Community*. trans. M. Hardt. Minneapolis, MN: University of Minnesota Press.

Agamben, G. (1995), *Idea of Prose*, trans. Michael Sullivan and Sam Whitsitt. Albany: SUNY Press.

Agamben, G. (1998), *Homo Sacer: Sovereign Power and Bare Life*, trans. D. Heller-Roazen. Stanford, CA: Stanford University Press.

Agamben, G. (1999), *Potentialities: Collected Essays in Philosophy*, trans. D. Heller-Roazen. Stanford, CA: Stanford University Press.

Agamben, G. (2000), *Means Without End: Notes on Politics*, trans. V. Binetti and C. Casarino. Minneapolis, MN: University of Minnesota Press.

Agamben, G. (2002), *Remnants of Auschwitz: The Witness and the Archive*, trans. D. Heller-Roazen. New York: Zone Books.

Agamben, G. (2004), *The Open: Man and Animal*, trans. K. Attell, Stanford, CA: Stanford University Press.

Agamben, G. (2004), '"I am sure that you are more pessimistic than I am ...": An Interview with Giorgio Agamben' *Rethinking Marxism* Vol. 16:2.

Agamben, G. (2005), *State of Exception*, trans. K. Attell. Chicago: Chicago University Press.

Agamben, G. (2005), *The Time That Remains: A Commentary on the Letter to the Romans*, trans. P. Dailey. Stanford: Stanford University Press.

Agamben, G. (2007), 'The Work of Man' in M. Calarco and S. De Caroli (eds), *Giorgio Agamben: Sovereignty and Life*. Stanford, CA: Stanford University Press. 1–10.

Agamben, G. (2009), *The Signature of All Things: On Method*, trans. L. D'Isanto and K. Attell. New York: Zone Books.

Agamben, G. (2009), *What is an Apparatus?: and Other Essay*, trans. D. Kishik and S. Pedatella. Stanford, CA: Stanford University Press.

Agamben, G. (2010), *The Sacrament of Language: An Archaeology of the Oath*, trans. A. Kostko. Stanford, CA: Stanford University Press.

Agamben, G. (2011 [1986]) 'Nota alla prima edizione', in P. Virno, *Convenzione e materialismo: L'unicità senza aura*. Rome: DeriveApprodi.

Agamben, G. (2011), *Nudities*, trans. D. Kishik. Stanford, CA: Stanford University Press.

Agamben, G. (2011), *The Kingdom and the Glory: For a Theological Genealogy of Economy and Government*. Stanford, CA: Stanford University Press.

Agamben, G. (2012), *The Church and the Kingdom*, trans. L. de la Durantaye. New York: Seagull.

Agamben, G. (2013), *Opus Dei: An Archaeology of Duty*, trans. A. Kostko. Stanford, CA: Stanford University Press (Homo Sacer II, 5).

Agamben, G. (2013), *The Highest Poverty: Monastic Rules and Form-of-Life*, trans. A. Kostko. Stanford, CA: Stanford University Press.

Agamben, G. (2014), 'What is a Destituent Power?' *Environment and Planning D: Society and Space* Vol. 32, 65–74.

Agamben, G. (2015), 'On the Limits of Violence' in B. Moran and C. Salzani (eds) *The Critique of Violence in Walter Benjamin and Giorgio Agamben*. London: Bloomsbury.

Agamben, G. (2016), *The Use of Bodies*, trans. A. Kostko. Stanford, CA: Stanford University Press.

Bibliography

Agamben, G. (2018), *Karman: A Brief Treatise on Action, Guilt, and Gesture*, trans. Adam Kotsko. Stanford: Stanford University Press.

Agamben, G. (2018), *Pulcinella: Or, Entertainment for Children*, trans. Kevin Attell. New York: Seagull.

Agamben, G. (2018), *What is Philosophy?*, trans. Lorenzo Chiesa. Stanford: Stanford University Press.

Agamben, G. (2020), *A Che Punto Siamo? L'Epidemia Come Politica*. Macerata: Quodlibet.

Agamben, G. (2020a), *Quando la Casa Brucia*, Macerata: Giometti & Antonello.

Agamben, G. (2020b), *La follia di Hölderlin. Cronaca di una Vita Abitante*. Torino: Einaudi (1806–1843).

Agamben, G. (2020c), 'Potenza Destituente e Critica della Realizzazione', *Pólemos. Materiali di filosofia e critica sociale* 1/Luglio.

Agamben, G. (2020d), 'Where is Science Going? An Interview with Professor Giorgio Agamben', *Organisms* Vol. 4:2.

Albertus Magnus (1894), *Atisbonensis Episcopi, Ordinis Praedicatorum, Opera Omnia, Volumen Xxx, Commentarii In Iv Sententiarum*. Paris: Ludovicus Vivès.

Althusser, L. (2014), *On the Reproduction of Capitalism. Ideology and Ideological State Apparatuses*. London: Verso.

Altini, C. (2014), *Potenza/Atto*. Bologna: Il Mulino.

Amato, P. et al. (2008), 'Pouvoir desitutant. Les Révoltes métropolitaines' – *La rosa di Nessuno* 3. Milan: Mimesis.

Ambrose (2002), *De Officiis*, trans. I.J. Davidson. Oxford: Oxford University Press.

Arendt, H. (1978), *The Life of the Mind*, M. McCarthy (eds). New York: Harcourt.

Aristotle (1991), *The Complete Works of Aristotle*, J. Barnes (eds). Princeton: Princeton University Press.

Austin, J.L. (1962), *How to do Things with Words*. Cambridge, MA: Harvard University Press.

Badiou, A. (2009), *Logics of Worlds: Being and Event II*, trans. A. Toscano. New York: Continuum.

Bartolus (1555), *Tractatus minoriticarum*, in *Opera*. Lyon: Lugduni.

Benjamin, W. (1978), *Critique of Violence*, in W. Benjamin, *Reflection. Essays, Aphorisms, Autobiographical, Writings*, trans. P. Demetz. New York: Schocken Books.

Benjamin, W. (1996), 'Capitalism as Religion' in *Selected Writings, Volume 3: 1935–1938*. Cambridge, MA: Harvard University Press, 288–91.

Benjamin, W. (2003), 'On the Concept of History' in *Selected Writings, Volume 4: 1938–1940*. Cambridge, MA: Harvard University Press, 389–411.

Benjamin, W. (2006), 'Theological-Political Fragment', in *Selected Writings, Volume 3: 1935–1938*. Cambridge, MA: Harvard University Press, 305–6.

Benveniste, E. (1948) 'L'expression du serment dans la Grece ancienne', *Revue de Histoire des religions*.

Benveniste, E. (1971), *Problems in General Linguistics*. Miami: University of Miami Press.

Berardi, F. (1970), *Contro il Lavoro*. Milan: Edizioni della Libreria.

Berardi, F. (2009), *The Soul at Work. From Alienation to Autonomy*, trans. F. Cadel and G. Mecchia. Cambridge: MIT Press.

Berardi, F. (2012), *The Uprising On Poetry and Finance*. South Pasadena (CA): semiotext(e).

Berger, P.L. and Luckmann, T. (1966), *The Social Construction of Reality A Treatise in the Sociology of Knowledge*. New York: Penguin Books.

Bey, H. (1991), *T.A.Z: the Temporary Autonomous Zone, Ontological Anarchy and Poetic Terrorism*. New York: Autonomedia.

Bey, H. (1994), *Immediatism*. San Francisco: AK Press.

Bey, H. ([1987] 2011), 'Post-anarchist Anarchy' in D. Rousselle and S. Evren (eds.) *Post-Anarchism: A Reader*. London: Pluto Press.

Bignall, S. (2016), 'On Property and the Philosophy of Poverty: Agamben and Anarchism' in D. McLoughlin (eds) *Agamben and Radical Politics*. Edinburgh: Edinburgh University Press, 49–70.

Boano, C. (2017), *The Ethics of a Potential Urbanism. Critical Encounters between Giorgio Agamben and Architecture*. London: Routledge.

Bonagratia (1929), *Tractatus de Christi et apostolorum paupertate*, L. Oliger (eds), in *Archivum Franciscanum Historicum* 22.

Bonefeld, W. (2011), 'Primitive Accumulation and Capitalist

Accumulation: Notes on Social Constitution and Expropriation', *Science & Society*, Vol. 75, No. 3.

Book of Acts, (1998), F.F. Bruce (eds). Grand Rapids: William B Eerdmans Publishing Co.

Butler, J. (1997), *The Psychic Life of Power Theories in Subjection*. Stanford, CA: Stanford University Press.

Campagna, F. (2013), *The Last Night: Anti-work, Atheism, Adventure*. London: Zero Books.

Capra, F. and Mattei, U. (2017), *Ecologia del diritto. Scienza, politica, beni comuni*, San Sepolcro: Aboca.

Castoriadis, C. (1997), *The Castoriadis Reader*, trans. D.A. Curtis. Oxford: Blackwell.

Chignola, S. (eds) (2012), *Il Diritto del Comune. Crisi della Sovranita', Proprieta' e Nuovi Poteri*, Verona: Ombre Corte.

Christiaens, T. (2018), 'Aristotle's Anthropological Machine and Slavery. An Agambenian Interpretation', *Epoché: A Journal for the History of Philosophy*, Vol. 23, Issue 1.

Cicero (1928), *De officiis*, trans. W. Miller. London: Heinemann.

Cinquemani, L. (2019), *Forma di vita. Dal pensiero destituente nella filosofia di Giorgio Agamben alla radicale nullificazione del dispositivo*. Rome: Aracne.

Clastres, P. (1979), 'Entre silence et dialogue', in R. Bellour and C. Clement (eds), *Claude Lévi-Strauss*. Paris: Éditions Gallimard, pp. 33–8.

Clastres, P. (1989), *Society Against the State: Essays in Political Anthropology*, trans. R. Hurley and A. Stein. New York: Zone Books.

Clastres, P. (2000), *Chronicle of the Guayaki Indians*, trans. P. Auster. New York: Zone Books.

Coccia, E. (2006), 'Regula et vita. Il diritto monastico e la regola francescana', *Medioevo e Rinascimento*, 20 / n.s. 17, 97–147.

Coccia, E. (2015), 'La Norma Iconica', *POLITICA & SOCIETÀ*, 1: 61–80.

Colectivo Situaciones (2011), *19 & 20: Notes for a New Social Protagonism*. New York: Autonomedia.

Couver, G. (1961), *Les Pauvres Ont-ils Des Droits*. Rome: Editrice Universita' Gregoriana.

Cover, R. (1986), Violence and the Word, *Yale Law Journal* 95.

Croce, B. (1899), *Pulcinella e il Personaggio Napoletano in Commedia*. Rome: Ermanno Loéscher & C.

Croce, M. (2015), 'Quod Non Est in Actis Non Est in Mundo: Legal Words, Unspeakability and the Same-Sex Marriage Issue', *Law & Critique* 26(1).

Croce, M. and Salvatore, A. (2013), *The Legal Theory of Carl Schmitt*. New York: Routledge.

Dardot, P. and Laval, C. (2019), *Common: On Revolution in the 21st Century*, trans. Matthew MacLellan. London: Bloomsbury.

De Angelis, M. (2007), *The Beginning of History: Value Struggles and Global Capital*. London: Pluto Press.

De Angelis, M. (2017), *Omnia Sunt Communia. On the Commons and the Transformation to Postcapitalism*. London: ZED Books.

De Angelis, M. and Harvie, D. (2013), 'The Commons', in M. Parker, G. Cheney, V. Fournier and C. Land (eds), *The Routledge Companion to Alternative Organisation*. London: Routledge, 280–94.

De Caroli, S. (2016), 'What is a Form-of-Life?: Giorgio Agamben and the Practice of Poverty', in Daniel McLoughlin (eds), *Agamben and Radical Politics*. Edinburgh: Edinburgh University Press, 207–33.

De la Durantaye, L. (2009), *Giorgio Agamben: A Critical Introduction*. Stanford, CA: Stanford University Press.

Debord, G. (1995), *The Society of the Spectacle*, trans. D. Nicholson-Smith. New York: Zone Books.

Deleuze, G. (1978–1981). *Lecture Transcripts*. Retrieved from https://www.webdeleuze.com/.

Deleuze, G. and Guattari, F. (1987), *A Thousand Plateaus: Capitalism and Schizophrenia*, trans. B. Massumi, Minneapolis, MN: University of Minnesota Press.

Derrida, J. (1992), 'Force of Law: The Mystical Foundation of Authority', in D. Cornell and M. Rosenfeld (eds), *Deconstruction and the Possibility of Justice*. New York: Routledge. 3–67.

Dickinson, C. (2011), *Agamben and Theology*. London: T&T Clark.

Elon, M. (2007), 'Punishment' in F. Skolnik, M. Berenbaum, T. Gale (eds), *Encyclopaedia Judaica*. Detroit: Macmillan Reference, Vol. 16, 734–40.

Fabini, U. (1991), 'Il Primato dell'Istituzione in Arnold Gehlen', *Scienza & Politica*, n.5.

Fabbri, L. (2011), 'From Inoperativeness to Action: On Giorgio Agamben's Anarchism', *Radical Philosophy Review* Vol. 14, No. 1.

Fava, A. (2015), 'Official Recognition of Pulcinella. The One who Saved the Commedia from Extinction by Securing its Continuity to the Present Day' in J. Chaffee and O. Crick (eds.), *The Routledge Companion to Commedia dell'Arte*. London and New York: Routledge.

Federici, S. (2011), 'Women, Land Struggles, and the Reconstruction of the Commons', *Working USA*, 14: 41–56.

Finley, M. (1974), *The Ancient Economy*. Berkeley: The University of California Press.

Fleming, P. (2015), *The Mythology of Work. How Capitalism Persists Despite Itself*. London: Pluto Press.

Foley D. and Duménil, G. (2008), 'Marx's Analysis of Capitalist Production', in M. Vernengo, E. Perez Caldentey and B.J. Rosser Jr (eds), *The New Palgrave Dictionary of Economics*. London: Palgrave Macmillan.

Foucault, M. (1998) *The History of Sexuality. Vol. 1, an Introduction*, trans. R Hurley. New York: Penguin.

Francesco D'Assisi (2004), *La letteratura francescana*, Vol. 1: *Francesco e Chiara d'Assisi*, C. Leonardi (eds). Milan: Fondazione Valla-Mondadori.

Frayne, D. (2015), *The Refusal of Work. The Theory and Practice of Resistance to Work*. London: ZED Books.

Fumagalli, A. (2017), *Economia politica del comune. Sfruttamento e sussunzione nel capitalismo bio-cognitivio*. Rome: DeriveApprodi.

Fusco, G.G. (2020), 'Exception, Fiction, Performativity', in G.G. Fusco, C. Cercel, and S. Lavis (eds), *States of Exception: Law, History, Theory*. Abingdon–New York: Routledge, pp. 15–33.

Geertz C. (2000), *Available Light: Anthropological Reflections on Philosophical Topics*. Princeton, NJ: Princeton University Press.

Gehlen, A. (1988), *Man, His Nature and Place in the World*, trans. C. McMillan and K. Pillemer. New York: Columbia University Press.

Gehlen, A. (2016), *Urmensch und Spätkultur. Philosophische Ergebnisse und Aussagen*. Frankfurt: Klostermann.

Gernet, L. (1984), *Le droit penal de la Grece antique* in Du Châtiment dans la Citè. Rome: Ecole Francaise.

Getman, J. (2008), 'Bartleby, Labor and Law' 10 *U. Pa. J. Bus. & Emp. L.* 717.

Girard, R. (2013), *Violence and the Sacred*, trans. P. Gregory. London: Bloomsbury.

Gorz, A. (1989), *Critique of Economic Reason*, trans. G. Hardyside. London: Verso.

Gorz, A. (2020), *Addio al Lavoro. Rome*: Castelvecchi.

Graeber, D. (2004), *Fragments of an Anarchist Anthropology.* Chicago, IL: Prickly Paradigm Press.

Graeber, D. (2018), *Bullshit Jobs. A Theory.* New York: Simon & Schuster.

Hardin, G. (1968), 'The Tragedy of the Commons', *Science, 162*(3859), 1243–8.

Harvey, D. (2004), 'The "New" Imperialism: Accumulation by Dispossession', *Socialist Register* 40: 63–87.

Heidegger, M. (1995), *The Fundamental Concepts of Metaphysics: World, Finitude, Solitude*, trans. W. McNeill and N. Walker, Bloomington: Indiana University Press.

Holman C. (2021), 'Pierre Clastres as Comparative Political Theorist: The Democratic Potential of the New Political Anthropology', *European Journal of Political Theory* 20(1): 67–94.

Holloway, J. (2010), *Crack Capitalism.* London: Pluto Press.

Horvath, A. (2010), 'Pulcinella, or the Metaphysics of the *nulla*: In Between Politics and Theatre', *History of The Human Sciences* Vol. 23, No. 2. 47–67.

Illich, I. (1970), *Deschooling Society.* New York: Harper & Row.

Illich, I. (1980), *Shadow Work.* Boston: Marion Boyars.

Jacobson, E. (2003), *Metaphysics of the Profane. The Political Theology of Walter Benjamin and Gershom Scholem.* New York: Columbia University Press.

Jappe, A. (2013), *Contro il Denaro.* Milan: Mimesis.

Jappe, A. (2019), *Le Avventure della Merce. Per una Nuova Critica del Valore. Rome*: Aracne.

Jesi, F. (2014), *Spartakus: The Symbology of Revolt*, trans. A. Toscano. Chicago: The University of Chicago Press.

Johansen, T.O. (2020), 'Minor Law: Notes Towards a Revolutionary Jurisprudence' in G.G. Fusco, C. Cercel,

S. Lavis, *States of Exception: Law, History, Theory*. Abingdon: Routledge.

Kant, I. (2002), *Groundwork for the Metaphysics of Morals*, trans. A.W. Wood, New Haven: Yale University Press.

Kant, I. (2006), *Anthropology from a Pragmatic Point of View*, trans. R.B. Louden. Cambridge: Cambridge University Press.

Kelsen, H. (1943), *Society and Nature: A Sociological Inquiry*. London: K. Kegan Paul, Trench, Trubner & Co., Ltd.

Kelsen, H. (1967), *Pure Theory of Law*, trans. M. Knight, Berkeley: University of California Press.

Kelsen, H. (1973), *Essays in Legal and Moral Philosophy*, trans. P. Heath, Dordrecht: Reidel Publishing Company.

Kjellén, R. (1917), *Der Staat als Lebensform*. Leipzig: Hirzel.

Kniss, K. (2019), 'Beyond Revolution, Beyond the Law: Christian Anarchism in Conversation with Giorgio Agamben'. *Political Theology*, 20:3.

Kotsko, A. and Dickinson, C. (2015), *Agamben's Coming Philosophy. Finding a New Use for Theology*. London: Rowman and Littlefield.

Kurz, R. (1991), *Der Kollaps der Modernisierung. Vom Zusammenbruch des Kasernensozialismus zur Krise der Weltökonomie*, Frankfurt am Main: Eichborn Verlag.

Kurz, R. (2014), 'The Ontological Break: Before the Beginning of a Different World History' in N. Larsen, M. Nilges, J. Robinson, and N. Brown (eds.), *Marxism and the Critique of Value*. Chicago, Alberta: M C M.

La Boétie, E. de (2012), *Discourse on Voluntary Servitude*, trans. J.B. Atkinson, D. Sices. Indianapolis: Hackett Publishing Company.

Lafargue, P. (2016), *The Right to be Lazy*, trans. L. Bracken. London: AK Press.

Laudani, R. (2013), *Disobedience in Western Political Thought: A Genealogy*. Cambridge: Cambridge University Press.

Laudani, R. (2016), *Il movimento della politica. Teorie critiche e potere destituente*. Bologna: Il Mulino.

Legendre, P. (1999), *Sur la question dogmatique en Occident: Aspects théoriques*. Paris: Fayard.

Legendre, P. (2001), *De la société comme Texte. Linéaments d'une anthropologie dogmatique*. Paris: Fayard.

Lewis C.T. and Short, C. (1958), *A Latin Dictionary*. Oxford: The Clarendon Press.

Linebaugh, P. (2007), *Magna Carta Manifesto: Liberties and Commons for All*. Berkeley, CA: University of California Press.

Loick, D. (2018), *A Critique of Sovereignty*, trans. A. DeMarco. London, New York: Rowman & Littlefield.

Loick, D. (2018a), 'Law Without Violence' in C. Menke, *Law and Violence. Christoph Menke in Dialogue*. Manchester: Manchester University Press.

Lucarelli, A. (2013), *La democrazia dei beni comuni*. Roma-Bari: Laterza.

Mackay, R. and Avanessian, A. (2014), *#Accelerate The Accelerationist Reader*. Cambridge MA: MIT Press.

Macpherson, C.B. (1962), *The Political Theory of Possessive Individualism: Hobbes to Locke*. Oxford: Oxford University Press.

Malevich, K. (1999), *La pigrizia come verità effettiva dell'uomo*. Genoa: il melangolo.

Marmont, G. and Primera G.E. (eds) (2020), 'The Politics, Ethics, and Aesthetics of Inoperativity', *Journal of Italian Philosophy* Vol. 3.

Marx, K. (1975), *Marx & Engels Collected Works Vol. 2*. London: Lawrence & Wishart Ltd.

Marx, K. (1976), *Marx & Engels Collected Works Vol. 5*. London: Lawrence & Wishart Ltd.

Marx, K. (1980), *Marx's Grundrisse*, D. McLellan (eds). London: Palgrave Macmillan.

Marx, K., (1990), *Capital. Vol. I*, trans. B. Fowkes. London: Penguin.

Mattei, U. (2011), *Beni Comuni: Un Manifesto*. Roma-Bari: Laterza.

May, T. (1994), *The Political Philosophy of Poststructuralist Anarchism*. University Park: Pennsylvania State University Press.

McLoughlin, D. (2016), 'Liturgical Labour: Agamben on the Post-Fordist Spectacle', in D. McLoughlin (eds), *Agamben and Radical Politics*. Edinburgh: Edinburgh University Press, 91–114.

Menke, C. (2018), *Law and Violence. Christoph Menke in Dialogue*. Manchester: Manchester University Press.

Moyn, S. (2004), 'Of Savagery and Civil Society: Pierre Clastres and the Transformation of French Political Thought', *Modern Intellectual History*, 1(1), 55–80.

Nadler, S. (1999), *Spinoza: A Life*. Cambridge: Cambridge University Press.

Negri, A. (2007), 'Giorgio Agamben: The Discreet Taste of the Dialectic' in M. Calarco and S. De Caroli (eds), *Giorgio Agamben: Sovereignty and Life*. Stanford, CA: Stanford University Press. 109–25.

Negri, A. and Hardt, M. (2009), *Commonwealth*. Cambridge MA: Harvard University Press.

Newman, S. (2001), *From Bakunin to Lacan. Anti-Authoritarianism and the Dislocation of Power*. Lexington: Lexington Books.

Newman, S. (2011), *The Politics of Post Anarchism*. Edinburgh: University of Edinburgh Press.

Newman (2016), *Postanarchism*. Cambridge: Polity.

Nietzsche, F. (1997), *Daybreak. Thoughts on the Prejudices of Morality*, trans. R.J. Hollingdale. Cambridge: Cambridge University Press.

Nizza, A. (2020), *Linguaggio e Lavoro nel XXI secolo. Natura e storia di una relazione*. Milan: Mimesis.

Noys, B. (ed.) (2012), *Communization and Its Discontents Contestation, Critique, and Contemporary Struggles*. New York: Autonomedia.

Noys, B. (2014), *Malign Velocities: Accelerationism and Capitalism*. Winchester: Zero Books.

Ockham, G. (1963), *Opus nonaginta dierum*, 2 vols, in *Opera politica*, R.F. Bennet and H. S. Offler (eds). Manchester: Manchester University Press.

Olivecrona, K. (1964), 'The Imperative Element in the Law', *Rutgers Law Review* 18.

Olivi, J.P. (1945), Ferdinand Delorme, 'Question de P.J. Olivi "Quid ponant ius vel dominium" ou encore "De signis voluntariis"' in *Antonianum* 2, 309–30.

Ostrom, E. (1990), *Governing the Commons*. Cambridge: Cambridge University Press.

Ostrom, E. (ed.) (2002), *The Drama of the Commons*. Washington: National Academic Press.

Palmer, F. (2001), *Mood and Modality*. Cambridge: Cambridge University Press.

Plessner, Helmuth (1970), *Laughing and Crying: A Study of the Limits of Human Behaviour*, trans. J.S. Churchill and M. Grene. Evanston: Northwestern University Press.

Postone, M. (1993), *Time, Labor and Social Domination: A Reinterpretation of Marx's Critical Theory.* Cambridge: Cambridge University Press.

Primera, G. (2019), *The Political Ontology of Giorgio Agamben: Signatures of Life and Power.* London: Bloomsbury.

Prozorov, S. (2014). *Agamben and Politics: A Critical Introduction.* Edinburgh: Edinburgh University Press.

Rauch, M. (2020), 'An-archē and Indifference: Between Giorgio Agamben and Reiner Schürmann', *Philosophy Today* 65:3.

Rifkin, J. (1995), *The End of Work. The Decline of the Global Labor Force and the Dawn of the Post-Market Era.* New York: Putnam.

Rogin, M.P. (1985), *Subversive Genealogy: The Politics and Art of Herman Melville.* New York: Alfred A. Knopf.

Rousselle, D. and Evren, S. (eds) (2011), *Post-Anarchism A Reader.* London: Pluto Press.

Russell, B. (2004), *In Praise of Idleness and Other Essays.* London: Routledge.

Salzani, C. (2013), *Introduzione a Giorgio Agamben.* Genova: il melangolo.

Salzani, C. (2013a) 'Introduzione' a Benjamin W. *Capitalismo come Religione.* Genova: il melangolo.

Scarry, E. (2009), 'The Declaration of War: Constitutional and Unconstitutional Violence', in A. Sarat and T.R. Kearns (eds), *Law's Violence.* Ann Arbor: University of Michigan Press.

Schauer, F. (2015), *The Force of Law.* Cambridge, MA: Harvard University Press.

Scheler, M. (2009), *The Human Place in the Cosmos,* trans. K. Frings. Evanston: Northwestern University Press.

Schmitt, C. (2008), *Constitutional Theory,* trans. J. Seitzer. Durham: Duke University Press.

Schmitt, C. (2014), *Dictatorship. From the Origin of the Modern Concept of Sovereignty to the Proletarian Class Struggle,* trans. M. Hoelzl and G. Ward. Cambridge: Polity Press.

Searle, J. (1969), *Speech Acts: An Essay in the Philosophy of Language*. Cambridge: Cambridge University Press.

Searle, J. (1983), *Intentionality: An Essay in the Philosophy of Mind*. Cambridge: Cambridge University Press.

Šerpytytė, R. (2019), 'Sulla "natura" della legge: "nómos" come "ornamentum"' *FILOSOFIA*, N. 64.

Sieyès, E.J. (2003), *Political Writings: Including the Debate Between Sieyès and Tom Paine in 1791*. Indianapolis: Hackett Classics.

Smith, J.E. (2012–2013), 'Form-of-Life. From Politics to Aesthetics (and Back)', *The Nordic Journal of Aesthetics* No. 44–5: 50–67.

Smith, J.E. (2016), 'Form-of-Life and Antagonism: On Homo Sacer and Operaismo' in D. McLoughlin (eds) *Agamben and Radical Politics*. Edinburgh: Edinburgh University Press, 189–206.

Spinoza, B. (2018), *Ethics. Proved in Geometrical Order*, trans. M. Silverthorne. Cambridge: Cambridge University Press.

Stiegler, B. (2009), *Acting Out*, trans. D. Barison, D. Ross, and P. Crogan. Stanford, CA: Stanford University Press.

Stirner, M. (1995), *The Ego and its Own*, D. Leopold (eds). Cambridge: Cambridge University Press.

Supiot, A. (2007), *Homo Juridicus*, trans. S. Brown. London: Verso.

Tarì, M. (2017), *Non esiste la rivoluzione infelice. Il comunismo della destituzione*. Rome: DeriveApprodi.

Tarizzo, D. (2010), *Vita, Un' Invenzione Recente*. Rome: Laterza.

Thomas, Y. (2021 [1988]), 'The Slave's Body and its Work in Rome: On Analysing a Juridical Dissociation' in Yan Thomas, *Legal Artifices: Ten Essays on Roman Law in the Present Tense*, trans. C. Schütz and A. Schütz. Edinburgh: Edinburgh University Press.

Thomas, Y. (2002), 'La valeur des choses. Le droit romain hors la religion', *Annales. Histoire, Sciences Sociales*. Volume 57, Number 6.

Tierney, B. (1997), *The Idea of Natural Rights: Studies on Natural Rights, Natural Law and Church Law, 1150–1625*, Grand Rapids: William B. Eerdmans Publishing Company.

The Invisible Committee (2015), *To Our Friends*, South Pasadena, CA: Semiotext(e).

The Invisible Committee (2017), *Now,* South Pasadena, CA: Semiotext(e).

Thucydides (1959), *The Peloponnesian War: The Thomas Hobbes translation*, Ann Arbor: The University of Michigan Press.

Thucydides (2009), *The Peloponnesian War,* trans. M. Hammond. Oxford: Oxford University Press.

VanDrunen, D. (2008), 'Natural Law, the Lex Talionis, and the Power of the Sword', *Liberty University Law Review:* Vol. 2, Issue 3, Article 14.

Vernant J-P. and Vidal-Naquet P. (1988), *Travail et esclavage en Grèce ancienne.* Brussels: Complexe.

Virno, P. (2011 [1986]), *Convenzione e Materialismo: L'unicità Senza Aura.* Rome: DeriveApprodi.

Virno, P. (2015), *L'idea di Mondo. Intelletto Pubblico e Uso della Vita.* Macerata: Quodlibet.

Viveiros de Castro E. (2010), 'The Untimely, Again', in Clastres P. *Archeology of Violence*, Los Angeles, CA: Semiotext(e), pp. 9–51.

Viveiros de Castro E. and Danowski, D. (2017), *The Ends of the World.* Cambridge: Polity.

von Jhering, R. (1913), *Law as a Means to an End*, trans. by I. Husik, Boston: The Boston Book Company.

Warrender, H. (1957), *The Political Philosophy of Hobbes: His Theory of Obligation.* Oxford: Clarendon Press.

Watkin, W. (2014), *Agamben and Indifference: A Critical Overview.* London: Rowman & Littlefield.

Weber, M. (2005), *The Protestant Ethic and the Spirit of Capitalism*, trans. T. Parson. London-New York: Routledge.

Weeks, K. (2011), *The Problem with Work: Feminism, Marxism, Antiwork Politics, and Postwork Imaginaries,* Durham, NC: Duke University Press.

Weinberger, O. (1973), Introduction: Hans Kelsen as Philosopher, in H. Kelsen, *Essays in Legal and Moral Philosophy*, Dordrecht: Reidel Publishing Company.

Whyte, J. (2009), 'I Would Prefer Not To': Giorgio Agamben, Bartleby and the Potentiality of the Law', *Law and Critique* Vol. 20.

Whyte, J. (2010), '"A New Use of the Self": Giorgio Agamben on the Coming Community', *Theory and Event:* Vol. 13, Issue 1.

Whyte, J. (2013), *Catastrophe and Redemption: The Political Thought of Giorgio Agamben*, Albany: State University of New York Press.

Widmer, K. (1969), 'Melville's Radical Resistance: The Method and Meaning of "Bartleby"', *Studies in the Novel* Vol. 1, No. 4: 444–58.

Williams, A. and Srnicek, N. (2013), 'Accelerate: Manifesto for an Accelerationist Politics' in A. Mackay and R. Avenessian (eds), *Critical Legal Thinking: Law and the Political*.

Wittgenstein, L. (2009), *Philosophical Investigations*, trans. G.E.M. Anscombe, P.M.S. Hacker and J. Schulte. Oxford: Wiley-Blackwell.

Wrobleski, H. and Hess K. (2006), *Introduction to Law Enforcement and Criminal Justice*, Belmont, CA: Wadsworth Publishing.

Zartaloudis, T. (2010), *Giorgio Agamben: Power, Law and the Uses of Criticism*. London: Routledge.

Ziebarth, E. (1895), 'Der Fluch im griechischen Recht', *Hermes* 30.

Žižek, S. (2006), *The Parallax View*, Cambridge MA: MIT Press.

Index

Index